New Learning
Elements of a Science of Education

In this, the era of the 'knowledge society', more is expected of education than ever before, yet disappointment in education seems pervasive. *New Learning* analyses the state of education today and presents an exciting vision of what schools *could* be like. It addresses the fundamental questions: what kinds of workers, citizens and individuals will our future need, and how can schools refashion themselves and become more relevant?

The focus of *New Learning* is on learners and their learning – the extraordinary diversity of their backgrounds and interests, and the dynamics of educational environments which can engage all to fully maximise the effectiveness of learning.

This book by internationally renowned experts Mary Kalantzis and Bill Cope is an imaginative, future-oriented exploration of contemporary education. It is an indispensable resource for educators, pre-service teachers, and anyone interested in the challenges and opportunities facing teachers and learners today. The supplementary website **NewLearningOnline.com**  includes extracts from books and interviews, case studies, keyword definitions and additional learning material.

Mary Kalantzis is Dean of the College of Education at the University of Illinois at Urbana-Champaign, USA, and formerly Dean of the Faculty of Education, Language and Community Services at RMIT University, Melbourne, Australia, and President of the Australian Council of Deans of Education.

Bill Cope is Research Professor in the Department of Educational Policy Studies at the University of Illinois at Urbana-Champaign, USA, and an Adjunct Professor in the Globalism Institute at RMIT University, Melbourne, Australia.

New Learning

Elements of a science of education

Mary Kalantzis and Bill Cope

CAMBRIDGE
UNIVERSITY PRESS

CAMBRIDGE UNIVERSITY PRESS
Cambridge, New York, Melbourne, Madrid, Cape Town, Singapore, São Paulo, Delhi

Cambridge University Press
477 Williamstown Road, Port Melbourne, VIC 3207, Australia

Published in the United States of America by Cambridge University Press, New York

www.cambridge.org
Information on this title: www.cambridge.org/9780521691246

First published 2008

Printed in Australia by Ligare

A catalogue record for this publication is available from the British Library

National Library of Australia Cataloguing in Publication data

Kalantzis, Mary, 1949–
New Learning: elements of a science of education / authors, Mary Kalantzis; Bill Cope.
ISBN 978-0-521-69124-6 (pbk)
Port Melbourne, Vic.: Cambridge University Press, 2008
9780521691246 (pbk)
Includes index.
Education – Australia.
Education – Study and teaching – Australia.
Learning.
Cope, Bill, 1957–
370.7

ISBN 978-0-521-69124-6

Contents

Preface

The art of teaching and the science of education

Teaching happens everywhere. Many people are naturally quite good at teaching. They explain things clearly. They are patient. And they have the knack of explaining just enough, but not too much, so the learner gains a sense that they are gradually mastering something, albeit with a more knowledgeable person's support. Parents are teachers. Friends are teachers. Sales, service and maintenance people are teachers. Co-workers are teachers. You can find the practice of teaching in action everywhere in everyday life. In fact, it is impossible to imagine everyday life without it. Teaching and learning are integral to our nature as humans.

Some people profess to be terrible teachers. They'd rather not have to explain to a novice how to do something. 'It's quicker and easier to do it myself', they say. Or, 'I just don't have the patience to explain things'. Such people are rarely as bad at teaching as they think and say they are. Everyone has been a learner and has had direct experiences of having been taught. Such everyday teaching is more art than science, more instinctive than articulate, and something that is never far beyond the range of anyone's capacities.

Teaching is also a vocation, a profession. People in the business of teaching are good at their job when they have developed and apply the dispositions and sensibilities of the person who is a good teacher in everyday life.

But there is much more to the teaching profession than having a natural knack, however well practised. There is also a science to education, which adds method and reflexivity to the art of teaching, and is backed up by a body of specialist knowledge. This science asks and attempts to answer fundamental and searching questions. How does learning happen? How do we organise teaching so it is most effective? What works for learners? And when it works, how do we know it has worked? The science of education attempts to answer these questions in a well thought-through and soundly analysed way.

Parents, friends and workers tend not to think as systematically about teaching and learning as professional teachers do. Scientific thinking and disciplined practice are what distinguish the profession of teaching from the art of teaching. If you want to be a teacher, you undertake training in the discipline of education.

This book is an introduction to the systematic thinking that is the science of education, designed for two audiences. One is a general readership including professional educators interested to reflect upon some fundamental questions about the nature of the profession, and the science that underpins that profession. Another is people embarking on a program that will lead to a teaching qualification. For both audiences, this book offers a distillation of key ideas of the discipline of education, and the body of knowledge upon which the discipline is grounded.

More than simply reflecting on the traditions of the discipline, however, this book ventures into a re-conception of education for our dramatically changing times. The title 'New Learning' points to the need to redesign the way we 'do' education as a social experience known currently as 'schooling', to meet the demands of our changing times and to benefit from the opportunities that these changing times offer us. Today's science of education needs to be able to 'read' contemporary social conditions and adjust our educational institutions and processes if it is to be truly useful. We want to suggest that a redesigned science of education is required today as a foundation of knowledge for a renewed teaching profession. As such, we hope this book will help experienced and beginning educational professionals to re-conceive the scope and shape of the profession of teaching and the science of education.

The meaning of 'science'

What is 'science'? The more profound and important the concept, the harder it seems to define, and the more it seems to be plagued by a wide, even contradictory, range of meanings.

Mention the word 'scientist' and the first thing that may spring to mind is a person in a laboratory coat, conducting an experiment. You might think of the chemistry, physics, geology and biology taught as subjects in school or university. This meaning of 'science' mainly refers to the natural and technological worlds.

Think a bit longer and you'll realise that term is also used to describe some of the 'social sciences'. By the time we come to realise that the word encompasses both the natural and social worlds, its scope is huge – from forests to politics, from physics to education.

If we tease out the underlying meanings of 'science' across such a broad range of domains of application, we might conclude that it refers to a privileged kind of knowledge, created by people with special skills who mostly work in research, academic or teaching jobs. It involves careful experimentation and focused observation. Scientists systematically explore phenomena, discover facts and patterns and gradually build these into theories that describe the world. Over time, we come to trust these as the authority of science.[1]

These meanings of science are quite unexceptionable. In this spirit, we might create a science of education that focuses on the brain as a biological entity and the mind as a source of behaviours (cognitive science). Or we might set up experiments in which we carefully explore the facts of learning in order to prove what works or doesn't work. Like the medical scientist, we might give some learners a dosage of a certain kind of educational medicine and others a placebo, to see whether a particular intervention produces better test results (randomised controlled experimentation).[2] This is the conventional view of science. And these kinds of thinking can be perfectly useful.

Often, however, we need to know more. It is indeed helpful to know something of how the mind works, but what of the cultural conditions that also form the thinking person? We need good proofs of which kinds of educational interventions work, but what if the research question we are asking or the tests we are using to evaluate results can only measure a narrow range of capacities and knowledge? For instance, what if the tests can prove that the intervention works – scores are going up – but some learners are not engaged by a curriculum that has been retrofitted to the tests? What if the tests only succeed in measuring recall of the facts that the tests expect the learners to have acquired – simple, multiple-choice or yes/no answers? A critic of such 'standardised testing' may ask, what's the use of this in a world in which facts can always be looked up, but problem solving and creativity are now more sought-after capacities, and there can be more than one valid and useful answer to most of the more important questions?[3]

For these reasons, we want to outline a broader understanding of the discipline of education, based on a broader definition of science. There's nothing wrong with doing science in its narrower senses, so long as this work is balanced with a 'bigger-picture' view of science.

'Science' comes into English from the Latin word *sciens* ('knowing'). However, our modern conception of science is not just any old knowing. It consists of a variety of specially focused things you do that distinguish everyday, commonsense knowing from an organised, ordered, socially and historically constructed knowing, which is regarded as trustworthy because of its authority, effectiveness and openness to critique and refutation. These special ways of knowing distinguish the everyday practitioner of an art from a professional. As we explain in further detail as this book unfolds, some of these special things you do to know when you are being scientific are experiential (including focused reflections of what you know from your everyday experience and careful observation in new and unfamiliar settings), others conceptual (carefully defining concepts and building theories that tie these concepts together into patterns of meaning), others analytical (explaining how things work as well as whom and what they are for) and still others applied (testing how knowledge works in practice, being creative and innovating). There are, in other words, quite a few different types of things you can do to know, in a way that is more systematic in its methods and reliable in its results than everyday, casual knowing.

The discipline of education is grounded in the science of learning, or how you come to know. It is a science that explores what knowing is, and how babies, then young people, then adults, learn. Education-as-science is a specially focused form of knowing: knowing how knowing happens and how capacities to know develop. It is, in a sense, the science of all sciences. It is also concerned with the organisation of teaching that supports systematic, formal learning and the institutions in which that learning occurs.

We want to make this special claim for the science of education for some practical as well as principled reasons. Too often, education is regarded as a poor cousin of other disciplines in the university – the natural sciences, the humanities and the other professions, for instance. It is regarded as something that enables other disciplines, rather than being a discipline in its own right. This is reflected in lower levels of research funding, student entry requirements and the destination salaries of graduates. Education seems to be less rigorous and derivative, its disciplinary base borrowed from other, apparently more foundational disciplines – sociology, history, psychology, cognitive science, philosophy – and the substantive knowledge of various subject areas such as literature, science and mathematics.

For sure, education is broader ranging and more eclectic than other disciplines. Education draws on a number of disciplinary strands – epistemology, or the philosophy of knowledge, the cognitive science of perception and learning, developmental psychology, the history of modern institutions, the sociology of diverse communities, the linguistics and semiotics of meaning – to name just a few of education's disciplinary perspectives. These and other strands come together to make the discipline of education.

More than the equal of other disciplines, however, education is the soil in which all the other disciplines grow. You can't do any of the other disciplines in a university or college except through the medium of education. No other discipline exists except through its learning – an individual learning the accumulated knowledge that has become that discipline, and the social learning represented by the whole discipline itself and its community of practitioners.

Education is the systematic investigation of how humans come to know. It is the science of sciences.

Towards a 'New Learning'

We set out to explore new territory in this book. It is our aim is to build a vision for the future of education – 'New Learning' – which does not simply reflect and reproduce the heritage institutions and practices of schooling. Social, cultural and technological change are throwing into question the relevance and appropriateness of heritage education. So, although our counterpoint is the educational processes of our recent past, the focus of this book is the design of New Learning environments that are more engaging, more effective and more appropriate to our contemporary times and our imaginable near futures. How do we create learning environments that work better and that provide more equitable outcomes for all?

Some foundational values and principles underlie the theory and practice of New Learning. The first is that diversity, understood in a broad and all-encompassing way, is a key feature of contemporary cultures that must figure at the core of our thinking about education. One-size-fits-all schooling may have worked in the past as a form of social control and a strategy for selecting the few into higher education. Today, such an approach to education is more and more widely acknowledged to be not working very well. For a host of reasons, it is not well suited to the needs of today's society. Our contemporary designs for learning must accommodate the differences in knowledge, life experience and motivation amongst our learners, as well as a wider range of rapidly changing occupational destinations, and a need that is just now being recognised: for highly creative problem solvers able to re-imagine and reinvent entire ways of living in order to address increasingly urgent social and environmental challenges.

The second foundational principle is that education must cultivate deep knowledge, hence the grounding of the theory of New Learning in epistemology, or the theory of the possibility, origins, nature and extent of human knowledge. The third principle is that education needs to develop and maintain a systematic focus on designing learning experiences and tracking learning processes. Our measure of success as educators is the effectiveness of learning as reflected in learner performance.

The fourth principle that makes this book different is its globalist content and aspirations. Our case for New Learning is grounded in a 'new basics' of education applicable anywhere in the world. These consist of the knowledge competencies, and sensibilities necessitated by changing technology, culture and economy in our times. Paradoxically, however, such a globalist approach is necessary, not only because the teachers and learners are facing more and more of the same dilemmas all around the world, but because one of the key dilemmas of the New Learning, as we see it, is diversity itself – amongst learners and between the settings in which learning occurs. If we can negotiate learner and contextual diversity at the local level, we can do it globally; and if we can do it globally, we will be able to do it better locally.

In this globalist spirit, we engage with theories and case studies from many parts of the world and many cultural traditions. One of the reasons we use this globalist frame of reference is practical. Nowadays, ideas and policies about teaching and learning circulate around the world faster than ever, influencing education at a local level. Also, practically speaking, people undertaking teacher education programs today are more likely than was ever the case in the past to end up teaching in different parts of the world in the course of their careers. Teaching has become an international profession. Teachers are migrants. Teachers are 'foreign' students when they do their first or second degrees away from home, or take international student exchanges as part of their degrees. Teachers take their students on visits to faraway places. Teachers go on extended working holidays, often as young people, but increasingly today after their families have grown up and as they are nearing retirement. More than ever in the past, teaching is becoming a peripatetic profession, a profession of global travellers and this is one of its great attractions. Formal teaching standards and registration require-ments are adjusting to accommodate such movement. If you are a lawyer, you can't easily move from one jurisdiction to another. But as a teacher, the world awaits. In fact, teachers are increasingly being recruited across borders. Your dif-ference may also be a virtue, no matter how distant the destination. Your native language skill – in Mandarin, or English, or Arabic – will mean that you are 'in demand' in many places other than your home country. Even if you are a speaker of a small or immigrant language, you are likely to find minority communities of speakers of your language in many of today's world cities, who need your special cultural and language knowledge.

In addition to these practical considerations, this book is globalist as a matter of principle. Given the differences amongst the learners in our classrooms and the increasingly interconnected world in which we are living, it is simply imperative that educators view their profession from a global perspective, and develop in themselves and their learners dispositions and sensibilities that are cosmopoli-tan and worldly-wise. The students in your class may have been born or end up spending their later lives around the corner or at the other end of the Earth.

Nor do we assume that everyone 'doing education' as a course of study will become a teacher in the conventional sense. Or that a teacher will remain in the one career for all of his or her life. Sometimes people studying education head off on professional tangents, using the skills they have learnt to become trainers, mentors, knowledge managers, coaches, counsellors and leaders in organisations and communities. Indeed, career flexibility is likely to become the norm. The benefits for the profession will be great – as professionally trained educators go out into the wider community and prove the mettle of the science and profession of their training, and as they return to education with experiences from other fields. For this reason, we pitch our arguments at a high level of generality. This book is not about the nitty-gritty of lesson plans and timetables and the organisational structures of schools as we know them. It is about the idea of learning, and how learning is organised in a carefully premeditated way in the human processes of education. Even more broadly speaking, it is about the creation of persons with new kinds of capacities for the 'knowledge society'.

Our exploration, then, is more than a distillation of the stuff of the discipline of education as we have come to understand it. It is that, for sure, but more. We outline a theory of New Learning, a different kind of learning for a future whose horizons are open. To support our case, we discuss the changing dimensions of work, citizenship and everyday life, which seem to be insisting upon a revolution in education. We explore learner diversity, equity, the nature of learning and the dynamics of pedagogy that will work in contemporary educational settings. We examine the changing nature of teachers' work, school organisation and the blurring of the boundaries between institutionalised education and learning that is lifelong and life-wide.

Our focus throughout is on the nature of learning, and thus learners. The word 'education' most commonly suggests something that has been designed for learners by teacherly types who know what will be good for them. In this conception, the institutions, systems, curricula, textbooks, assignments and assessment procedures of education often seem to have been created by experts positioned on high and handed down to learners. This perspective is characteristic of the old teaching. Such an approach may have had its place in the past, and its perennial limitations, too. But it often appears out of place today for the learners who will be the workers, citizens and persons-in-community of the near future. Our version of New Learning changes the balance of agency, granting that learners play a much more active role in the process of learning than was allowed in the past. So, in this book we set out to view education's designs from the learner's perspective.

This focus on learning, in its turn, requires a new view of teaching. Teachers are professionals who diagnose learner needs; design learning experiences appropriate to these needs; monitor learner performance; and create learning pathways based on this performance. By focusing on today's learners, the New Learning also works towards the creation of a new kind of teaching professional doing a different kind of job.

Not that the past should be disregarded – on the contrary, the New Learning stands upon the deep knowledge of the discipline and the long and wide experiences of educational practice. It does not discard, but extends and develops the theories and practices of the education and the body of knowledge that underpin the discipline. Even though our primary aim is to imagine the new, in the words of 17th-century physicist Isaac Newton, we can only do this because we are 'standing on the shoulders of giants'.

How this book is organised

This book outlines the elements of the science of education. It is a distillation of the main ideas at the core of the discipline, that body of knowledge that concerns itself with human learning. As such, it is just as concerned with the art of teaching and the very practical processes of engaging with learners. It is supplemented by a website (www.NewLearningOnline.com) ◉ that includes extracts from key texts, keyword definitions and learning tasks.

Guiding narrative (in this book)

This is our outline of the science and discipline of education. Each chapter is divided into three stages: education and social life in the modern past, changing education in recent and current times and the theory and practice of a New

Learning. This division is roughly chronological – roughly, because much of the past remains present. We live in a state of what might be called 'uneven change'. In this sense, the three stages in each chapter are more importantly analytical than they are chronological, each stage representing a perspective or approach. Each chapter works its way though a number of dimensions of education. One chapter after another, the main narrative cycles around this threefold stage structure, progressively building a many-dimensional picture of the trajectory of change in education and a wide variety of educational paradigms or ways of thinking.

Navigational aids (in this book)

This book covers an enormously wide ground. For practical reasons, we provide three kinds of navigational aid to help you through the text. Each chapter begins with an Overview, which summarises the main points. The main narrative is then divided into small parts with a structure of subheadings so you can locate particular ideas easily. There are three main subheadings in each chapter, covering the three stages in the argument and culminating in our case for New Learning. Within each of these three sections, we come back to the various dimensions of the area of education discussed in that chapter. Finally, each chapter ends with a summary table that captures the three stages in the argument (the columns) and shows the intersections with the various dimensions of education discussed in the chapter (the rows).

Breakout boxes (on the web)

We want to expose those coming newly to the discipline of education to different points of view representing a range of theoretical perspectives across the discipline of education, from different eras and from different parts of the world. These are mentioned and cited at relevant points in the text, and can be found on the web at NewLearningOnline.com . Some of these texts address theoretical questions (and are often difficult to read if you are unfamiliar to the disciplinary genre they represent – but being intellectually challenged, even to the point of having to move beyond your comfort zone, is a part of the learning process). Other texts are more practical and descriptive, and thus more accessible. Either way, these are original sources. We wanted you to hear people speaking in their own voices, rather than tell you what we think they are saying.

Keywords (on the web)

It is in the nature of science to create a technical language that is more precise in its meanings than everyday language. This technical language may at first seem unclear, particularly when precise meanings are confused with commonsense meanings. For this reason, every chapter has a keywords section where you can look up technical terms that have been introduced in that chapter. This glossary of keywords, laid out in the order in which they are presented in the book, is to be found at NewLearningOnline.com.

Knowledge processes (on the web)

This book introduces many of the ways in which teachers can help learners engage with learning. It also suggests that you try them out as a learner and teacher yourself. We want to encourage you to be a knowledge-maker and a learner. For this reason, each chapter has supporting 'knowledge processes', to be found at NewLearningOnline.com. Here, we suggest lines of inquiry and research you might pursue to build your own understanding of the science of education. In other words, this section is an invitation to be a scientist yourself, to build your own knowledge.

Notes

1. For an introductory discussion of the meaning of 'science', see Chalmers 1976. See also: Phillips and Burbules 2000
2. See, for instance, National Center for Education Evaluation and Regional Assistance 2003; Shavelson and Towne 2002
3. For a critique of a narrowly 'evidence-based' view of the educational sciences, see: Schwandt 2005; Erikson and Gutierrez 2002; Popkewitz 2004

Acknowledgements

As much as this book is a recap of things we have been doing, thinking about, talking about and writing about for several decades, it is also a social product. Where does one begin to describe the influences that have come to bear on writing a book like this, and the people who have helped us in the process? The following is a list of the most direct connections, at the expense of not doing justice to the influences of the wider intellectual and social context.

Our educational journey began in a small Catholic primary school in western Sydney, Australia. Lately, we have become very conscious that much of what we are saying now we started thinking back then – in the curriculum work we did with the support of, and in collaboration with, Mark May, Wendie Batho, Kerry Stirling and Allan Coman. We are also conscious of the degree to which the joint work with our 'genre', then 'Multiliteracies', colleagues has shaped our thinking from the 1990s till today – Courtney Cazden, Norman Fairclough, James Gee, Gunther Kress, Allan Luke, Carmen Luke, Jim Martin, Sarah Michaels and Martin Nakata.

We started this book when we were at RMIT University in Melbourne, and so we wish to thank our co-researchers and colleagues there – Ellen-Jane Browne, Peter Burrows, Rachael Dunstan, Kieju Suominen and Nicola Yelland. The idea for this book arose while Mary was President of the Australian Council of Deans of Education, and the series of reports produced together with the other Deans and the assistance of Executive Officer, Andrew Harvey. We want to thank Gunther Kress for his wise advice on an earlier version of this manuscript. We've ended up finishing the book in Illinois, and here we want to thank Nick Burbules, Candace Clark, Lizanne DeStefano, Rosemary Onyango, Michael Peters and Fazal Rizvi for their collegiality and support. We also want to thank Helen Smith for her meticulous and thoughtful reading of the manuscript. Thanks, finally, to Peter Debus, who helped us shape this project when he was at Cambridge University Press, and Glen Sheldon and Kate Indigo, who have seen it through to completion.

Our children, Phillip, Diana and Peter, have travelled with us on this journey, in some moments wondering where it was going, in others getting on board themselves. Phyllis Cope asked how the book was getting on almost every day during its writing, but sadly did not live to see it finished. We dedicate this work to that foundational site of learning, our family.

Mary Kalantzis and Bill Cope
University of Illinois at Urbana-Champaign, USA
12 November 2007

Part A

Introduction – Changing Education

Chapter 1

New Learning

Overview

In this chapter, we reflect upon this peculiar moment in the profession of education. Certainly, education seems more important than ever before. Politicians talk about the knowledge society; business people discuss the new economy; and parents worry about the role a good education will play in their children's futures. Despite this, educators struggle to find the resources to meet increasing expectations.

What is this thing, 'education', that is expected to do so much? In its most visible manifestation it consists of institutions – schools, colleges and universities. Education is also a social process, the relationship of teaching and learning, where one person helps another to learn. As a professional practice, it is a discipline. As a body of knowledge and way of knowing the world, it is a science.

Education in all its aspects is in a moment of change, or transition. The idea of 'New Learning' contrasts what education has been like in the past, with the changes we are experiencing today, with an imaginative view of the possible features of learning environments in the near future. What will learning be like, and what will teachers' jobs be like?

Being an educator in 'interesting times'

These are strange times for education – or, in the words of the often-quoted Chinese saying, 'interesting times'.

On the one hand, we are told on an almost daily basis that education is of paramount importance. It was always important, but somehow, today, it is more important than ever.

Take parents, for instance. At all income levels and everywhere in the world, parents know that education is critical in shaping their children's destinies. They have always known this, but it seems more crucial today and the pressures to succeed feel even greater. And they are right. There is no stronger predictor of affluence and wellbeing later in life than one's level of education. Education is the most achievable route to social mobility.

Meanwhile, growing anxieties about globalisation and technology are creating both new opportunities and new divisions. Persistent issues of equality of access are coming to the forefront of people's concerns, at the local level and around the world. New fears about identity and security are emerging just as the spirit of freedom and choice appears more lively and insistent. This is the stuff of conversations in the street.

Meanwhile, in the broader public discourse, people are talking about the 'knowledge society', the 'new economy' or the 'knowledge economy'.[1] Take the world of work: it's not just that knowledge-heavy professions are employing more people – in information and communications technologies and services, in health, in human services and in education itself. Even traditionally manual industries such as manufacturing and agriculture now require 'knowledge workers': people with technical and scientific knowledge and skills, and who also have the social skills required to operate effectively in a diverse workforce, to interact in collaborative teams, to provide better service relationships to customers, to use networks effectively and to be more sensitively aware of the broader human and environmental impacts of their actions.[2]

Education is not only expected to address the challenge of changing skill and knowledge requirements; it is also expected to provide solutions for inequality, poverty and prejudice, as well as to enable social justice, cohesive sociality, job skills, scientific discoveries, wealth creation, personal fulfilment and self-realisation. Our political leaders make promises like these every day. Their rhetoric shows just how wide and deep are the expectations placed on education today. [*See*: Political Leaders, Speaking of Education.[3]]

However – and this is the 'strange' aspect of our times – educators are getting conflicting messages about education's value. For every moment in which it seems our society is valuing knowledge and education more highly than it did in the past, there is another moment in which it appears that education is devalued. Education falls prey to perpetual funding crises, often linked to taxpayer revolt, small government conservatism and the shrinking size of government budgets. (A significant crisis, given that modern Western schooling has mostly been publicly funded.) How, then, do we improve teacher–student ratios in public schools? How do we bring teacher salaries closer to those of other similarly qualified professionals in equally demanding jobs? How do we fund the new essentials of learning – a laptop computer for every learner – or new areas of learning to address difficult areas of social concern, such as sexuality and drugs, or specialist aides who can assist teachers in an era in which we are properly much more sensitive to individual learner needs as a consequence, for instance, of dyslexia or autism? The answers to these questions are more straightforward for affluent communities, who have the tax revenue to be able to spend more on education or who can afford to pay higher school fees under the 'user pays' principle.

A comparison with the social cost of health care is relevant here. In 2003, Organisation for Economic Cooperation and Development (OECD) countries spent 8.8 per cent of their total national incomes on public and private expenditures on health, up from 7.1 per cent in 1990 and 5.0 per cent in 1970. The absolute figures are much higher, because of the substantial growth in national incomes over these years.[4] These increases reflect the cost of developing and making widely available new medical procedures, technologies and pharmaceuticals, and to employ many more medical professionals. Even with this level of expenditure, there is a long way to go to make the possibilities of modern medicine available to all. Some people and communities are able to afford the latest medical services; others are not. Meanwhile, costs continue to rise, and so do demands for universal access.

However, the story is different for education. On average, total public and private expenditure on education in OECD countries has not kept up with national income. Across OECD countries in 2002, 6.1 per cent of national income was spent on education, slightly less than the proportion of national income spent on education in 1995 – and this, despite the fact that young people were staying at school longer.[5]

As a society, we don't yet seem to have realised that education adequate to today's social requirements requires a significant additional social investment. It's just too easy for taxpaying generations (who seem more prepared to pay for health as they are getting older, either from their own resources or by using public resources) to suggest that the user – and in the case of children, this means the parent – should pay for education. As public education fails to meet parents' increasing expectations, in many parts of the world there is a drift away from public schooling. Even parents who find private schooling hard to afford are feeling the pressure and investing in private schooling for their children. If you want a full-service school – every child with a laptop, up-to-date curriculum and personalised attention with specialist support – the only choice available, it seems in many cases, is to go to a private school and pay fees. The consequence of shrinking public education is that significant groups of the population, indeed the majority of the populations of developing nations, are missing out on a decent education. Education, despite its promise, ends up contributing to the vast breadth of inequality on a global scale.

This, then, is a peculiar moment for education. Education is more important to society and individuals than ever before – nobody would deny that. But as a society we seem reluctant to invest in it sufficiently to perform the bigger and more significant role it is now expected to play. If education is so important, and so much more important now than it ever has been in the past, then, as a society, we need to make a commitment to invest considerably more, not just in current educational arrangements, but also developing new ideas and then producing evidence to back our claims that the investment is worthwhile. It is our role as educators to advocate for education, to make a claim for the allocation of social resources required in order to meet expanding expectations.

On learning and education

What is this thing 'education' – a concept that is now so prominent in public conversation? The word has traditionally been used with reference to three things.

First, education refers to *institutions*, which first appeared along with the emergence of writing as a tool for public administration (to train, for instance, 'mandarins' or public officials in imperial China, or the writers of cuneiform in ancient Mesopotamia/Iraq); to support religions founded on sacred texts (the Islamic *madrasa*, or the Christian monastery); and to transmit formally developed knowledge and wisdom (the Academy of ancient Athens, or Confucian teaching in China).

It should be said that before the invention of writing the speakers of first or indigenous languages had elaborate education systems – processes by which oral tradition was remembered, spirituality inculcated and the laws of the human and natural world taught. However, the roots of modern educational institutions can be traced to the invention of writing.

Until recently, the practice of institutionalised education, and of writing, was meant to be for the few. It was only in the past two centuries in the West, and in the 20th century in developing nations, that education began to take its modern, universal, compulsory, mass-institutional form: now immediately recognisable in almost every corner of the Earth. When politicians say they are going to support education, they almost always have institution building in mind – new or extended schools, colleges or universities in the forms that have emerged to dominance everywhere in the world over the past two centuries.

Second, education refers to *curriculum*: the substantive content of learning and its organisation as subjects and topics.

Third, education refers to *pedagogy*, or the planned and deliberate process whereby one person helps another to learn. This is what first peoples did through various formalised rites of passage, from child to adult to elder – learning law, spirituality and nature. It is also how teachers in the era of modern, mass-institutionalised education have organised the learners in their classrooms and their learning.

This three-part meaning of education connects several related concepts – 'pedagogy', or the microdynamics of moments of teaching and learning; 'curriculum', or the learning designs for particular areas of knowledge; and the overall institutional setting in which pedagogy and curriculum are located.

Bringing these three aspects of education together as something that can be known, analysed, configured and reconfigured, is the *science of education*: a discipline or body of knowledge about learning and teaching – about how these practices are organised, theorised, in different times, from different political and empirical perspectives. This is education as a subject of study, analysis and transformation.

And what of 'learning'? Learning is much bigger than education. Humans are born with an innate capacity to learn, and over the span of a lifetime learning never stops. Learning simply happens as people engage with each other, interact with the natural world and move about in the world they have built. Indeed, one of the things that makes us distinctively human is our enormous capacity to learn.

Other species learn, too; from the tiniest of insects to the smartest of chimpanzees.[6] But none has institutions of education, practices of pedagogy or underpinning knowledge foundations that might be called 'disciplines' or 'sciences'. As a consequence, the main way in which other species develop over time is through the incremental, biological adaptations of evolution. Change is natural. It is slow.

Education makes human learning unlike the learning of any other creature. Learning allows humans to escape some of the determinations of nature. It gives humans the resources with which to understand themselves and their world, and to transform their conditions of living, for better or for worse.[7]

Education is a peculiarly human capacity to nurture learning in a conscious way, and to create social contexts that have been specially designed for that purpose – the institutions of education. Within the institutions of education, curriculum is a consciously designed framework for learning a body of knowledge, be that a discipline or a coherent set of social competencies or capacities. And within curriculum, pedagogy is the conscious creation of activities to facilitate learning.

Everyday learning happens naturally, everywhere and all the time. Education – the institution, its curriculum and its pedagogies – is learning by design.

What's 'new' about 'New Learning'?

In part, this book describes education today – what goes on in schools, the role of the professional teacher, what it is like to work in a school as an organisation, the psychology of learners, the job of instructional design, how to manage a classroom and the assessment of learner outcomes. These are the practices of education today, built on the familiar foundations of our yesterdays.

However, we also want to consider a renewed mission for education in these 'interesting times'. Huge changes are afoot, in the world outside of formal educational institutions and in the kinds of learners that fill those institutions. Perhaps at times the people who manage and staff the institutions of education do not feel a need to change. But often they do need to, whether they feel that need or not.

Hence, the idea of 'New Learning'. In order to build a view of what's happening in education today, we need a broader view of learning – of what people need to know and do in the contemporary world outside the walls of formal educational institutions, regardless of what their teachers might consider good for them in their usual teaching practices, and beyond what practitioners of the discipline of education might be in the habit of prescribing from their books of received wisdom. New Learning is located in that peculiar territory of anticipation, where a 'might' becomes a 'can', becomes a 'should', becomes a 'will', and maybe, all being well, eventually becomes an 'is'.

Here are eight dimensions of learning today that may prompt us to formulate a theory and practice of New Learning.

Dimension 1: The social significance of education

When our political leaders use the rhetoric of the 'new economy' and 'knowledge society', they tell of a large and significant social transition. Knowledge is now a key factor of production: an economic and thus social fundamental. All the talk of the 'knowledge economy' moves education to the heart of the system, as a crucial part of the fabric of economic and social progress. This applies to individuals as much as it does to economic and political society – more than ever, education serves as an essential ingredient of personal ambition and success, even a key determinant of one's earning capacity.[8] It is also presented by political and community leaders as a mechanism for ensuring social equity, so the 'have-nots' get a chance to achieve the success that was previously limited to the 'haves'.

Dimension 2: The institutional locations of learning

More and more learning is happening outside of traditional educational institutions – on the job, at play, through the media, on the World Wide Web. This produces a crisis of relevance for schools, colleges and universities. They have long been the sites of pedagogies that 'teach about' the wider 'outside world'; for instance, through the sciences of the natural environment or the geographies of human communities. The school curriculum divides the world into subjects that take on the appearance of being self-sufficient, rather than the partial and specific views of the world that they are. And when this world is changing so rapidly, the disconnect between content and the world itself grows ever greater. This is not to say that educators should second-guess the specifics of the future to make their subjects more directly relevant – that is near-impossible and indeed not the point. Rather, institutionalised education needs to become less of a site for 'learning about' bodies of content knowledge, and more a set of experiences of 'learning in and for' a world whose future shape we cannot predict. In order to become relevant once more, educational institutions should reappraise the traditional boundaries of discipline content, perhaps moving to teach through new modes and subject configurations, to recognise and accredit things that have been learnt outside of the program and classroom, and to take their teaching mission outside the comfort zones and habits of their institutions.

Dimension 3: The tools of learning

The new media that have transformed so much of our personal, community and working lives require a change in the tools of the teaching trade. In the past, education systems have been relatively slow to respond to the new media, let alone to lead the way in their development and the development of innovations in teaching and learning. Since the turn of the new century there has been a flurry of activity around the role of 'ICT' (information and communications technology) in schools, but not yet to the extent that the new media are being used to promote discernible changes in the mainstream schooling experience. Distance learning, learning at home and work, community integrated learning, learning with other learners who are not sitting in the same classroom – the new media allow us to blur the boundaries that neatly enclosed traditional classrooms and learning institutions. Amongst the new tools, the digital learning media loom large, presaging a change that could be as large and as revolutionary as the mass application of the classroom in earlier modern times – itself a learning architecture and communications technology. [*See*: One Laptop Per Child.[9]]

Dimension 4: The outcomes of learning

What kinds of capacity will the New Learning promote? Compared to the form of learning that is characteristic of our recent past, the New Learning is about learning by doing as well as learning by thinking: about the capacity to be productive in the world as well as knowing that world; about action as well as cognition. If the older learning tended to be individualised and cognitive (with educational performance measured by the stuff in one's head that gives one a competitive advantage, in exams, then jobs, then life), the New Learning adds the dimensions of practical capability and collaborative social learning so that thinking is also connected with an ability to act and to be adaptable, responsive and flexible in a world of diversity and change. One can be a resilient individual, but that resilience has to connect with the sophisticated sociability of collaborative learning, group work, emotional empathy and an holistic understanding of the global as well as local consequences of one's actions. The New Learning anticipates a different kind of learner.

Dimension 5: The balance of agency

The 'balance of agency' refers to the mix of teacher and learner subjectivities in the learning process. In the learning of the earlier modern past, teachers told and asked, and learners listened and answered. Syllabuses and textbooks presented the contents of the disciplines, which learners recounted in tests – getting it 'right' or 'wrong'. The balance of agency was heavily skewed towards the knowledge authorities of teacher, curriculum designer and textbook writer. The teacher's subjectivity was dominant; the learner's was subservient. This *seemed* right for a world in which bosses were bossy, political and military heroes led, the mass media propagandised, we consumed mass-produced commodities supposed to be good for us, cultural icons were revered and narratives were to be listened to and appreciated. It no longer seems so right in a world in which agency rather than obedience is becoming regarded as a key to economic and social achievement. The New Learning affords a shift in the balance of agency in the same direction that is evident in the world at large. This is an evening-up of balance, so that learners are as much makers of their own knowledge as the receivers of it, and teachers are designers of learning as much as they are knowledge experts. In fact, what teachers do in the New Learning is to 'design-in' a greater share of learner responsibility for learning and learners for each other in the learning process. This helps to form the sorts of subjectivities that are effective in a world in which workplaces use teamwork and a self-motivating workplace culture to get the best out of people, in which we need to take responsibility for our own level of civic participation, in which we can choose our own interpretations of the world from hundreds and thousands of media channels, in which we are fussy about what we consume, in which (in video games, for instance) we have become characters in the narrative who can influence its outcomes, and in which there is a pressing need for a proactive and critical 'take' on the way we live our lives and interact with our environment. As the balance of agency shifts within the broader society, schools and their teachers need to transform the most basic terms of pedagogical engagement to make a useful contribution to the emerging social world. Indeed, teachers may not have much choice but to change the fundamentals of their pedagogy if they are not to frustrate and bore young learners whose dispositions are very different to the children and young people of earlier generations. [*See*: James Gee, Video Games are Good for Your Soul.[10]]

Dimension 6: The significance of difference

One of the most striking aspects of this shift in the balance of agency is the increasing significance of differences amongst learners to the process of learning. By collectivising individual learner subjectivities under the label of 'pupil' and having all 'pupils' move through the curriculum at the same pace, all doing the same things, and forcing pupils to move towards a norm or standard, earlier modern schooling tried to maintain a veneer of sameness. To a large extent, however, and somewhat ironically, it achieved this veneer by creating a form of difference; by ranking learners against an average or norm, such that many learners – those who fell 'below' the 'norm' – literally failed. When we take subjectivity and agency into account, we encounter a panoply of human differences that cannot be ignored in the configuration of educational experiences – material (class, locale), corporeal (age, race, sex and sexuality, physical and mental characteristics) and symbolic (culture, language, gender, family, affinity, persona). In fact, not dealing with difference means excluding those who don't fit the norm. It means ineffectiveness, inefficiencies and thus wasted resources in a form of teaching that does not engage with each and every learner in a way that optimises his or her performance outcomes. It also cheats the learners who happen to do well: those whose learning styles and habits happen to be accommodated in the one-size-suits-all curriculum, by limiting their exposure to the intellectual and personal experience of cultural differences and different ways of knowing so integral to the contemporary world.

Dimension 7: The relation of the new to the old

Notwithstanding the trajectory of change, one of the peculiar things about the New Learning is that none of the old has gone away. Didactic teaching of subjects-in-themselves is alive and well today in the form of 'back to basics' curriculum, teaching to standardised tests, stimulus–response approaches to e-learning, and in teaching fundamentalist religious doctrine: a 'back to the future' view of what we need to do to address the difficulties of our times and the uncertainties of our future. These are as much features of education today, indeed are more dominant in many educational systems, as is the New Learning. Sometimes, what is presented as new is in fact old; and sometimes what is presented as traditional is new insofar as it is a reaction to contemporary social anxieties. Didactic teaching may at times even still have a place. There may be moments when it is appropriate. Rote learning, for instance, may still work, at least in part, at certain times and in certain places for certain kinds of knowledge. Moreover, insofar as didactic teaching may be connected with some traditional cultures, in a society that values social pluralism, we are obliged to respect it, so long as it does not disadvantage learners or produce outcomes that are incompatible with democratic pluralism itself. Moments of older learning are, in other words, an integral part of the world of the New Learning.

Dimension 8: The professional role of the teacher

To juggle all these relations – of agency, diversity, learning outcomes, institutional locations – this is the challenge for the new teaching professional. And 'professional' is the operative word. The 'old' teacher was constructed as a person who habitually took and followed orders; whether as a public servant or member of a religious order. The new teacher is an autonomous, highly skilled, responsible manager of student learning. The old teacher shut the door of the classroom and, apart from the periodic visit from an 'inspector', this was his or her private fiefdom. The new teacher is both grounded in the community and a corporate player, a collaborator and a member of a self-regulating profession. The old teacher was an instrument in a bureaucratic system or religious hierarchy. The new teacher is not simply a public servant or someone bound by bureaucratic accountabilities, but a learner – a designer of learning environments, an evaluator of their effectiveness, a researcher, a social scientist and an intellectual in their own right.

Designs for social futures

Our picture of the New Learning emerges as we trace contemporary trends in education. In this sense, it is an evolving description. However, it is also a series of prescriptive ideas, suggestions about the ways we might do things differently in education. It is an agenda for the future of education, requiring the creation of educational systems that are in many respects very different from those of the recent past, and the formation of professionals with new skills and sensibilities. The New Learning suggests we develop strategies to meet the needs of communities of learners living in social conditions that are changing dramatically.

Precisely what shape will the New Learning take? No single answer to this question is possible. In this respect, our proposal for the New Learning is a series of open possibilities and agendas in the plural. 'What might we do?' That is the question. Even asking the question puts the educator in a quite definite position as an engaged intellectual and professional. Any answer is contingent on a whole set of factors that require purposeful and deliberative responses designed to meet learner aspirations. We explore alternatives as this book unfolds and in our practices try out a range of possibilities, wherever we are.

Professional educators of tomorrow will not be people who simply enact received systems, standards, organisational structures and professional ethics. In this time of extraordinary social transformation and uncertainty, educators need to consider themselves to be designers of social futures, to search out new ways to address the learning needs of our society, and in so doing to position education at an inarguably central place in society. In fact, powerful educational ideas – about how people act and build knowledge in context and in collaboration with others, for instance – could well become leading social ideas in currently more privileged areas of endeavour, such as business and technology. Perhaps, if we can succeed at putting education at the heart of the designs for society's future, we might even be able to succeed in our various campaigns to ensure that education is just, empowering, creative and adequately resourced.

The mission of educators is the mission of this book. Our case is built on the proposition that we are on the cusp of a revolution in education that will change at the core the structures of its institutions, the practices of its professionals and the experiences of learners. Some of this is happening now in the opening decades of the 21st century. Some of it may take decades to evolve. Whatever direction the revolution takes, professional educators must position themselves as significant players – imagining alternative scenarios and designing and testing alternatives. Educators will also need to become advocates in the public arena and within their educational communities in order to make sure that their new designs for education work demonstrably, to get the recognition and resources they need, and to be sure that their innovations take firm institutional hold.

In order to make our case for a New Learning, we will tell stories that trace the broad trajectory of educational change. Although we go back further than this at times, the primary reference point will be our earlier modern past. Learners of this recent past experienced a novel, mass social phenomenon: a peculiar world of classes, and lessons, and teacher talk, and textbooks, and activities, and tests, and marks, and school reports. Roughly speaking, this began to happen on a mass scale in the now-developed countries in the 19th century and the now-developing countries in the 20th century. We will go back and examine these experiences, not because they could be considered an inevitable part of the human experience, but because they are so recent, and at the time were so novel. Nor do we examine them to disparage them, as though we should throw out all of the old to make way for the new. Rather, we need to go back and consider them again because our educational habits can all too easily cloud our vision of what is possible, what a New Learning could be like. It's too easy to regard our own experiences and the experiences of our modern past as universal, permanent and inevitable. They are not. It is easy to think we are doing something new because we are using new tools, or seem to have broken out of the four walls of the traditional classroom. But the pedagogy we are using may still be deeply influenced by an earlier age. [*See*: The Fun They Had.[11]]

For many learners today, earlier modern or industrial-age schooling is still a reality, anachronistically in places in which the industrial age itself has now mostly passed, and where work and community life are heading in the direction of the 'knowledge economy'. Such heritage education is also to be found in places in which people still live off the land and have barely joined the industrial age, in the so-called 'developing' world. There may be little other alternative in those places in terms of the skills of the teachers, the facilities available and the legacy understandings of education in the wider community. But the education that the learners are getting in these conditions may not serve their best interests in the imminent future.

The danger is that if schools do not change in some fundamental ways, they may find themselves mired in a crisis of declining credibility. Children and young people are astute, and their senses of boredom, frustration and irrelevance will translate into 'discipline' problems and truancy. Parents may come to realise that these schools are not working for their children, and if they can afford it, they'll be scouring the market for alternatives that seem to be worth the money. Not that these parents' judgements will always be correct. Paradoxically, they may often end up choosing schools whose back-to-the-future air of discipline and rigour reminds them of their own school days – contemporary versions, in other words, of an earlier era of schooling. These parents may end up disappointed if and when these schools do not deliver what is appropriate to the contemporary world.

Meanwhile, employers may find themselves complaining about the quality of new entrants to the labour force. These employers might not be able to articulate terribly well what's wrong with the young people coming out of school. They may only be able to express it in terms of superficial symptoms, such as the failure of the school to teach spelling and grammar, but may nevertheless correctly sense a deeper problem.

However inchoate the community arguments at times, the complaints seem to be more deeply felt today. Education faces a crisis of public confidence. If professional educators do not take a lead in the revolution in education, they will find other forces in the community taking the lead, and the outcomes may not be what they expect or consider best from a professional point of view. As a profession, teachers and their professional organisations need to take a clear and prominent stand in this debate, as advocates for the transformation of our institutions of education.

It is easier to chart the territory of the past and heritage teaching practices than it is to predict the future. We can describe the old teaching more easily than we can articulate the New Learning. The familiar shape of the old teaching is easier to capture in our mind's eye than something that is still emerging and uncertain. If the future is unsure, old teaching is a rock of certainty to which we may feel we can safely retreat. Except, of course, if we find that retreat is no answer, and that a back-to-the-future approach does not really solve the fundamental problems faced today in schools and their communities.

The New Learning we are proposing is not a destination, but a challenging journey. The debate about our educational futures is so volatile and stoops at times to such populist depths, that we can't be sure how the coming revolution in education will unfold and what shape the New Learning will take. The consequence is that the New Learning is not an agenda that can be clearly formulated; still less a specific prescription. Rather, our New Learning is an open call to read the transformations going on in the world, to imagine the corresponding transformations that may need to go on in education, and to plan ways in which educators might lead these transformations rather than fall victim to changes over which they feel they have little or no control.

Summary

Changing education	The modern past: Mass-institutional education	More recent times: 'Progressive' educational modernisation	New learning: Innovations anticipating the near future
Dimension 1: The social significance of education	. . . always important in imparting basic skills and social discipline.	. . . more important as an economic force, as a path to participation and as a means of personal enablement.	. . . a central part of the emerging 'knowledge society'.
Dimension 2: The institutional locations of learning	. . . located mainly in formal institutions – schools, colleges and universities.	. . . happening more and more outside of formal institutions.	. . . something that happens everywhere: at work, at play, through the media; mixing formal, semi-formal and informal learning.
Dimension 3: The tools of learning	. . . based on tools of teacher talk, textbooks and student workbooks.	. . . using a broader range of instructional media.	. . . communicated in part though new media – such as the Internet and other new media – that don't need the students to be in the classroom and 'on the same page'.
Dimension 4: The outcomes of learning	. . . grounded in subject content, the things you know.	. . . increasingly focused on learning how to learn.	. . . grounded in capabilities, or the things you can do, including the capacity to find out what you don't know.
Dimension 5: The balance of agency	. . . a relationship of authority in which teacher and text transmit knowledge to learners.	. . . a relationship in which learners are more actively engaged.	. . . a relationship in which teachers facilitate active knowledge making by learners.
Dimension 6: The significance of difference	. . . a place where one-size-fits-all curriculum seemed easiest and best.	. . . a place where differences are increasingly recognised.	. . . a place where it is clear that effective teaching for learner differences makes a difference in outcomes.
Dimension 7: The relation of the new to the old	. . . an institution that was quite consistent and predictable.	. . . an institution that is challenged by the increasing variety of approaches to education.	. . . a series of places where there are many forms of learning, new as well as revived versions of older learning approaches.
Dimension 8: The professional role of the teacher	. . . a workplace where teachers were loyal workers who took orders and taught the curricula they were given.	. . . a workplace where teachers are expected to take more responsibilities.	. . . a workplace of responsible, self-managing professionals, who are also intellectuals and social scientists.

Notes

1. Kalantzis 2004; Peters and Beasley 2006.
2. Cope and Kalantzis. 1997a.
3. See a sample of political leaders speaking at NewLearningOnline.com
4. Organisation for Economic Cooperation and Development (OECD) 2003
5. OECD 2005
6. Deacon 1997
7. Christian 2004
8. OECD 2005
9. http://laptop.org/ See extract at NewLearningOnline.com
10. Gee 2005. See extract at NewLearningOnline.com
11. Asimov 1951 (1973). See extract at NewLearningOnline.com

Chapter 2

Life in schools

Overview

*This chapter characterises three different kinds of educational experience –
didactic, authentic and transformative.*

*Didactic education is relatively old, with roots as old as writing. However, it comes
to global and near-universal prominence as the primary mode of learning in the mass-
institutionalised education that emerged almost everywhere in the world in the 19th
and 20th centuries. The experience of didactic education is still common today, for
a variety of social, cultural and, at times, practical reasons. Mass, institutionalised
education allowed parents to work while schools took care of children, imparting the
basics of reading and writing, but perhaps more importantly inculcating in children
a sense of discipline and order. Didactic teaching had teachers and textbooks telling,
and learners getting their lessons right or wrong. In the didactic classroom, the
teacher established a pattern of relationships in which students learnt to accept
received facts and moral truths, to comply with commands given by the teacher and
to absorb the knowledge authority of the curriculum. In these classroom settings,
they learnt to get used to a balance of agency in which they were relatively powerless
to act autonomously or to make knowledge themselves.*

*Authentic education movements emerged in the 20th century, in part as a reac-
tion to the culture of order and control characteristic of didactic education. The
major principles of authentic education are that learners should take a more active
part in their learning, and that this learning should be closely and practically connected to their life experiences. Authentic education is more child-centred, focusing
on internalised understanding beyond formal repetition of the 'right' answers. But*

17

does it necessarily have the effect of changing a child's life chances? Or is it at times overly 'practical', accepting that unequal life chances are inevitable? Authentic education's critics argue that, all too often, it does not fulfil the promise of education.

Transformative education focuses on the learner and learning. As such, it sets out deliberately to transform students' life chances and play an active role in changing social conditions. It changes the balance of agency in learning relationships by encouraging learners to build their own knowledge in a supportive learning environment, to work with others in lateral knowledge-making relationships (peers, parents and community members), to negotiate local and global differences, and to extend the breadth and scope of their education beyond the walls of the traditional classroom.

Understanding these educational traditions matters in part because each is woven, sometimes unconsciously, into everyday classroom practices. Educators should know the power of each, its historic and cultural purposes, when and how to deploy it, and when it works or when it fails learners and society.

Thinking of change, thinking of paradigms

A paradigm is a model, a way of viewing reality, or a worldview. This book analyses education in terms of three educational paradigms. In this chapter, we call these paradigms 'didactic', 'authentic' and 'transformative' education. The paradigms are presented roughly in the order in which they first appeared on the educational scene. However, we don't want to give the impression that this is a neatly ordered progression. We trace the general trajectory of change, and use only the broadest of brushstrokes to render the complexities of history manageable. More importantly, we regard these three paradigms as alternative ways of thinking about education. At any point in time and in any educational setting, not everything will fit neatly into one or other paradigm.

In building a picture of the paradigms, we have constructed a model, an abstraction of three broad kinds of educational experience, in order to make the educational story we are telling easier to navigate. The overall story may be one of gradual and uneven change. However, all three paradigms are alive and well today, in the imaginations of educators and the communities they serve, and in the complexities of our educational practices.

Didactic education: The modern past

The bell has just rung and the children begin to file into the classroom, 30 or so of them. 'Quietly,' says the teacher, as they make their way to their places. Watching over the scene, she stands beside her desk on a small platform at the front of the room.

The children's desks are in straight rows, bolted to the floor. They all sit and face the teacher, and the teacher surveys the little sea of faces, eye to eye, one to all and all to one. The walls are bare except for some lettering charts and a map supplied by the Department of Education.

'Sit up straight, children. Be quiet. Open your grammar textbooks at page . . .'

Such a scene has been the repeated experience of most children since the advent of mass-institutionalised education. Some children have cried inconsolably at the first sight of their school, later reconciling themselves to its structures and strictures. Others have reacted to the peculiar goings-on of the classroom with a mixture of fear and anger and irony, daydreaming of better things, or making their own mark on the place by carving their name into the desk, or 'mucking up'.

'Today we are doing . . . nouns and verbs.'

The door is closed. This is the teacher's private space, her own fiefdom. 'My classroom,' she says. 'Our teacher,' say the students, in deference to her authority.

'A noun is a naming word. A verb is a doing word.'

She writes this neatly on the board, under the date. This is the lesson for the day.

'Now, let's all say this together,' she says.

'A noun is a naming word. A verb is a doing word.'

The class recites in unison, in that funny singsong lilt children seem to have invented just for teachers. The kids who are mucking up can be sure the lilt is sarcasm. The others are just sweetly singing what they imagine must be the teacher's tune.

'Harry, give me an example of a verb.'

Harry recoils in horror. He had chanted the chant but his mind was elsewhere, hoping that the law of one in 30 would spare him cross-examination just one more time. But it hasn't, and his number's up.

'Umm . . . I don't know an example', he splutters, ' . . . Miss'.

Inwardly, he fears, 'she'll fail me', and 'the other kids will think I'm dumb'.

'Then can somebody else give me an example of a verb?'

Judy shoots up her hand.

'Yes, Judy.'

'Run is a verb. The fox runs. Runs is what the fox is doing,' she says in triumph. Judy's good at the game of schooling and plays to win.

'Yes, well done, Judy.'

Such is her momentary victory, a manifest triumph of one over 30. Judy doesn't need to know what verbs are going to do in her life. It's the moment of symbolic victory that matters.

And so the class continues.

This kind of teaching we call 'didactic', a word which finds its way into English from the Greek 'to teach'. At times, it still has a relatively neutral meaning, when one speaks of teaching methods – 'foreign-language didactics' or 'music didactics'.

In English, however, its meaning has also come to have a particular loading. Being didactic means to spell things out explicitly but perhaps a little too laboriously, or to present a view of what seems true or right or moral, but in a way that at times sounds dogmatic. So, the teacher tells and the learner listens. Didactic teaching turns on what the teacher says rather than what the learner does. The balance of agency weighs heavily towards the teacher's side. The teacher is in command of knowledge. Their mission is to transmit this knowledge to learners, and learners, it is hoped, dutifully absorb the knowledge laid before them by the teacher. 'Didactic' implies a heavy handed 'teacherliness'.

Not that this is always a bad thing. In fact, being explicit can be an effective way of teaching. There are often times when clear instructions from the teacher remove ambiguity and provide a useful way forward for a learner.

Didactic education was, until the recent past, the dominant educational experience for the majority of school students. In fact, it remains dominant in many places. Modern, mass-institutionalised education is only now reaching the poorest parts of the world. When school finally does arrive in these places, its primary mode in the first instance is likely to be didactic, usually because of limited resources and teacher training. And even in those places in which modern, mass-institutionalised education has been around for a long time, didactic education lives on. We'd hazard a guess that most classrooms in the world today operate more or less in the didactic mode for a fair proportion of the school day. Maybe the desks have been unbolted from the floor and some of the children's work has been displayed on the wall as small concessions to a newer way of learning, but teachers in many of today's schools still perform to the script of didactic teaching.

At its worst, didactic teaching is dreadfully predictable and deadeningly banal. However, even in New Learning contexts, the didactic mode may sometimes have a place – in certain places and for certain moments, at least. That moment might be when a learner enters a new, well-established and authoritative area of knowledge. When you're beginning quantum mechanics, there's no point in trying to argue with it. It's best to listen to the teacher, at least until you get your head around it. Didactic teaching may also have its place in areas of learning that require reverence in particular communities, such as fundamentalist readings of religious texts. In order to be a person of manifest faith in some cultural settings, you need to absorb the messages presented by the text; not to question them. Or didactic education may be a useful method at certain moments for dealing with particular subject matters – learning by rote vocabulary items of a foreign language, the periodic table or mathematical formulae, for instance. Or it may be the stamp of integrity of a school that prides itself on a certain kind of rigour and discipline, where teachers get straight to the point and deliver directly to the tests that supply credentials for conventional success. This may work, or at least be seen to work by anxious parents. In other words, didactic teaching may be a part of the practical world of New Learning, a world of varied approaches to teaching, diverse learning styles and cultural pluralism.

To analyse the nature and form of didactic education, we will examine eight dimensions: *architectonic, discursive, intersubjective, socio-cultural, proprietary, epistemological, pedagogical* and *moral*. These dimensions help us understand the design and form of education in a comprehensive and rounded way.[1] Each dimension has been selected because it sheds light on a key component of the experience of teaching and learning – location and space, communication, identity and relationships, personal backgrounds, power, ways of knowing, ways of teaching and ethics.

Dimension 1: Architectonic meanings are those expressed by a physical setting; they are the spatial designs that shape the way people relate to each other.

Dimension 2: Discursive meanings are expressed through the patterns of person-to-person communication.

Dimension 3: Intersubjective meanings are created in the interaction of one person's will – their interests, motivations and drives – with another.

Dimension 4: Socio-cultural meanings emerge from the ways in which a person's life experiences are negotiated in a particular setting.

Dimension 5: Proprietary meanings are formed in relationships of ownership and control.

Dimension 6: Epistemological meanings are those arising from the ways in which knowledge is represented and created.

Dimension 7: Pedagogical meanings are the ways of making knowledge that are configured in learning relationships.

Dimension 8: Moral meanings underlie the establishment of a balance of power between those who control and those who are controlled.

Together, these dimensions help us explain how education is understood, planned, delivered and experienced.

Dimension 1: Architectonic

Here we are in a physically bounded space, having divided however many children in the school into groups of 30 or so and putting them into more-or-less identical boxes – their classrooms. This is an architecture created to serve a communications design. The room is big enough for this many children to listen to the teacher without the need for audio amplification, and for the teacher to be able to talk over them all when they need to be silenced. There's something about ratios in the rough range of one to 20 and one to 40 – this seems to provide the optimum efficiency range for teacher–learner interaction in the traditional classroom. Any more and the class is too big to manage; any fewer and too many teachers need to be hired. So, the teacher stands at the front of the class and the learners face the teacher. This spatial arrangement shapes the nature of interactions and the system of teaching. The desks are set up to ensure eye contact from each student to the one teacher. Student-to-student contact is in lateral vision and not to be encouraged – knowing glances perhaps to another kid who may be tempted to pursue some tangential interest, or even to muck up, perhaps as an exhibition of defiance of the teacher's authority or to embroil you as co-conspirator. Or you might look askance out of temptation to 'copy' another learner's work or check where they are up to. Whatever the motive, there's an air of the forbidden in lateral views. The proper view is to look to the teacher – many to one – so their authority can be heeded – one to many. The overall feeling of this classroom, the way it works for learners and the way the teacher operates, is determined to a significant degree by the way its space is configured. This is how the classroom space more or less does its educational and social job. These bounded, physical structures frame a particular set of educational and social purposes.

Dimension 2: Discursive

Teaching – and this didactic mode of teaching, in particular – is the talking profession. Teacher–learner talk, however, is an unequal exchange. The teacher starts the classroom conversation by way of exposition. 'Today we are going to . . .', followed by a lecture in which she tells the learners what she knows and what they are supposed to know. She engages the students via question-and-answer routines. Often, they are 'guess what's in the teacher's head' routines, as strange and counter-intuitive as her hoped-for answers, once revealed, often seem. Only one student can speak at any one time. 'Put up your hands. One person at a time, please.' Or the whole class recites in unison. 'Say after me . . .'. Or the students quietly do their work, reading or writing. Or the students take a test – in another, eerier kind of silence – in which they will do well or badly, depending on whether they have managed to figure out the tricks of the arcane game of multiple choice, or whether they have been able to second-guess what the assessing teacher wants to hear. For most of the day, even the most voluble of students sit in silence; unless, that is, they decide to break the communicative protocols of the place. 'Shoosh, quiet please.' 'Talking in class' is a phrase of approbation, and if excessive, deserving of punishment. In the corner of the room? Outside in the corridor? A trip to the headmaster's office? Lateral peer-to-peer communication is unmanageable in a practical sense, and when it does occur, it is most likely considered to be 'off task'. Quite simply, this classroom discourse is teacher-dominated and presented in the standard form of the single official language, with no concession to the home languages or dialects of the learners. The teacher orchestrates all conversational turn-taking, expecting the few responses that come from students to be within a narrowly prescribed range (getting the responses she expects, her 'right' answers). [*See*: Winston Churchill's School Days.[2]]

Dimension 3: Intersubjective

In the didactic educational experience, the teacher's will must prevail. The best student is the silent, bodily constrained, undifferentiated, listening student; or the student who answers the question in the right way; or the student who doesn't miss mouthing a word in the whole-class recitation; or the student who quietly does the work without talking to the kid beside them – surely, that can only be because they want to copy the neighbour or talk about something off-task. Communication with other students is limited by the teacher's directions, as are movement and touch. Their incentives are rewards. The teacher says, as a sign of approval – 'Good boy, well done'. Or the reward is the good marks the student might get in the end. Alternatively, there's immediate and direct punishment for transgressing the rules of the intersubjective game, or just bad marks, which speak for themselves. [*See*: Yan Pho Lee's School Days.[3]]

Dimension 4: Socio-cultural

The teacher in the didactically ordered classroom does their work as though all students' backgrounds are the same, or can be assumed to be the same, or, with the good influences of uniform education, can be made more or less the same. The teacher talks to the middle of class, hoping that the 'above-average' kids will not get too bored and the 'below-average' kids will pick up enough to be engaged and learn something. All the students should be on the same page – literally. They should all do the same work and move ahead at the same pace. All students should cover the same content, doing the same activities in the same way and sitting for the same test at the end. And this, regardless of who they are, what they know already, what their interests are, what their motivations and aspirations are. The key to the traditional classroom is simultaneity. One-to-many is easiest if it's one to 30 identically replicated learning experiences – doing the same thing at the same time. If the students are not the same, the least the school can do is operate on the wishful thinking that for all practical purposes they are the same, and if they are not, influence them to be the same by treating them the same, rewarding 'good work' and 'right answers'. In this context, divergence from the ideal norm is seen to be deviant or to represent a deficit in some way. [*See*: George Orwell's School Days.[4]]

Dimension 5: Proprietary

'My classroom,' says the teacher, meaning a private space within which she is in control of 30 or so learners. Except for the occasional 'inspection' and the marks sent home to parents at the end of the year, this is a barely examined space. There are no parents, no other teachers, no students other than the 30 in her charge, no public documentation of what goes on in the classroom other than teacher grades on the student's report card and the odd piece of work that a student may take home. And 'my work', says the student. 'No copying please,' says the teacher as a precaution against the learner's collaborative instincts. 'In your own words' is the instruction when a student is tempted to copy a text that seems to have already struck the right chord. The student's work is individualised and private. Each produces their assignment or completes the test for an audience of one, the assessing teacher. The main official or public trace of the student's work is a recorded score. Thus, power is exercised by the authorised teacher, the behaviour protocols established and the forms of curriculum and assessment they impose.

Dimension 6: Epistemological

Teachers and textbooks tell students the facts, rules and theories of disciplinary knowledge. 'Verbs are doing words.' 'The Normans conquered England in 1066.' 'The square of the length of the hypotenuse of a right-angled triangle equals the sum of the squares of the lengths of the other two sides.' This is knowledge, pure and simple, singular and uncontroversial. It is neatly divided into 'subjects', disciplines that are complete in themselves and systematically arranged from what is regarded as the easier stuff to the harder stuff. Just as neatly as it is compartmentalised by theme, each subject is placed into temporal cells in the grid arrangement of the school timetable. So, at the appointed time at each designated stage in the unfolding of a discipline, teachers present authoritatively, textbooks tell definitively, students repeat in unison. Student work regurgitates these hopefully well-received truths, and the test is final proof of what they've learnt and what they haven't. Then, on to the next bit. Little or no time is left for learners to make knowledge, even to inject a perspective or idea of their own, except when their minds wander into daydreams or their pens into doodles. Writing is privileged as a knowledge source. And the source of definitive knowledge is clear from the direction of knowledge flows, the origins of the written text and the writer–reader authority relations that follow – from the syllabus, to the textbook, to the teacher, to the learner. The sources of written authority are people outside of the sphere of learner activity, and outside of the classroom. 'Know as others say you should know,' is the underlying message. To remove any possibility of transgression, the student's knowledge has to be verified by the teacher's test (measured against the teacher's exposition and the textbook), or the external examination (measured against the system-mandated syllabus). This is a 'transmission' approach to knowledge. It is an approach, moreover, which assumes that definitive disciplinary knowledge can be learnt once and is sufficiently durable to be learnt for life. The underlying assumption is that disciplinary knowledge, and the society it serves, is relatively stable. So, when your formal education is over, you will have learnt just about all you'll need from the institutions of education. Engagement and performance are thus narrowly prescribed. The rest you can safely learn in the school of life. [*See*: Charles Darwin's School Days.[5]]

Dimension 7: Pedagogical

In the traditional classroom of mass, institutionalised education, students are receivers and absorbers of knowledge. It is presupposed that learning is

memory work, absorbing facts, rules and 'correct' answers by rote. School knowledge is a kind of shopping list of things-to-be-known. The teacher is a didact,
the mouthpiece of official knowledge. So students drill 'times tables', memorise
spelling lists and learn by rote the facts and dates of history for regurgitation
in tests. When something is actually learnt, it is often because the learner has
been more active than the pedagogue would care to admit in connecting the presented knowledge with thier own identities and destinies. [*See*: Audre Lorde's
School Days.[6]]

Dimension 8: Moral

The architectonics of classroom space, the discourse of classroom talk, the intersubjective patterns of reward and punishment, the socio-cultural dynamics of
sameness, the proprietary spaces of teacher and student work, the epistemology
of knowledge transmission and the pedagogy of didactic presentation – these all
add up to a certain kind of moral economy. They amount to a set of practical
relationships of social interchange with moral force. It seems hard to argue with
the fact that, in this particular classroom and this particular school, that's the way
things are and have to be. And, it always seems (at least within a narrow frame
of reference), with good cause. The moral economy of didactic education might
be considered inappropriate and ineffectual today (which it certainly is at some
times, in some respects, for some students), but it has always had a rhyme and reason, a practical rationale behind its design. If the underlying lesson of the didactic
teaching is about the nature of knowledge (accepting received truths unquestioningly), then it was a lesson appropriate for a society that expected its workers
to take the supervisor's orders at work, its citizens to conform and its wives to
obey their husbands at home. Much of the time, however, didactic teaching does
not even achieve this. More often than not, and for the majority of students, its
classrooms are experienced as places of passivity, boredom and failure. However,
even this makes a certain kind of sense. Perversely perhaps, poor results at school
serve as a kind of moral lesson. They happen to serve a greater good. The lessons
of failure are absolutely learnt if you end up in a job that is drearily unskilled, not
requiring much beyond work discipline and the capacity to put up with boredom.
If that's where you end up, it must have been your own fault for not doing better
at school, or so the conventional story of school results would have you believe.
To live a good life is to know your place in the world, and school will help tell
you this. This type of moral economy worked perfectly well for a society in which
learners were destined to belong to traditional workplaces requiring deference to
authority and whose skill requirements were minimal, predictable and stable. It
was well suited to the creation of homogeneous and submissive citizenries in the
service of the old nation-state. It was appropriate to the development of compliant
personalities. There was even a logic of sorts in having a large number of learners

'fail' at school; it was a way of rationalising lack of opportunity for a large part of the society. [*See*: Mahatma Gandhi's School Days.[7]]

This world has now gone. Or it is going, given the impacts of social change and new technologies. This kind of schooling is becoming less and less relevant to the needs of learners – any learners, in any part of the world. Its moral economy is fast becoming an anachronism.

Or so one would think. However, didactic education is far from irrelevant and far from dead. In affluent, developed-world contexts, anachronistic as it may seem, it often matches the self-understanding of 'proper schooling' of parents and older community members. It teaches discipline, respect, hierarchy, order, self-restraint and all manner of other moral virtues. It teaches capacities that are supposed now to be neglected, like memory and fastidiousness for detail. Parents who can afford it are often willing to pay a premium for schools that offer this kind of experience. And in the wider society, 'back-to-the-future', populist politicians promise the public that they can and will return schools to the halcyon days when 'standards' were clearly spelt out and rigorously tested. Just because these politicians seem to be making the most noise, does not mean that their analysis of what individuals and society need from education today is correct.

Moreover, even in the world of the New Learning, there are moments when elements of didactic education may be of some value, or at the very least when it deserves some measure of our respect. Didactic education may be useful when learners are entering a new field with an established body of knowledge. It may be appropriate to certain doctrinally grounded religions, whether we agree with their mission and their messages or not. New Learning is in some senses antithetical to didactic education. In other senses, New Learning recognises the historic role of didactic education in the development of modern education systems, and allows that didactic education may have enduring validity as one of a number of strategic approaches to education. New Learning also respects didactic education as a cultural choice in an open and pluralistic society.

Authentic education: More recent times

Almost from the moment it was applied to mass-institutionalised schooling, didactic education attracted its share of critics, from popular culture (the image of the stern school teacher) to the ranks of the education profession itself. 'Progressivists' began to ask questions like, 'Isn't there more to knowledge than the "black-and-white" rigidity of right and wrong answers? What kinds of persons are formed by schooling that instils the idea that knowledge is the stuff you are told by authority figures? What's the moral lesson of teaching that requires the passive acceptance of received knowledge on the assumption that it is unquestionably correct? How useful to real life are the formal academic disciplines? And how effective is learning that does not fully engage the learner?'

So began a shift in focus from didactic teaching to a view of education in which the learner takes a more active part in their learning and which is regarded as truer to the needs of the learner, and society's needs. At its root, this shift was part of an interconnected series of economic and cultural changes, as well as a developing sense that didactic education may even be a kind of betrayal of 'human nature'. [*See*: Jean-Jacques Rousseau on Emile's Education.[8]]

One of the ironies of didactic teaching was that it reduced the role of the teacher to little more than a bureaucratic functionary. The teacher became a mere intermediary in a chain of knowledge command, an interlocutor sandwiched between syllabuses and textbooks, on the one hand, and learners, their answers and the tests they had to sit, on the other. Intellectually and professionally, nowhere near as much was expected of teachers as today. Often, they started work with little or no training – a year or two in a teachers' college or as an apprentice to their place of employment. Certainly, the teachers' training was much less than the university or college degrees that are required today. When the focus shifts from teaching to learning, the role and standing of the teacher as a professional are enhanced, and the minimum level of training they need goes up.

The shift in focus from teaching to learning was first articulated at about the turn of the 20th century. In Rome, Maria Montessori created learning environments, at first for children with disabilities and from very poor neighbourhoods. In her 'Children's House', one little group of learners could be found working with a 'contraption' consisting of coloured rods of different sizes to represent fractions. Another group of learners would be working with a map of the world on which the countries were wooden jig-saw puzzle pieces. Not all learners had to be doing the same thing at the same time; the teacher did not have to assume that all learners were at the same level and had the same interests; and, most importantly, learners were actively engaged in their learning processes.[9] [*See*: Maria Montessori on 'Free, Natural' Education.[10]]

Meanwhile, in the United States, John Dewey had created a laboratory school associated with the University of Chicago, in which students learned by 'direct experience'; making things, doing things, experimenting and solving real problems. Named 'progressivism' by way of contrast to traditional, didactic teaching, this approach to education was learner-centred instead of academic, discipline-centred; it was focused on processes of learning rather than the content of teaching; and was interested in the development of the whole child more than teaching school subjects with their rigid content and artificial disciplinary boundaries. Dewey's underlying philosophy was 'pragmatism'. In schools, pragmatism meant solving real-world problems through active discovery and testing hypotheses through practical experience.[11] [*See*: John Dewey on Progressive Education.[12]]

Sometimes, educational progressivists went so far as to suggest that better schools could influence the creation of a better world, a world of creative workers, active citizens and responsible personalities – this was called 'social reconstructionism' because it envisaged an active role for education in building a new society.

The twentieth century, however, soon put an end to any such optimism. Its social convulsions threw up a succession of horrors: two world wars; the communism/capitalism divide; economic recessions and depressions; and barbarous holocausts. The waters of progressivism and social reconstructionism seemed forever muddied by other political and moral agendas. The result was that, over the course of that painful century, not as much changed in education as the progressivists and reconstructionists may have hoped in their more optimistic moments.[13]

The term 'progressivism', although widely used, is not in itself a useful descriptor of what this kind of education is and does. It simply implies that it represents progress beyond the more traditional forms of education that it was attempting to supersede. The term has little semantic value other than to reflect a judgement of improvement and superiority. 'Authentic' is a more useful descriptor for this kind of education, of what it is in principle and the way it works.

Progressivist education is 'authentic' in several respects. It is authentic in the sense that learning is not merely abstract and formal, as are the 'disciplines' of didactic pedagogy. It works hard to make itself relevant to the lives of learners. It has demonstrably practical uses. It is also authentic insofar as it is learner- or child-centred, true to the interests and motivations of the learner in preference to the dictates of the teacher, syllabus and textbook. Finally, it is authentic for its focus on truly internalised understanding over formal correctness; knowing the processes of reasoning behind a mathematical formula, for instance, not just producing the right answer.

Returning to the eight dimensions we introduced earlier to characterise didactic education, this is what authentic education looks like:

Dimension 1: Architectonic

Characteristically, the physical spaces in which authentic learning takes place are modifications of the classrooms of the didactic regime, with a less fixed placement of desks, and a less formal classroom configuration. Teachers may open up classroom space to allow for movement and student interaction. They might replace desks with tables to allow more student activity. If the tables are clustered and learners face each other, they might work in groups. In some classrooms, and particularly for younger learners, the space may be divided into different functional or resource areas located around the room. Children's work might be used to decorate the walls – a celebration of the efforts of students and their central presence in the life of the classroom. However, the size and shape of the classroom rarely change and the overall arrangement is still roughly one teacher to 30 students. Children may also get out of the classroom to some degree, on excursions and for outdoor activities, but the centre of activity is mostly grounded in the classroom itself.

Dimension 2: Discursive

The arrangement of the room allows for more student dialogue, but within the practical bounds of the classroom. Small groups may talk as they work amongst themselves. This had been discouraged in the design of the traditional classroom of didactic education. Some use of colloquial language is allowed and attempts are made to teach both mother tongues of native speakers and the official language of the school and the wider society.

Dimension 3: Intersubjective

More opportunities are created in which students are allowed to be themselves. This is a child-centred environment, in which active engagement with knowledge is encouraged, with 'inquiry learning', experimentation, problem-solving and other learner-centred activities. Students' opinions and points of view are solicited and activity outputs consist of complex, student-designed objects such as 'projects' or 'assignments'. Now the teacher is more a facilitator of student learning. There is increased recognition of cultural and social diversity and the effects learner differences have on wellbeing and learning outcomes. Some traditional punishments, such as corporal punishment, are abandoned or made illegal. However, traditional systems of reward often remain, in the form of assessment regimes. [*See*: A. S. Neill's Summerhill.[14]]

Dimension 4: Socio-cultural

There is growing acknowledgement of student differences, with some self-paced and individualised learning taking place. In the first instance, however, such individualisation is mostly designed along the dimension of 'ability' or psychologically defined universal stages of development.[15] Cultural, gender and other differences are subsumed, and appear to be factors that create an educational 'deficit' for some students. The school can try to 'make up' for these deficits by creating and offering special, remedial programs that help initiate outsiders or those not performing to the standards of mainstream curriculum. This is done in order to initiate them into a common culture of learning and, via this route, into the broader mainstream of society. Alternatively, there might be some move towards a tokenistic recognition of differences, along the lines of a superficial multiculturalism, which, in the case of ethnic diversity, for instance, celebrates national days or gets students to do country studies as an add-on to the mainstream curriculum. Such gestures to student differences, however, are constrained by classroom architecture and timetable demands. Practically speaking, having to teach this particular subject at this particular time, one teacher to 30 students, requires a degree of uniformity. This means that there are still pressures towards sameness, although these are mostly more subtle than they were before – underlying assumptions in the learning content and the best ways to learn that content.

Dimension 5: Proprietary

The classroom of authentic education is opened up in a partial redistribution of the ownership of knowledge and control of space. Students get involved in some group work. This, however, is not the primary form of work, nor the work that is valued when determining 'results'. The teacher increasingly brings outsiders into the space of the classroom, engaging them in the learning process: other 'team' teachers, professional teachers' aides, parent-helpers and community members whose knowledge or expertise is relevant to the learning. The boundaries of the class remain neatly defined, however, and the learning relationship remains one that is almost exclusively between the teacher and the 30 children.

Dimension 6: Epistemological

The syllabus of authentic education is not so rigidly focused on content as didactic teaching. Rather, it speaks in terms of generalised learning outcomes in key learning areas. Textbooks are less central because they are supplemented by other things ('real world' texts, discussions, experiments, excursions, problems-to-be-solved). Where textbooks are still used, they are often written differently, providing task suggestions that promote active engagement rather than factual and theoretical 'answers'. Although there are more images, diagrams and other forms of visual representation, written text on the printed page continues to predominate. The old timetable may still be there, slicing time and place in order to divide the discipline areas, but with some deference now to 'integrated units', whereby a particular topic or series of activities is tackled from multiple disciplinary perspectives. Cross-disciplinary perspectives may be added to a subject such as 'language across the curriculum' in science or mathematics. In addition to the old disciplines, new areas of concern are added to the curriculum, from AIDS education to driver education. This creates a bewildering range of pressures on schools, either in the form of the 'crowded curriculum' whereby schools are now simply expected to cover too much essential ground, or the 'shopping mall curriculum' in which students are provided too much choice and each choice is too narrowly particular. The overall result, however, is that the sources, flows and nature of knowledge have changed. The balances of agency in the educational process have shifted, giving more scope for teachers to create curriculum relevant to their learners (thus allowing that the teacher will be a knowledge source, to some degree at least), and allowing that learners will be, at the very least, partial co-constructors of knowledge. This shifts the focus of learning away from learning things students are expected to learn, in the direction of learning how to learn, or from learning content to the process of learning.[16] In a changing world, knowing how to know is as important as the content of knowledge itself.

Dimension 7: Pedagogical

Learning now is more active, more experiential. The focus becomes learner inquiry rather than teacher- and textbook-transmitted knowledge. Developmental psychology tells of generic stages of 'readiness' in which children have the cognitive capacities to construct understandings of the world at particular levels of sophistication.[17] A distinction is made between a true understanding and mere repetition of what one has been told. This means being able to figure things out for yourself, explaining cause, effect and logical relations, rather than learning something off by heart and coming up with the right answer. [*See:* Rabindranath Tagore's School at Shantiniketan.[18]]

Dimension 8: Moral

Authentic education is concerned with creating citizens who will actively participate in their social world, workers and community members who will be able to deal with a good deal of social change over their lifetimes, and persons with open, inquiring minds. The moral economy of authentic education is one that offers learners the opportunity to become members of multiple social worlds. Individual choice and self-realisation, the ideals of a certain kind of liberal–democratic, 20th-century modernity, emerge as dominant themes.

At the beginning of the 21st century, there could well be a larger number of classrooms in the world still cast in the mould of didactic education than there are classrooms whose educational processes could be described as 'authentic'. However, the influences of authentic education have been enormous. Broad generalisations will always be proven faulty by striking counter examples, but as a general rule it would be true to say that the shift from didactic to authentic education has been more pronounced in the kindergarten and primary or elementary years than in high schools, in the humanities more than mathematics and the sciences, in affluent schools more than poorer schools, in the developed world more than the developing world.[19] These generalisations are also confused by a more complex reality in which one program in a school will operate with a predominantly didactic orientation to education and another with a more authentic orientation, or one teacher compared to another, or even one teacher in one moment of teaching compared to the same teacher in another moment.

How do we evaluate authentic by way of comparison with didactic education? Whatever its superiority over didactic education claimed by its progressivist supporters, authentic education has its own intrinsic limitations, whether in its turn-of-the-20th-century form or its contemporary forms such as more recent 'constructivist' approaches to education, which we discuss in Chapter 8.

'Authentic to what?' one might ask as an initial question. To this, progressivism might reply, 'Whatever is immediately needed and useful'. Whatever teachers negotiate with learners and whatever communities might seem to need or think they need. Something new or the same old stuff if teachers and parents have warm memories from their own school days of spelling lists and times tables and stories of nationalistic heroism. And if it's something new, it might be carefully differentiated curriculum for different kinds of learners, Shakespeare in the subject English for those who might become doctors and lawyers, and 'Communication Skills' for those who are going to become somebody's clerical assistant and who may need to be taught how to write a half-reasonable curriculum vitae. 'Communication Skills' sounds good and is doubtless 'relevant', but the kids know what being placed in this course really means when they call it, in tones of publicly unspeakable contempt, 'veggie English'.[20] In cases such as this, authentic education could, despite its best intentions, mean streaming society in new and more subtle ways in the name of relevance. The 'democratic' of this kind of democratic schooling can easily translate into a kind of populism, a series of seemingly democratic moves that have the effect of keeping the social order just the way it is, and that is unfairly unequal. If and when this is the case, authentic education takes a course that, in the final analysis, stays true to the cultural logic of an unequal society. It doesn't enable learners by producing different social outcomes for them, and it doesn't do anything to the world other than reflect the way it is. It represents a view of the world that is ultimately agnostic, neutral, disengaged. It's just a somewhat kinder, gentler way of achieving unequal social outcomes than didactic education.

To which the proponents of didactic pedagogy might retort that they have more to offer – the rigorous, hard stuff of traditional education that will teach you the 'basics' you need to get you the marks you need to succeed.

Transformative education: New Learning

If the pace of change in schools seemed glacial over the course of the 20th century, there are reasons to believe that it is about to quicken in the 21st. Some of the reasons for this may be attributed to external factors. It is nearly impossible for schools today to avoid addressing new technologies, globalisation, diverse classrooms, the changing nature of work and citizenship, and the shifting dimensions of human subjectivity, identity and personality. Schools increasingly have to speak to these broader social realities simply in order to remain relevant. [*See*: Bill Gates on US Schools.[21]]

Amongst the changes educators face, some come from the changing sensibilities of students and teachers. In the developed world at least, today's children and young people come from the video game, MP3 and digital television generation.[22] They are the products of child-centred upbringing in a consumer society. They will simply not put up with traditional classrooms in the way earlier generations did, even if at times these older generations only barely tolerated them. Nor will today's teachers put up with working environments that challenge their profes-sionalism by dictating the script of what they will teach, when they will teach it and how they will teach it – hence the widespread unease and resistance across the teaching profession to the return of externally imposed, high-stakes tests.

Meanwhile, new possibilities for teaching are also opened up by the Internet and e-learning. In its initial phases, e-learning has often appeared to replicate the worst of old teaching. But a newer phase of e-learning is creating new learning spaces in which teachers and learners challenge and transform the social relations of traditional classrooms and didactic pedagogies.

Educators need to be keen observers of change. This is the only way we can keep our teaching, and our schools, up to date and relevant. But, more than this, we must be agenda-setters and change-makers. We have the power to transform our classrooms and our schools. As we embark on these transformations, we also make our own contribution to the transformation of the broader society. Better learners will better contribute to the making of a better society.

If we were to choose a single word to characterise the agenda of the New Learning, it is to be 'transformative'. New Learning, for us, is thus not simply based on a reading of change; it is also grounded in an optimistic agenda in which we educators can constructively contribute to change.

If knowledge is indeed as pivotal in contemporary society as the 'new economy' commentators and politicians claim, then educators should seize the agenda and position themselves as forces of change. Not only is the education of the near future likely to drift further and further away from its roots in the industrial era. So it should. And 'should' means that we have a professional responsibility to be change agents who design the education for the future.[23]

After a century of progressivist attempts to improve on didactic education, the 'New Learning' needs to be authentic and more; it should also be 'transformative'. Being authentic may produce a better fit between education and society, but leaves society fundamentally the way it is. It sets out to reflect the realities of the world more than to change them. It does not necessarily move the learner in terms of intergenerational mobility or life trajectory. Transformative education builds on many of the insights of authentic pedagogy, to be sure, but ups the ante. Its aims are no less than to change the life chances of the learner and to change their world.

The transformative education that we identify is emergent rather than some-thing to be found anywhere in a fully developed form. It is an idea that builds upon and extends the insights into the nature of learning and the role of edu-cation in society to be found at moments in both didactic and authentic educa-tion, whilst attempting to move beyond some of their limitations. It is for us a work-in-progress. It is, if you like, an act of imagination for the future of learning and an attempt to find practical ways to develop aspects of this future in the educational practices of the present. The transformative education that we advocate is an open-ended struggle rather than a clear destination, a process rather than a formula for action, and something that recognises the educational legacies of the past in order to design better educational futures.

The third part of each chapter of this book describes certain dimensions of our 'New Learning' proposal. 'Transformation' is a key aspect of that vision for a New Learning, which this book articulates. The idea of transformation stands in contradistinction to, at the same time as it builds upon and develops, the heritage practices of didactic and authentic education. In one sense, this is an exercise in the broad integration of ideas across the science of education, articulating a theoretical framework for the discipline.

This exercise, however, is also a very grounded and practical one. As educators – teachers and people who have worked with teachers in training and in-service professional development – we have ourselves struggled with the practical question of the design of our educational futures in the various projects with which we have been involved, from Social Literacy in the 1980s,[24] to Multiliteracies in the 1990s,[25] to Learning by Design in the 2000s.[26] The ideas of New Learning and transformation are, for us, not just schematic and theoretical. They are vividly and insistently practical, the stuff of what you do with your learners on Monday morning.

So what do we think a transformative education might achieve? At its best, transformative education embodies a realistic view of contemporary society, or the kinds of knowledge and capacities for knowing that children need to develop in order to be good workers in a 'knowledge economy', participating citizens in a globalised, cosmopolitan society, and balanced personalities in a society that affords a range of life choices that at times feel overwhelming. It nurtures the social sensibilities of a kind of person who understands that they determine the world by their actions as much as they are determined by that world. It creates a person who understands that their individual needs are linked inextricably with responsibility for the common good as they are connected into ever-expanding and overlapping social networks.

Make of this what you will, be that a sensible conservatism (sensible for being realistic about the contemporary forces of technology, globalisation and cultural change) or an emancipatory view that wants to make a future that is different to the present by addressing its crises of poverty, environment, cultural difference and existential meaning. In other words, the transformation may be pragmatic (enabling learners to do their best in the given social conditions); or it may be emancipatory (making the world a better place).

What follows is an outline of some aspects of the landscape of New Learning and its transformative view of education, some of which may be happening now, or be about to happen, or which might happen sooner or later.

Dimension 1: Architectonic

Imagine this scenario: what if students could do their work anywhere, not just in the classroom to which the school timetable has sent them, but in small syndicate rooms, in the library, in somebody else's classroom, in locations out in the community where knowledge is made and used (a local library, a gallery or museum, a workplace, a community organisation), or in a group of students who decided to work at one of its members' homes? What if they are connected with teachers, information and other learners globally and locally, seven days a week, 24 hours a day through any number of electronic devices?

Impossible, you might say. What about the teacher's duty of care? How would the teacher know what each student was doing? Where they were? What they were exposed to? To which we might respond, nowadays you can know where every child is, no matter where they are, and as well as any teacher did, perched up on their little platform surveying the traditional class. Every child in this scenario has a mobile phone, which is also a personal digital assistant (PDA) and has a global positioning system (GPS) facility that tells you exactly where they are within a range of error of one metre. (This happens to be about the same margin for positional error as in the traditional classroom.) It means they can talk to you and you can talk to them. And you can know exactly what they are doing because they are constantly committing their work to a server-based content sharing system and messaging around this work. Every email and instant phone message is collected in a message spool for an assignment, and this can tell every little step in the developmental 'story' of that work.[27] The teacher can just as easily as ever 'see' what the learners are doing, and automated systems can alert them when students stray beyond agreed locations, or outside of negotiated task parameters. This is particularly helpful in the case of jointly constructed student work, because it is now possible to see exactly who has done what in a collaborative piece of work.

This is a new communications design, and one that means that students do not have to be co-located within a classroom. In fact, the physical classroom for 30 kids and one teacher may become an anachronism, a throwback of industrial-era schooling. [*See:* The MET: No classes, no grades and 94% graduation rate.[28]]

What on earth are we going to do with all those old school buildings now? Authentic education made the best of heritage infrastructure, unbolting the desks from the floor and rearranging the rooms in ways that had never been envisaged by their architects. Up to a point, we can knock down the internal walls in old schools and put up new ones that divide the space in different and more varied ways. We can wire (or wireless) up the school so the dominant communications dynamic is not room-by-room, one-voice-at-a-time audio. But there may be a limit to how far we can go with this. And when we reach this limit, we might need to build completely new schools in which spaces are multifunction, multipurpose, flexible and varied. [*See:* Class Work.[29]]

If we trace the trends to their logical conclusion, sometimes it may be just too hard to redesign the old schools. In these cases, we might have to regard the old buildings as a real-estate problem rather than an educational one. Perhaps developers with some flair for recycling might turn them into community drop-in centres, apartments or shopping arcades and so help fund the building of brand new schools for the future.

Dimension 2: Discursive

Traditional teaching discouraged lateral communication between students. The New Learning thrives on enormous amounts of lateral communication between learners – face-to-face talk, Internet and mobile telephony, online chat, instant messaging, email and messaging around text, image, sound and video in content creation and sharing environments. In the old classroom this amount of lateral interaction would have turned out to be unmanageable 'noise'. The teacher could not possibly have listened to it all at once. The stuff that would have been noise is now 'visible', as the teacher selectively views interactions and intelligent computer 'agents' automatically monitor student interactions and progress and send the teacher alerts if anything seems out of order. It also allows for multiple languages, multimodality, invented discourses and special communication means for those with disabilities, thus expanding exponentially access and potentials for expression of meaning.[30]

In this environment, the orienting axis of communications has changed from vertical to lateral. Learners become teachers of each other. And teachers become equals in the learning exchange. This equality, however, is primarily discursive. It brings teachers onto the same level as learners as conversationalists. Teachers are not, of course, their students' equals in terms of teachers' greater responsibility for building scaffolds for student learning based on their deep professional understanding of the science of education, or in terms of their respected positions as bearers of authoritative knowledge, or in terms of their duty of care to ensure that learning environments are welcoming and safe. However, there is a subtle but important discursive shift from the teacher's authoritarian stance in the traditional classroom to their authoritative position in the New Learning. The old teaching discourse of command becomes the new learning discourse of dialogue between experts and novices.

Along the way, the neat mathematics of teaching changes. It does not always have to be one to 30, teacher to students. Sometimes it will be one to one, other times one to a small group, other times one to 100 (when lots of learners access an online resource created by a teacher, or watch a teacher's video, or listen to a large group presentation, either live in-person or live online). Still other times it will be two or more to however many – in the case of team teaching or jointly created learning resources. The overall teacher–student ratios might stay the same. (It is hard to imagine that resourcing for education will suddenly improve, although educators should continue, insistently, to make the claim that a knowledge economy is only as dynamic as the investment it is prepared to make in education.) It's just that the economies of scale may be much more variable. The average of one to 30 does not necessarily have to change. It just no longer means that this has to be the same one to the same 20 or 30, or always in this kind of ratio, or always in the one place and always at the one time. Alternatively, if the human resources of educators are used more efficiently by means of new discursive economies (learners only accessing teachers when they are needed, otherwise working in crafted, self-paced learning environments, learning with peers and learning in community), there may be scope to increase teachers' salaries to a significant extent, with or without additional resources being devoted to education.

Dimension 3: Intersubjective

Authentic education went some of the way to change the intersubjective balance of agency between teachers and learners. It granted learners a significant role in constructing their own knowledge through experiential, inquiry or activity based learning. But the teacher was still very much in command and the systems of reward and punishment remained little changed. At best, individual learners could do their own work, at their own pace and in their own way, perhaps with some support and assistance from a group.

The New Learning places an additional premium on learner engagement, starting with the careful identification of learner needs, identities, expectations, aspirations, interests and motivations. If the learner fails to engage with these raw materials of subjectivity or agency, they will not learn. Critically, however, these things are not individual (the 'activity' notion in authentic education), but the stuff of social relationships (hence an 'interactivity' notion in the New Learning). Successful learning occurs in a social context that affirms the learner's identity and in a social setting that supports their interests, values, perspectives and contributions. The deepest learning occurs in an environment of reciprocity and sociability. This is a context in which learning is a matter of negotiation, rather than imposed subject contents, and where students are meaning makers as much as they are meaning receivers. It is also a context in which new incentive and evaluation systems need to be designed into the learning experience – work that is truly interesting and engaging from the learner's point of view; collaborations with others that include the social expectation that you should give your all; communication of the work to other learners, parents and the broader community, perhaps through web-based portfolios; and assessment of published portfolios by qualitative review rather than a single mark and by peer reviewers rather than, or in addition to, the teacher.

Above all, these new intersubjective relations mean that teachers – and this is sometimes intimidating for those who were schooled in the old teaching or even some forms of authentic education – need to let go of the old position of command they have become so used to holding. They will need to see themselves more as collaborative researchers, designing and tracking, purposeful, transformative

interventions. This will require supportive networking and professional collaborations – with other teachers, community partners and with learners themselves.
Allow the learners to take greater responsibility for their learning. Allow that they
might know, or be able to find out, things that you the teacher would not necessarily know. Allow that trust will breed responsibility. And allow that things will go
wrong, but that the balance of benefit as measured on a scale of the effectiveness
of learning, will be worth it. [*See*: Discovery 1, Christchurch.[31]]

Dimension 4: Socio-cultural

In the New Learning, learners' different attributes are fundamental. Effective
learning will not occur unless the professional educator finds a way to deal with
these differences. They are myriad: material (class, locale), corporeal (age, race,
sex and sexuality, and physical and mental characteristics) and symbolic (culture,
language, gender, family, affinity and persona). And they are profound, representing at times huge gulfs between one learner and the next – in values, style, affect,
sensibility and disposition. We discuss these differences in detail in Chapter 5.

In response to these differences, the New Learning spends time finding out
about learners' prior experiences, interests and aspirations. It allows that different learners can be working on very different things at the same time. It allows
for different learning habits – some learners will feel more comfortable learning
by immersion in experience, willing to wait for a 'big picture' view to emerge;
others will want to start with the abstract map of the big picture, then try to fit the
experiential pieces into that map. New Learning identifies and negotiates alternative learning pathways to common goals, appropriate to students' capacities as
formed by prior learning, meeting their needs and satisfying their interests.

Getting beyond the subtle and often not-so-subtle homogenising and assimilationist tendencies of didactic and authentic education, the New Learning is
inclusive (no child left unbelonging) and pluralist, respecting and building upon
the personal experiences and cultural knowledge each learner brings to learning
and to high performance. It fosters the sensibilities and develops the skills for
affirming one's own and others' identities and negotiating differences in order to
succeed. It is locally grounded, yet outward looking towards a global context.

Dimension 5: Proprietary

In authentic education, the classroom is still a relatively private, enclosed space.
Learners mainly do their own, private work, albeit with higher levels of individu-
alisation and self-direction than was the case in the didactic teaching. In the New
Learning, the physical walls are broken down (literally, or metaphorically).

No longer 'lone rangers', teachers work more closely together as members of an
integrated community of professional collaborators. They work closely with other
teachers in team teaching. They document, publish and share the lesson plans
and learning resources they have developed. They work with aides to assist students with identified needs requiring a specialist outside of the teacher's range of

expertise. They involve parents closely. They involve community experts – on site, online, or hosting learners off site – who can make a contribution to the learning.

The teacher of the old, cloistered classroom becomes a thing of the past. No longer is the classroom an enclosed, private, even secret space. What the teacher does with 'their' class is no longer simply a matter of spoken words that disappear into the ether the moment they are uttered. Instead, they become a very different kind of worker, a collaborative professional whose knowledge and experiences are always being complemented and corroborated by other professionals. Their every pedagogical word is transparently on the record and open to scrutiny – the e-learning sequences they have created for their learners, the email conversations with their students about their work.

Student learning activities become more open and collaborative, too. In authentic education, student learning may be more individualised and self-paced than in didactic teaching. It might be a complex, multidisciplinary self-directed project or assignment that the student is doing. But it still mostly has to be 'your own work'. ('Don't copy' and 'it's a problem if your parents help' . . . too much or too obviously, that is.)

There's still a place for individualised activities and private learning spaces in the New Learning. That's not because individualised learning is an end in itself. In fact, making this an end itself ('my marks' for 'my work') seems to encourage students to play the system by cheating or plagiarising. The audience for the meaning-maker in individualised learning should not just be the audience of one, the assessing teacher who gives the work a '54' (which we get to know means 'passable but not very good') or a '76' ('pretty good but not brilliant'). Rather, the audience for every student when they make meanings should be other learners (the class as a learning community), parents and the wider world. This is what happens when the work is published to the Internet, simultaneously into the learner's own portfolio and the class 'bookstore'. This way, private vertical communication flows are replaced by lateral, public, community oriented flows. Learners speak to an audience of many. If you dare to plagiarise, it is not just the teacher you are trying to deceive, but your peers and the world – and it's more likely your peers who will find you out. The world of easily accessible digital text makes it easier to plagiarise, and also harder to get away with, because there are more people who might pick it up and because the sources are more public and easily traceable.

Beyond individualised teaching, the New Learning opens up space for collabo-rative learning, reflecting the changing shape of today's workplaces and learning communities beyond the formal institutional settings of education. Collabora-tive work is produced in pairs or small groups; students thus learn how to think and act as team players. The collective outcome is greater than the sum of the individuals' contributions. So, the learners become good communicators, good readers of others' differences, good at negotiating, good at compromising and good at producing knowledge that is jointly owned. In didactic teaching as well as in authentic education, collaborative work was hard to manage for the most practical of reasons. How could an assessor ever know whose contribution was whose, without watching every learner's every move? With the versioning, messaging and tracking systems of today's networked content management environments, however, it's possible to know exactly who did what and when. If you're not pulling your weight, it will be obvious to the other learners and the teacher.

The nice twist is that, as soon as learners become good at collaborative learning, they start to do individualised learning in a new way. If you're new to something, you find experts (persons, published information) who will give you explicit support and advice (assisted competence – see Chapter 10). If you're comfortable with something and think you can figure it out more or less for yourself, you'll be confident enough to use, assemble and acknowledge a variety of other sources of information and inspiration (autonomous competence – also Chapter 10). Even individualised activity becomes collaborative. This is how the active learning processes of authentic education turn into the interactive learning processes of transformative education. [*See*: Ivan Illich on 'Deschooling'.[32]]

Dimension 6: Epistemological

In didactic teaching, teachers and textbooks told. They expounded, bit by laborious bit, the facts and theories they thought learners needed to know in order to master a discipline. Transformative education encourages ways of thinking based on a different understanding of how knowledge is most effectively and powerfully made, particularly in today's social settings and those of the conceivable future. The base point is not teacherly or textbookish regurgitations of knowledge, but working with real-world texts, issues, ideas and problems. Students research the facts, test them and corroborate them. Indeed, facts only become facts when they have passed a number of tests – of apperception (how well have you observed?), plausibility (do the facts make sense?) and applicability (do they fit with other facts and do they work?). These tests are for the student to apply, never to take a single source at its word and never to accept that a fact is a fact just because someone says so. Then, putting the facts together, hypotheses are developed, theories are created inductively and then tested deductively against the facts. Thus, as we argue in greater detail in Chapter 8, learners become reflexive knowledge makers rather than knowledge receptors. This way, the disciplines become not so much bunches of facts and theories, but approaches to knowledge creation: scientific, historical or literary, for instance. And knowledge is constructed from multiple sources, based on variable perspectives, knowledge orientations and approaches to problems.

Underlying is a profound shift in the direction of knowledge flows. Learners become co-designers of knowledge, developing habits of mind in which they are comfortable members of knowledge-producing and knowledge-sharing communities. And teachers build learning experiences that engage with learner subjectivities, developing and negotiating learning scaffolds that can be customised for different individual learners or groups of and extend learners and so build on and extend learners' identities and senses of destiny.

Along the way, discipline boundaries may need to be blurred, to the extent even of breaking out of the constraints of the old, subject-divided timetable. The New Learning becomes increasingly interdisciplinary, requiring deeper engagement with knowledge in all its complexity and ambiguity.

If we are to avoid the difficulties of the 'crowded curriculum' or the 'shopping mall curriculum' in this context, we may have to re-conceive the core of learning or 'the basics'. We may even need to move towards more general and more comprehensive education, with just a few key areas such as technology (science, mathematics, applied sciences), commerce (enterprise, innovation, working together) and humanities (cultural understandings, capacities for intercultural interaction and boundary crossing). Even though this is a moment of particularity, change and diversity in all areas of knowledge and human experience, it may well be that formal education needs to become more centred and more focused on a few core areas of learning. Perhaps, each of these core areas should be studied at a higher level of generality than the traditional subject areas, should be relevant to a broad range of students with quite different life aspirations, and should be applicable in very different contexts? This may prove to be the essence of a 'new basics'.[33]

Finally, the source of valid knowledge is no longer primarily linguistic as it was in the heritage practices of didactic teaching, and even more narrowly, the written word. It is also multimodal, where the visual (diagram, picture, moving image), gestural, tactile and spatial are considered to be just as valid knowledge sources as writing. This reflects the deeply integrated, synaesthetic meanings of our contemporary communications environment.[34] Learners, moreover, can build and represent knowledge using a variety of meaning modes and mixes of mode. Why should a diagram be of less knowledge value than a theory-in-words? Or a documentary video of less value than an essay?

Dimension 7: Pedagogical

Didactic education focused on fixed content knowledge: undeniable facts and theories-to-be-applied. This knowledge was supposed to last for life. Applied today, this kind of education becomes instantly redundant. Knowledge today is constantly changing, and particularly in areas of dramatic social transformation such as computing, biotechnologies, identities/sexualities or socio-historical interpretation. Indeed, old disciplinary approaches often foster rigid ways of thinking that are counter-productive for the workers, citizens and persons of today and the near future.

The New Learning is less about delivering a body of knowledge and skills that will be good for life and more about forming a deeply knowing kind of person. This person will be aware of what they don't know, capable of working out what they need to know and be able to create their own knowledge, either autonomously or in collaboration with others.

In the New Learning, learners not only become creators of knowledge. They also represent the fruits of their creativity to each other. Their learning becomes the grist for the mill of other learners.

As much as they develop disciplinary or content knowledge, they also develop knowledge about their knowledge making, and learning about how they learn. These include habits of mind, which are often called 'meta-cognition' – the thinking about thinking alongside the pragmatics of thinking that makes that thinking all the more powerful. This includes consideration of one's own thinking processes, knowledge strategies and continuous self-monitoring reflection on one's learning. In these ways, not only do learners become co-designers of knowledge (on the epistemological dimension). They also become co-designers of learning (on the pedagogical dimension).

And so, the role of the teacher-as-pedagogue also changes. No longer do they stand and deliver. No more are they primarily the fonts of disciplinary knowledge. Their roles have expanded and they are now not only knowledge experts but also designers of learning environments, builders of learning scaffolds, managers of student learning and researchers of learner performance. [*See*: 'I did it all by myself.'[35]]

Dimension 8: Moral

Education always creates 'kinds of persons'. What is the moral economy of accepting as given somebody else's facts and theories, just because they are presented as authoritative? Didactic education formed people who had learnt rules and could be relied on to obey them; people who would take answers out to the world rather than regard the world as an ever-unfolding series of problems to be solved; and people who thought they had 'correct' knowledge in the private spaces of their heads rather than people who can always approach a new situation as flexible and collaborative learners. As we argue in the chapters that follow, these orientations to the world are inadequate to the demands of changing work (Chapter 3), citizenship (Chapter 4) and personhood (Chapter 5). The New Learning imagines a kind of person who is able to navigate constant change and deep diversity, learn-as-they-go, solve problems, collaborate, innovate and be flexible and creative. This kind of person will not be traumatised by change, suffering from 'future shock' or retreating into the narrow safety of original community. Rather they will be able to take control as an agent of social design in the spaces in which they live and work. The guiding metaphor for their social life is the networked 'we': humanly interconnected, discerning, agile and flexible. [*See*: Paulo Freire on education which liberates.[36]]

The results of this New Learning will not be student scores spread neatly across a normal distribution curve, a few learners at the bottom, most clustered around the middle and a few at the top. Why would you want to condemn some students to simplistic numerical failure on narrow criteria and elevate others whose social capacities need not necessarily warrant such an elevation? There is no room for failure and marginalisation in the school of the New Learning. Poor results are anathema for individuals and society.

Children will grow up to do different things in their lives, and as adults may make comparable, though varied contributions to their world. That should be the basic assumption of education, and reward and credentialling systems need to make this abundantly clear. When learners leave school they should not be branded with a spread of exit scores statistically derived from narrow or inappropriate for the 21st-century norms of success and failure. Any such measure is unsatisfactory, whether your number happens to tell of success, or mediocrity or failure.

At the failure end of the spectrum, the stakes are higher than ever – even affluent societies cannot afford a dysfunctional underclass. At the success end of the spectrum, maybe the 'smart' ones are just smart at playing the game of school. Are we simply rewarding those who play the system rather than those who are creative and innovative? Is this the kind of person we really want as the worker and citizen of the future? Instead of these bald numerical scores, perhaps students should leave the various stages in their learning with complex and rounded stories of what they have actually done in their lives and their learning, stories that can be read in their fullness by other educational institutions, employers and the community.

In this chapter, we have told a story of tradition and change, from the didactic education to authentic education, to our proposal for the transformative world of New Learning that is only now emerging and the shape of which is not yet clear.

We have painted this picture of change in the broadest of brushstrokes. History, however, is rarely a succession of neatly defined periods. Today, you will find educational settings anywhere in the world that predominantly reflect one of these three approaches or paradigms for learning. And within one of these sites you may find moments and incidents that reflect one approach in one moment, and another approach in another moment. You will find patterns of variation from country to country, from school system to school system, from school to school, from classroom to classroom, from teacher to teacher, from discipline area to discipline area and even from one moment to the next within the life of one classroom. Sometimes one approach – didactic, authentic or transformative – will seem appropriate for the time and the setting. Other times it will not.

In this book, we try to imagine what a new phase of education would be like, and to look for signs of things to come in the innovative educational practices of today. This, we believe, is not simply an act of imagination, a wilful utopianism. Given the changes occurring today (globalisation, community diversity, new technologies, changing work, and the formation of new kinds of persons with different sensibilities), the New Learning of which we are speaking may soon become a necessity.

Unless, that is, we allow schools to slip into a crisis of irrelevance. We'll know when such a crisis arrives, because it will translate into employers' complaints about graduates, into discipline problems at school, into a general community anxiety that schools are not teaching learners what they need for the contemporary world. On these indicators, in many places, this crisis has already arrived.

Summary

Life in schools	Didactic education: The modern past	Authentic education: More recent times	Transformative education: New learning
Architectonic dimension	The classroom of 30 students facing one teacher.	Making the most of old classrooms, changing the arrangement of the room.	Flexible spaces, no physical boundaries; life-wide and lifelong learning.
Discursive dimension	Teacher-dominated classroom talk, most learners silent for most of the time.	Some student-to-student dialogue.	Horizontal, learner–learner and learner–teacher dialogue, with the teacher in an authoritative position.
Intersubjective dimension	Authoritarian systems command with teacher as mouth-piece; teachers command and learners obey.	Learner-centred activities.	Learner-surrounded interactivity; multiple teacher–learner relationships.
Socio-cultural dimension	All 30 learners regarded as the same; one-size-fits-all curriculum.	Some individualised and self-paced learning; deficit or tokenistic views of difference.	Inclusive learning, educational pluralism.
Proprietary dimension	Private spaces: 'my classroom' (teacher) and 'my work' (learner).	Opening up the classroom, some group work.	Collaborative learning – anywhere, anytime.
Epistemological dimension	Transmission of correct facts and definitive theories from teachers to learners.	Generalised learning outcomes and relevant curriculum.	Learners as co-designers of knowledge.
Pedagogical dimension	Learners as passive receptors of knowledge: facts, theories, truths, civic values.	Experiential learning, learning how to learn; students as inquirers.	The teacher as a designer of pedagogy; the learner as co-designer of learning.

(cont.)

(cont.)

Life in schools	Didactic education: The modern past	Authentic education: More recent times	Transformative education: New learning
Moral dimension	Discipline and conformity lead to success; and blame yourself for failure.	Inquiring minds and participating citizens; 'opportunity' to access the 'mainstream'.	Kinds of persons who can navigate, discern, change, negotiate deep diversity, create and innovate.

Notes

1. Histories of modern education tell this story in graphic detail. See, for instance, Cuban 1993; Tyack 1974
2. Churchill 1960 (1930), pp. 17–18, 19, 23. See extract at NewLearningOnline.com
3. Lee 1887 (1914). See extract at NewLearningOnline.com
4. Orwell 1968 (1953), pp. 385–86, 411. See extract at NewLearningOnline.com
5. Darwin 1892, pp. 8–11. See extract at NewLearningOnline.com
6. Lorde 1982 (1996), pp. 14–16. See extract at NewLearningOnline.com
7. Gandhi 1949, pp. 5–6. See extract at NewLearningOnline.com
8. Rousseau 1762 (1914), pp. 6, 80–81, 126, 131. See extract at NewLearningOnline.com
9. Montessori 1912 (1964); 1917 (1973)
10. Montessori 1912 (1964); pp. 14, 15, 21–22, 27, 28, 62–63, 65, 66, 86. See extract at NewLearningOnline.com
11. Dewey 1902 (1956); 1915 (1956); 1916 (1966); 1938 (1963); Dewey and Dewey 1915
12. Dewey 1915 (1956). See extract at NewLearningOnline.com
13. Bramfield 1965
14. Neill 1962, pp. 20–21, 42–43, 20, 39, 53–54. See extract at NewLearningOnline.com
15. Piaget 1976
16. Bruner 1977; 1966
17. Piaget 1971
18. Elmhirst 1961 (1925), pp. 69–70, 71–72. See also: Thompson 1998. See extract at NewLearningOnline.com
19. Cuban 1993
20. Kalantzis, Mary, Bill Cope, Greg Noble and Scott Poynting 1991, p. 222
21. Gates 2005. See extract at NewLearningOnline.com
22. Gee 2000
23. Kress 1995
24. Kalantzis and Cope 1989
25. Cope and Kalantzis 2000b
26. Kalantzis and Cope 2005
27. See www.ClassPublisher.com
28. http://www.bigpicture.org. See extract at NewLearningOnline.com
29. Smith, Kalantzis and Cope 2006. See extract at NewLearningOnline.com

30. Cope and Kalantzis 2004, pp. 198–282
31. http://www.discovery1.school.nz/ See extract at NewLearningOnline. com
32. Illich 1973, pp. 20, 37–38, 78, 34–35, 78–81, 104. See extract at NewLearningOnline.com
33. Kalantzis and Cope 2001
34. Kress 2000b, pp. 182–202
35. Burrows, Cope, Kalantzis, Loi, Suominen and Yelland 2006a. See extract at NewLearningOnline.com
36. Freire 1972, pp. 45–46, 52–53, 56–57. See extract at NewLearningOnline.com

Part B

Contexts – Changing Conditions for Learning

Chapter 3

Learning for work

Overview

Education prepares people for productive working lives – one of education's most important reasons-for-being. The types of work available in society influence the type of education that is considered most suitable. This chapter describes three main ways of organising work that have emerged since the beginning of the modern, industrial era, characterising these as 'Fordism', 'post-Fordism' and 'productive diversity'. It examines the main dimensions of each of these forms of work: technology, management, workers' education and skills, and markets and society.

'Fordism' (named after Henry Ford, inventor of production-line manufacture) is a model of work in which the production process is divided into simple tasks, management is authoritarian and hierarchical, and uniform products are mass produced for mass consumption. For this kind of arrangement of work, didactic teaching is generally appropriate and sufficient.

The concept of 'post-Fordism' speaks to the gradual and uneven changes in the organisation of work in the later part of the 20th century towards automation, multi-skilling, teamwork, increased horizontal communication and human interaction in the workplace. This form of work is, by and large, better served by authentic education.

The concept of 'productive diversity' signals for us changes currently taking place in the organisation of work in what is now widely known as the 'knowledge economy': changes which locate value in human skills, relationships, culture, knowledge and learning, and in which working arrangements are more likely to

have people with different skills working together, within enterprises and in organi-
sational networks. Such organisations, we suggest, relate more carefully to diverse
suppliers, clienteles and working environments, both locally and globally. Repre-
senting an optimistic view of the near future of work, people who are going to
work in this kind of workplace are best served, we also suggest, by transformative
education.

Not only does this chapter investigate one of the 'outside' aims of schooling,
it is also about the inside of schools as organisations themselves. Schools are
places in which teachers and learners work. At various times and in various places,
schools themselves have reflected Fordist, post-Fordist and the productive diversity
approaches to work.

On work and education

'Do well at school and you'll get a good job,' many a teacher or parent has told a
child. What they mean is that higher levels of knowledge, skill and qualifications
are linked to better-paid employment. They are right – level of education is a
reliable predictor of adult earning capacity.

In the modern era of mass, institutionalised education, school performs a social
role of sifting and sorting people into different kinds of jobs. One aspect of this
role is simply functional: ordinary workers need some basics in order to function
effectively in the workplace. Sometimes those basics are rudimentary literacy and
numeracy skills; at other times they are a set of dispositions inculcated at school –
punctuality, a capacity to understand orders and a willingness to comply. Until
recently, a relatively small number of workers also needed to have higher-level
knowledge and skills, and so received the additional training required for them
to be tradespeople or professionals.

More than providing skills for work, schooling's promise also goes to the heart
of the meaning and purpose of modern society. Education is one of the core
commitments of an unequal society. Although not everyone will end up with jobs
that are equally good, everybody has a chance to do well at school and get a good
job – or so the argument goes amongst people convinced that the way society
works today is as good as it gets. Roughly speaking, the kind of job you have
reflects how well you have done at school, and if you haven't done well enough
at school to get a good job, you have only yourself to blame. On the other hand,
many social scientists would argue that chances are not that evenly balanced –
not everybody comes from social circumstances that provide access to equally
well-resourced education. In this socially critical view, society and education are
not so fair at all. However, whether you want to rationalise or critique an unequal
society, the education-to-work nexus is a critical part of the explanation of how
society works to distribute resources.

In this chapter, we examine the connections between education and three paradigms of work and its organisation in modern societies. The first two are widely known as Fordism and post-Fordism, named after Henry Ford, who pioneered assembly line production. The third, which we have named 'productive diversity', is the subject of our research and development work into education for the workplace.[1] It is an optimistic view of the way work may be organised in the near future, based on emerging trends in work organisation today. Productive diversity is a perspective whose practice also is compromised by the structures of inequality, but nevertheless attempts to move realistically in the direction of a more equitable society.

All three paradigms of work are alive and well today, depending on the sector of the economy in which an enterprise operates, whether the workplace is a traditional industrial setting, or even in different places and at different moments within a single, contemporary workplace. At different times and in different places, the earlier Fordist or post-Fordist approaches still seem to make a certain kind of sense, even if at times that sense can be explained in terms of inertia or resistance to change. At other times they seem anachronistic or unjust.

In each of the three sections of this chapter, we explore the connections between work and education according to the following dimensions:
Dimension 1: Technology
Dimension 2: Management
Dimension 3: Workers' education and skills
Dimension 4: Markets and society

Fordism: The modern past

Fordism takes its name from Henry Ford, an iconic as well as a truly influential figure in modern industrial production and organisational management. Here, we analyse the dimensions of Fordist work using the example of his motor car factory.

Dimension 1: Technology

The year is 1920. Ford's automobile factory is the biggest manufacturing plant the world has ever seen. One car, the famous Model 'T' Ford, comes off the end of the production line every minute. The scene is characterised by smokestacks, starting sirens and the relentless movement of the production line.

A massive press stamps crankcases from flat pieces of steel; another produces the 95 tubes for the radiator in one stroke.[2] It's a noisy, smelly and frenetically busy place. The machines of mass production are bigger than any that have ever been built before – more imposing and more productive than ever before. So is the factory system into which they are placed: the huge, integrated corporation undertaking a variety of interconnected tasks.

Henry Ford becomes a rich man, and this because he owns all that physical plant, the fixed capital. This is his technology. The workers do the work, he owns the plant, and for this reason, the profits are his for the taking. [*See*: Henry Ford on his car factory.[3]]

Dimension 2: Management

The modern industrial plant, says Henry Ford, requires the most rigid of discipline. It is 'so highly specialised and one part so dependent on the other that we could not for a moment consider allowing the men to have their own way'.[4]

The Fordist factory runs on strict lines of command. It is uncompromisingly hierarchical. Beyond the work that every person does is the hidden hand of the engineer who designed the machine, and behind him the orders of the boss. The whole workplace is structured like a giant pyramid, with departments, and divisions within departments, and branches within divisions, and sections within branches. At each layer of the hierarchy, a lesser boss reports to a bigger boss one level up in the hierarchy. The ultimate source of all the orders is Ford himself, at the head of a vertical chain of command. This is where the buck stops, and where the profits go.

Nothing beyond minimal exertion and thinking is expected of the vast majority of the thousands of workers in Ford's factory. All you have to do, indeed, all you can do, is take orders.

The underlying management principles of modern industrial plants like Ford's are perhaps articulated most clearly by Frederick Winslow Taylor. He devises a set of principles that he calls 'scientific management'. By measuring 'time and motion' of the workers, the manager can devise new ways of getting them to do more work in less time. Taylor is insistent this is not something the workers can work out for themselves. It is the function of the manager to work it out and then tell the worker what to do. [*See*: Frederick Winslow Taylor on 'scientific management'.[5]]

Dimension 3: Workers' education and skills

The skills and capacities required of most workers in Ford's factory were minimal. Technical knowledge was handed down to the many on the factory floor by the few who sat in offices designing the product, configuring the production line and engineering the ever-finer division of labour. Henry Ford claimed that only one per cent of his workforce needed more than one year of training. The rest, he was proud to say, did not need much at all in the way of human skills and capacities.[6]

This was the ingenious paradox of Ford's factory: his workers were producing one of the most complicated products ever created, but the human skills required of almost all of them were minimal. A factory of predominantly unskilled workers was producing an item of unprecedented technological sophistication. This was achieved by refining the division of labour, creating more and more tasks or steps on the production line, each of which required less and less skill.

In 1908, just before the introduction of the Model T, the average length of the task cycle of a Ford assembler was 8.56 hours, as each person worked on a large component of the car. Cars were built using methods not unlike those of the coach builders who had for centuries built horse-drawn vehicles, employing skilled artisans who knew how to work with wood and metal, how to make a wheel, an axle and the body of a vehicle. After the introduction of the moving assembly line in 1913, the average task cycle went down to 1.19 minutes.[7] One worker put this particular panel in place and the next person on the production line tightened that particular nut. Which worker, which panel or nut, and where on the production line, were all determined centrally, in a technological sense by the engineers, and in an organisational sense by the managers. The worker was told what to do, or more likely shown what to do, given that the workforce was predominantly immigrant and not necessarily proficient in English. From the point of view of the organisation, human beings were reduced to a lowest common denominator as unskilled bodies with raw working capacities. From the point of view of the organisation and the production process, all human beings were the same; they had the same basic physiological capacities.

The results appeared to be nothing short of miraculous. In the 1913 financial year, the 14 366 workers in the Ford Motor Company produced 168 304 Model T Fords. In 1914, 12 880 workers produced 248 307 Model T Fords.[8] In one year, each worker produced nearly 12 cars. In the next year, each worker produced more than 19. And from one year to the next, the skill level of the workers did not increase. The skill was in the giant, interconnected arrangement of machines that was the production line.

Getting a job in Ford's factory, the largest and most sophisticated workplace the world had ever seen, was relatively easy. If you were a new migrant to the United States who spoke very little English, the supervisor could tell you what to do by showing you with a few gestures. You could start on the production line just by being put there and being shown which nut to tighten where.

It didn't matter that the next person on the line spoke a different language from you – which they often did in the Ford factory, filled as it was with unskilled immigrant workers – because vertical communications were all that mattered, and these were minimal. In fact, horizontal communications were viewed with great suspicion by employers like Henry Ford. They might breed complaint, and complaint could lead to unionism, and unionism to revolution, and revolution to communism. The massive co-location of living, breathing, thinking human beings created a new community capable of articulating what was inhuman about their experience of work, seeking improvements through union action. At times, they might even dare to dream of a paradise on earth, freed of the hardships they experienced in earning their daily bread. [*See*: Karl Marx and Frederick Engels on industrial capitalism.[9]]

What kind of education system would work best for the Fordist factory? The schools of the first phase of mass-institutionalised education were themselves workplaces in the Fordist mould – places where teachers and students worked in conditions not dissimilar in their general social arrangement to the workplaces of the modern industrial system. The state determined the syllabus; the teachers led their students through the textbooks; and the students were assessed against the correct answers, which had been centrally determined by the educational bosses. From a managerial point of view, the first modern schools were like Ford's factory – they had a command structure in which teachers had little scope to teach anything and in any way beyond what they had been ordered to do by the education system, and students had to learn what they were told. The classroom was a place of surveillance and discipline, where students were taught to take the orders of teachers and uncritically to respect authority. [*See*: Michel Foucault on the power dynamics in modern institutions.[10]]

The classroom of didactic teaching was itself a site that prefigured for children many aspects of the world of adult work. In the era of Fordism, the syllabus systematically divided the curriculum into its component parts (not unlike the task cycles of Ford's production line), transmitted it to students bit by bit, and then assessed to see what the student had learnt.[11]

As discussed in Chapter 1 during our exploration of didactic education, this type of education produced two possible outcomes, both of which made a certain kind of sense in the era of Fordism. A few did well at school, got good grades and were put into the top stream. These few were destined to become the managers and the engineers. Perhaps taken to the level of diploma or even occasionally a university degree, this education was a once-in-a-lifetime opportunity to learn professional or trade knowledge that would last for life. Any other learning could be left to life experience.

The majority did not do so well at school. 'If only I had done better at school . . .', they might say to themselves, wistfully, believing for a moment that they really had the chance of a better job. At best, school had taught them a few values – punctuality, discipline, to take orders and to respect received knowledge. School might also provide them with a few 'basic' skills, such as the minimal reading, writing and arithmetic sometimes required to make their way in modern work. [*See*: Going to school in Richmond, 1900.[12]]

Dimension 4: Markets and society

'Any colour you like as long as it is black', said the phlegmatic Mr Ford, who paid his workers five dollars a day. This was good pay, he said, and enough to be able to afford the $500 Model T motor car. The economies of scale of mass production made it possible to produce consumer goods cheaply enough to create a mass market for them. Churning out the same product in huge numbers, day in and day out, Ford was able to produce a cheaper and cheaper car – so cheap, in fact, that even the lowliest of his workers could afford one.

Consumers, in this view, were conceived as a uniform mass market. Henry Ford had worked out what was good for the consumer – a basic car, always black – and was determined to give them what he thought was good for them. Mass production begat mass consumption, and with this came a series of cultural assumptions about the universal and homogeneous interests of modern people. As their needs were identical, the product could be identical. The same, Ford determined, was good for all and good enough.

In 1915, Henry Ford set up the Ford English School. All foreign workers in his factory had to attend. The first sentence they were taught was 'I am a good American'. One of the school's graduation ceremonies was described thus:

A great melting pot (labelled as such) occupied the middle of the stage. A long column of immigrant students descended into the pot from backstage, clad in outlandish garb and flaunting signs proclaiming their fatherlands. Simultaneously from either side of the pot another stream of men emerged, each prosperously dressed in identical suits of clothes and each carrying a little American flag.[13]

Immigrants – the poor and the hopeful – would come to the United States and start work in Ford's enormous factory. People of different cultures, languages and nationalities would all work together in the factory in the same kinds of ways, mostly earning the same pay. Ford proudly called this the 'five-dollar day'. In the end, they would have the choice of buying the same $500 car. In so doing, they would assimilate to the American Way of Life. Underlying Fordism was a philosophy of cultural uniformity.

At most, cultural and linguistic differences were used as a divide-and-rule tactic, deliberately putting workers who spoke different languages beside each other on the production line, for example. Gender differences were addressed in the Fordist workplace with a similarly two-sided ambivalence. In one moment, the Fordist organisation was gender blind (women and men are equally capable of working on the production line); in another, men did the managing or, if they were at the bottom of the hierarchy, they did men's work. The women, before they married at least, became secretaries and tea ladies or – perhaps, if they weren't to work in a factory – nurses or school teachers.

Although people entering industrial work for the first time experienced new-found affluence, this was a deeply unequal society. Women may have felt liberated as they earned their first pay packet. Immigrants fleeing poverty and war-stricken countries found themselves able to purchase small but previously unthinkable luxuries. But while they became more affluent in minor ways, their bosses became wealthier in fabulous ways, profiting hugely from the productivity of their workers and the scale of the mass markets for which they were producing. The relatively good times, however, never seemed to last that long, as the whole system period-ically lurched into recession and war. It was at these times particularly that the system looked less attractive to ordinary workers. This was when they began to think of unions, of social democracy or even of a communist utopia in which the workers took control of the factories and distributed the fruits of their labours equally amongst themselves.

There are parallels and functional connections between didactic teaching and Fordism. This was the social context in which mass-institutionalised schooling emerged. Didactic education on a mass scale and Fordist work are social inno-vations born of the same historic moment. We might find Fordism and didactic education working together to create modern social orders and subjectivities in a variety of places and times. Even today, there are places where Fordism and didactic education remain explicable and viable. At other times they appear to be anachronistic flashbacks to a world that is all-too-familiar but in dire need of renovation and renewal. [*See*: Keeping Learners in their boxes.[14]]

Post-Fordism: More recent times

In times of bewildering change, diversity and uncertainty, we can easily find ourselves stumped for words to adequately describe what we are experiencing. So, social scientists have invented a number of 'post' terms – 'post-industrial' to describe technologically advanced economies, 'postmodern' to describe the state of our cultural affairs and 'post-colonial' to describe the cultures and modes of governance in now-independent countries of the 'developing' world. In the same vein, 'post-Fordism' describes a form of work organisation that is in many impor-tant respects quite different to Fordism. Post-Fordism tries to respond to many of the inherent problems and deficiencies of Fordism.

The gradual and uneven shift into working conditions that can be described as post-Fordist demands different skill sets and dispositions. This transition also influenced the circulation of ideas about the organisation of schooling, throwing into question the premises and ongoing relevance of didactic teaching. Maybe a vague sense of the changing times (less than any explicit edicts) gradually created a different kind of education to supply the new workplace with a new kind of person.

Dimension 1: Technology

Toyotashi, outside Nagoya in Japan, is one of the archetypical sites of post-Fordist work. Throughout its relentlessly urban and industrial landscape are scattered a number of large Toyota plants. In Plant No. 5, we stand watching the production line roll past, making cars at a pace and with a smooth efficiency that, were he there, doubtless would even have inspired that harsh task-master, Henry Ford.

But this is where the resemblance ends. Instead of mass production, the logic of production is now one of differentiation. Every other car on the production line is not just a different colour, it is also a different model. A computerised inventory system passes the windshield to the robot, which gently places it into the correct vehicle on the line. However, around these simple motions – just as simple as the motions of the worker making Ford's Model T – is a deep shift in technological process and organisational logic.[15]

The technological feel of Toyota's Toyotashi Plant No. 5 is one of lightness and adaptability. Cybernetic information systems guide the robots and the inventory system. These information systems are based on the notion of self-monitoring 'feedback loops'. Data is constantly circulating, the information system watching and checking, evaluating and predicting, what has just been done and what needs to be done next. The production process is open to continual software re-adjustment. It is based on principles of responsiveness and flexibility. Just-in-time inventory demands accurate communication of information and rapid responsiveness of suppliers.

Production-line workers now need high levels of skill to be able to deal with the complexities of the technology. The workers on the factory floor all belong to teams, constantly interacting with each other and the information systems, identifying as a group, reading the information flow and taking responsibility by intervening in this flow when necessary. These technological and human relationships are often also called 'flexible specialisation'. [*See*: After Fordism: Piore and Sabel on flexible specialisation.[16]]

Dimension 2: Management

The Toyota Company was founded in 1937. Amid the chaos of postwar Japan, in 1949 the company faced a series of crippling strikes and nearly collapsed. That year, Eiji Toyoda, an engineer and nephew of the founder, visited Ford's Rouge Plant in the United States. He decided that American-style mass production was not for Japan. Toyota had never been a mass manufacturer. Total production in the 12 years since it was founded was 2 685, compared with an output of 7 000 per day at Rouge. Japan had a small domestic market. There was a shortage of capital. There were no immigrants available who might work in substandard conditions.

This is how Japan's 'lean production' system came into being. Compared with mass production, the new Toyota system was based on smaller batches, less capital, shorter product development time, smaller inventories and, instead of vertical integration where all the divisions of the enterprise came within the control of one company, 'just-in-time' sub-contractual relationships with independent suppliers – meaning that the supplier was always there, ready to supply the component immediately it was ordered.

A degree of worker control was also conceded in the Toyota plant. Strong unions were given an official role in the running of the organisation. Teams were assigned responsibilities, including power to stop the line. An approach to problem solving was established, which involved every person so that problems once resolved never happened again. A suggestion scheme elicited workers' ideas. And a 'total quality management' system showed up mistakes instantly, or better still, prevented them from happening before they needed to be rectified. Beyond the organisation, a closer relationship was established with car dealers, so that production of specific models could be finely tailored to meet demand.[17]

Eiji Toyoda's measures reflect an important moment in the history of work and management in the 20th century. In the last part of that century, this new production system was established in many parts of the world. By the 1980s, even the United States was keen to copy the lessons of Japan's extraordinary postwar economic success story. This is how the authoritarian, Fordist, top-down management system came to be replaced in many workplaces by an approach that involves teamwork, and worker empowerment and responsibility.

At the smallest group level in the organisation, workers are organised into self-managing teams in a working culture based on 'shared values'. Team leaders are typically selected on the basis of interpersonal skills as well as technical capabilities, including their sensitivity to every team member's needs and capacities, and their ability to support team members so they could give of their best. The leader is meant to be a mentor or teacher more than an authority figure.

In addition to the emergence of new skills in demand, a consequence of this devolution of decision making and control to self-managing teams is a 'flattened hierarchy'. If teams can make decisions for themselves, so the argument goes, why do we need all those layers of middle management to make decisions for them? Indeed, the workers often understand their jobs better than their bosses and so have the capacity to make better-informed decisions, to the benefit of the whole enterprise.

Throughout the enterprise, the machine-like command structures of Fordism are replaced by the guiding metaphor of organisational 'culture'. Work is like a community in which, ideally, the workers identify with the 'mission and vision' of the organisation, and internalise its 'organisational values'. They are able to act autonomously and responsibly on behalf of the organisation because they have an intuitive feel for it and intrinsic interest in its success.

Or, at least, that's how the post-Fordist story goes, as told in countless training sessions, meetings, retreats and business-planning workshops. Workers may wish to question the extent to which the story rings true, or the extent to which their status as workers is elevated within company cultures. However, there is no doubt that the objective conditions of production and forms of work organisation have changed markedly from those of the Fordist enterprise.

An effect of the rise of post-Fordist work organisation is a shift in the balance of agency in the workplace. Teamwork shifted the site of some decisions about production from senior management to shop-floor team leaders and team members, integrating workers into the enterprise decision-making processes. If workplaces are sites of governance and consent, post-Fordism fundamentally changes the organisational politics of work. The autarchy of Fordism is replaced by the guided democracy of post-Fordism in which the 'empowered' worker assumes the objectives of the organisation on their own volition – hence the post-Fordist rhetoric of vision, mission, identifying with the culture of the organisation, team building and shared values. Systems–structure–command talk is replaced by motivation–culture–responsibility talk. [*See*: Peters and Waterman, 'In search of excellence'.[18]]

Dimension 3: Workers' education and skills

Ford had reduced the skill level required of every worker to a bare minimum, based on the principle of the division of labour into smaller and smaller components. In the post-Fordist factory, however, more of the unskilled jobs are taken over by machines as part of the process of increasing automation of production. This means that fewer unskilled workers are needed than before, and also that the skills required by the smaller number of skilled production workers have changed quite markedly. Society does more industrial manufacturing than ever before, but it needs fewer process workers. These changes also create a sense of fear that jobs are being taken by machines. Where, then, will the new jobs be? The answer to this question comes in part in the rise of service and 'knowledge' industries that create new areas of employment – including, for example, the rise of 'customer-relations' and marketing positions in manufacturing as customised production becomes increasingly oriented to consumer choice. Even in the traditional manufacturing and agricultural sectors of the economy, the skill levels required in order to operate sophisticated machinery steadily have risen, thus reversing the trend to de-skilling, which was a characteristic feature of Fordism.

Post-Fordist 'multi-skilling' becomes the order of the day. Contrary to the de-skilling characteristic of Fordist production processes (in which a complex task is broken down into multiple, narrower and simpler tasks, each of which can be completed by having minimally trained workers follow routine instructions), workers in the post-Fordist enterprise need to be able to undertake a broader range of complex tasks. They need to be flexible enough to shift from one task to another at different times during the production process – a form of work that became known as 'multi-tasking'. Technologies, moreover, are shifting more rapidly than ever. The broader and deeper your skills and knowledge base, the more readily you will be able to adapt in an environment of constant change.

The most immediate and direct impact of this change on education is felt as employers and governments recognise the need for a more highly skilled workforce, and turn again to their education systems to meet this demand. Since the middle of the 20th century, the numbers of people going on to higher levels of technical and professional education have increased markedly. In fact, the proportion of the population in the education system at any one time has grown more rapidly than total social investment in that system. Hence, the squeeze on resources that is so often felt in education, despite its growing (and acknowledged) significance in the development of a more highly skilled workforce.

The change from a Fordist to post-Fordist form of work organisation is not just about increased level of technical work skill. The post-Fordist workplace calls for different dispositions – for workers who can act autonomously and responsibly, who can troubleshoot and come up with creative solutions, who do not feel like they know the answers but have the resources to find things out and who can work effectively as team members. What kind of education will best serve this post-Fordist workplace? Didactic teaching may have produced the 'right' kind of person for the Fordist workplace, but this kind of person is not necessarily as well suited to the new work order of flexible specialisation.

Authentic education starts 'where the student is at' and 'builds motivation'; it facilitates individualised or student-centred 'inquiry'; and it encourages 'discovery' learning and 'problem solving'. In these respects, authentic education promotes classroom practices that are better aligned to the subjectivities suited to the post-Fordist workplace. [*See*: Dewey on education for active workers.[19]]

The historical connections between the rise of post-Fordist work and authentic education may be messy and complex. Teachers did not come to work one day to find instructions to create a new kind of person for the new regime of post-Fordist work. History rarely works in such obvious ways, with such clear relations of cause and effect. It is enough simply to note the compatibility of post-Fordist work and authentic education, and a broad parallelism on their development paths. The two are fellow travellers in a long, slow and uneven process of social change.

Dimension 4: Markets and society

The shift towards post-Fordist forms of work was accompanied by some enormous social transformations. What motivated people to go to work and what was supposed to make them 'tick' at work changed enormously. An economy of person-to-person command has been replaced by an economy of self-motivation. But this works only so long as the workers' goals align with those of the bosses. Hence, the corporate emphasis on training in teamwork, to develop a corporate culture, instil the organisation's vision and inculcate its mission.

Even though its forms of organisation and work processes are different to those of a 'Fordist' enterprise, the post-Fordist enterprise is still a place of relative cultural uniformity. This uniformity, however, is based now on pressures rather than commands to conform – to fit into the team and share its values, to express belief in the organisation's mission and to 'clone' to its corporate culture. This is a softer form of assimilation than Fordism whereby, if you don't fit in, you find yourself hitting a 'glass ceiling' rather than the street.

In the realm of consumption, too, although there's an appearance of wider choice, this is often only superficially the case. The car you go out to buy might be any colour or style, but underneath there's not that much product choice, let alone the choice not to consume. If you don't live near public transport you still need a car and there's no escaping the wage–consumption cycle. Meanwhile, despite the seemingly egalitarian talk of teams and cultures, at best, workers get slightly more affluent, while bosses get very much richer. Relative inequality grows.

Fordism also remains comfortably alongside post-Fordism in a relationship of uneven development. As developed countries move towards 'new economy' work-places, the sweatshops and the dirtiest of industrial production are shifted to poorer regions within a country or to the developing world. It seems, at times, that post-Fordism in one place needs Fordism in another. This symbiotic rela-tionship means exclusion from the more advanced post-Fordist forms of work and consumption around enduring and systemic divisions between the devel-oped world and the developing world; the rust belt and the sun belt; higher-paid workers and lower-paid workers; and those who can afford to consume in fancy niche markets and those who can only afford generic, mass-produced goods. [*See:* Richard Sennett on the new 'flexibility' at work.[20]]

Post-Fordism's limitations are also authentic education's limitations. Workers are more in control of what they do at work; but the agenda is set by the internalis-ing objectives of the boss and assimilation to the cultural feel of the organisation. Learners are more in control of their learning, but what is being learned is still the one right answer from the academic discipline, or content that is 'relevant' to your supposedly inevitable social destiny.

Productive diversity: New Learning

'Productive diversity' is a term we use to describe what every now and then comes after post-Fordism, particularly in those moments when the flaws and limitations of post-Fordism are addressed and or partly overcome. It is a term that emerges from our work and others' about the changing nature of work.[21] Productive diver-sity works on finding practical solutions to what doesn't work in post-Fordism. Each moment of the new demonstrates what could come next and what, it seems at times, should come next.

Productive diversity stands for a number of things: workplaces that foster autonomy and responsibility, that devolve power, that honour the differences amongst their members – that establish, in short, new working relationships and balances of agency. Productive diversity straddles the actual and the possible, the emergent and the ideal. It builds on the foundations of realism about today but with a strategically optimistic view of what may be possible tomorrow.[22] What we have called 'New Learning' is the kind of education that will best serve a world of work characterised by productive diversity.

Dimension 1: Technology

The flexible specialisation that comes with post-Fordism changes the way in which the modern factory operates. The technologies of productive diversity centrally depend on information and communications systems, not only in the new knowledge industries, but to transform manufacturing and primary industries, too. [*See:* Daniel Bell on the post-industrial society.[23]]

Whereas the first stage of the computer revolution advanced the level of automation possible in the traditional workplace, the second wave changes the workplace itself. To take just one aspect of change: the architect, the banker, the designer, the teacher no longer have to go to fixed geographical locations to do their work. They can do it online, for periods of time at least. They can work in virtual teams whose members do not even have to be in the same country. Perhaps they are members of huge organisations; perhaps they are sole traders or micro-businesses. Either way, the boundaries between work and home, personal and organisational, local and global, become blurred.

Being at home is by no means a retreat into familiar cultural territory. The teacher in a Melbourne home may be tutoring a child in China in English; the architect in London may be working with a design and construction team in Jakarta; and the banker in Beijing may be organising transactions between manufacturers in China and stores in Europe. Differences are closer to home than ever – literally as well as metaphorically. The industrial systems of Fordism and post-Fordism created neighbourhood diversity, insofar as they attracted migrant labourers from many cultures to manufacturing towns and cities. The information systems of productive diversity remove all physical barriers to direct engagement with diversity, from the intimacy of the home office to the ends of the Earth.

The new technologies, moreover, bring with them new economies of distribution. There is no cost advantage in proximity. If you can afford the computer and the Internet connection, emails, downloads and Internet telephony are virtually free. New media forms abound – blogs and wikis and bulletin boards – providing closer views of disaster, images of human travesties that in an earlier era could have been covered up, and terrorist-eye-views of acts of violence. These are disruptive technologies, unsettling centralised models of commerce and displacing them with highly devolved production of information, culture and services.

Such changes are deep. Economists have even had to rethink the nature of value. In the industrial era, value was in physical capital, and technologies were embodied in machines. The factory was more or less worth the value of the land on which it stood and the cost of building the plant. In the 'knowledge economy', the capital value of an enterprise is increasingly located in what economists call 'intangibles' – brand, product or service design, reputation, business systems, customer relationships and loyalty, intellectual property, human skills and the capacity of the organisation to capture, systematise, preserve and apply knowledge. These intangibles are more important to the viability of an enterprise today than physical capital. [*See*: Yoneji Masuda on the information society.[24]]

The fundamentals of value today are in human skills, relationships, culture, knowledge and learning. Complex and changing technological and human expectations require flexibility, creativity, innovation, initiative.

The reasons why the primary source of value has shifted from physical to human and cultural capital can be traced in part to the nature of the new technologies. These technologies are more infused with human meaning than ever before, their human interfaces drenched with textuality, visual symbolism and representational and cultural force. The irony here may not be that today's large changes in human society are technologically determined; quite the reverse, it may well be the case that we are finding new ways to humanise the machine.

Dimension 2: Management

Fordism is a system of top-down hierarchical control. Post-Fordism is a system of soft power. You might get sent off to a training course designed to build teams, to improve communication skills or enhance mutual understanding between team members. Such courses may have outdoor or physical activities, possibly involving an element of adventure and risk. In this artificial environment, all the differences seem to fall away. You develop 'shared values'. Your organisation may also develop vision and mission statements. It is, of course, always striving to be the best company, producing the best products or providing the best services. You are expected to believe it, and even better, to have come to that conclusion by yourselves. You 'clone' to the organisation's culture. You personify the organisation by sharing the 'passion' for all it does. You project the aura of good feeling that surrounds the organisation by saying 'have a nice day' to the customers.

The effect of this approach is cultural homogenisation in the workplace. The organisation seems to be saying to newcomers something like this: 'We will welcome you into the corporate fold providing you take on our shared values and cultural style, providing you become like our image of ourselves. We want you to fit in. If your differences are noticeable, then we will deal with them by not making an issue of them. For your part, just leave them outside each time you enter the corporate door.'

The major problem with this approach is that cloning or cultural assimilation is never this simple. Rarely can people completely hide their differences. It is also often counter-productive even from an organisational point of view. The organisation wantonly neglects potentially invaluable competencies, experiences and networks. 'Glass ceilings' develop that restrict that contribution of genuine talent just because people don't fit the existing corporate style, or when they are excluded by 'old boy' or insider networks. The organisation says it values everybody, but if you're a woman, or a member of an ethnic minority, or if you are different in some other way, it may just happen that you don't get the recognition and the promotions achieved by those who conform more closely to its dominant cultural image.

This becomes a system of soft power. The problem is that, despite its egalitarian words, post-Fordism often turns out to be just another system of exclusion. As soon as it is put in place, it runs into serious trouble on a number of fronts. In a world of increasingly diverse local communities, the organisation does not necessarily attract the best recruits, instead restricting itself to a narrow demographic that reflects its equally narrow cultural self-image. Within the organisation, the mediocre seem to float to the top just because they are well connected and happen 'to fit'. Meanwhile, other people who know their jobs extremely well, perhaps better even than the team leaders and managers, are excluded. In an era of globalisation and locally differentiated niche markets, this makes little sense. An organisation that is good at dealing with its own diversity will be better able to deal with a world of diversity. Its members will not expect the next employee, or next customer, or next supplier to have the same culture.

The post-Fordist organisation also breeds a culture of uncritical conformity. People are isolated as critics or trouble-makers when they might have a valid point of view that the organisation should be addressing. The critical non-conformists may be the people to whom a genuine 'knowledge organisation' should be listening most attentively. Besides, does anybody really believe the overblown rhetoric of vision and passion and shared values? Post-Fordism often creates a suppressed underground culture of people who know the critical truth and grumble about it privately to each other, but who never get the chance to contribute what they know.

We advocate productive diversity as a response to the inherent deficiencies of post-Fordist work organisation, deficiencies that become self-evident as soon as the organisation is established. Instead of attempting to force cultural homogeneity upon members of the organisation whose lifeworld origins are diverse, the productive diversity organisation attempts to capitalise on the talents of diversity. Valuing diversity is an important part of team building; not just to ensure the contribution of all involved, but also to draw on the resource of diversity – different points of view, styles of communication, ways of working, interests and life experiences. These may be based on gender, ethnicity, cultural aspirations, life experiences, interests or any other of a broad range of differences.

This approach to organisational culture encourages the development of habits of mind through which people are constantly prepared for the unpredictability of engagement with others whose lifeworld experiences are varied; and which recognise the value of those differences and negotiate them effectively. This represents a fundamental shift in the culture metaphor: from one which was, in systems described as post-Fordist, consciously or unconsciously founded on a notion of cultural commonality, to one where negotiating diversity is the key dynamic. Diversity here spans the customisation of products and services for niche markets, working the dynamics of teams drawn from a globalised labour force, building networks with other organisations whose occupational cultures are very different, and building cross-cultural collaborations and alliances.

The organisation that embraces the tenets of productive diversity replaces the soft power of post-Fordism with a more honest and genuine devolution of power in the organisation. Power is vested in the hands of the organisation as a whole: the people who belong to it and the clients who relate to it – in all their diversity. This is a system of stakeholder control. Management is through participation, negotiation and collaboration. It is also an approach that values dissent. In fact, people in this kind of organisation turn dissonance into a productive force. This could even extend to the point of dealing with bigger-picture ethical issues of inequality, sustainability and customer interests before they become a serious threat to the very existence of the organisation.

So deep is this change that it extends even to the nature of personality. The society of rigid, hierarchical Fordist organisations engendered relationships of command and compliance in all social agencies, not just in the workplace (the bosses and supervisors whose orders were to be obeyed), but also in homes (the heads of households who made decisions and disciplined) and in schools (the headmasters and teachers, mandated curricular content and tests of definitively correct answers). For every command personality, there had to be a multitude of unquestioning functionaries, and the system depended upon their compliance. The ideal worker was compliant; the ideal learner in the classroom of disciplined knowledge was compliant.

Today, the command personality is an anachronism. The devolution of social and cultural responsibility to the furthest reaches of the organisation is now a prerequisite to high performance. This is a time of self-regulation, which demands good citizenship at every level, from the corporation as good citizen to the members of the corporation themselves working as good citizens within its structures. [*See*: Peter Drucker on the new knowledge manager.[25]]

Dimension 3: Workers' education and skills

The working world of productive diversity raises the knowledge and skills expectations of its members still further than that of the post-Fordist organisation. Technologies change at a quickening pace, which means that workers need to be constantly updating their content knowledge and skills. What you learnt at school, college or university soon becomes out of date, which means that you need to take

another degree, or a refresher course, or a training program, or to teach yourself through an e-learning program, or to learn the latest version of a software
package from help menu and with 'over the shoulder teaching' by co-workers.[26]
Because both expertise and technical knowledge has a shelf life that is becoming shorter and shorter, learning and skills development have to be lifelong and
life-wide.

The skills of productive diversity are also deeply interpersonal: how to collaborate with colleagues whose life experiences and skill sets are different and
complementary to your own; how to share knowledge as a teacher as well as a
learner; and how to relate to clients and provide them with products and services
 that address their varied needs and interests. [*See*: Working at Google.[27]]

Meanwhile, the very nature of 'career' changes. Gone is the stable pathway,
based on seniority or even a simple idea that merit means conforming to a uniform
standard. Jobs don't last so long; people swap employers, and even industries,
more regularly. Careers head off on unanticipated tangents, and one's credentials
come to be made up of accumulations of divergent experiences that previously
might have been regarded as bizarre. What a worker takes with him or her from
one job to the next is a 'portfolio' of experiences, and the more varied and broadly
focused this portfolio, the more rounded and valuable they will appear to a new
employer.

The changes in the nature of work that we have described in this chapter have
enormous implications for education. The main game is now knowledge and
relationships – the stuff of human rather than fixed capital. They are things that
are made by learning. For this reason, learning has become pivotal to the whole
 economy. [*See*: Educating for the knowledge society. [28]]

The economy of the changing present and near future requires people who
can work flexibly with shifting technologies; who can work effectively in the new
relationship-focused market and community environment; and who are able to
work within an open organisational culture and across diverse cultural settings.

We have characterised the kind of education suited to the new nature of work
as 'New Learning', or transformative education. Preparing tomorrow's knowledge
worker is one of the principal tasks for contemporary educators. The success of
teachers and educational communities as they undertake this task will be reflected
in the performance of economies and the welfare of nations.

Dimension 4: Markets and society

'Any colour you like, so long as it's black,' said that heroic command personality,
Henry Ford. Today, there can be no such entrepreneurial heroism because the
customer is 'always right' and products and services need to be customised to mesh
with the multiple identities of niche markets. These markets are differentiated
according to age, gender, ethnicity, sexual preference, style, fashion and taste. So,
we have the big SUVs, the smart sports cars, the spacious family cars, the micro

cars for crowded cities, hybrid cars for the environmentally conscious, cars of any hue and trim – so many permutations, in fact, that an individual order sometimes has to be placed before a vehicle is even manufactured.

In the era of post-Fordism, product differentiation was often no deeper than the coat of paint and a few accessories. In the era of productive diversity, consumer 'needs' have been transformed to the point where consumers are drawn to representations as much as they are to physical entities. Here, the play of the product is about the consumer's identity and not just practical utility. The product is now a complex thing comprising design, aesthetics, image, concept, brand association, service values – and utility – but not first and foremost. The use-value of the transaction is cultural as much as it is utilitarian. This is also why organisations increasingly find that they need to trade on the intangibles of image, ethics and the making of moral meaning.

In an optimistic view, the transition to post-Fordism and then productive diversity may well indicate that we are on a social course whereby expanding expectations take us beyond the gross inequalities of past and current economic systems. The logic of equity, as anticipation and disappointment, may lead people into wider expectations and to demand real change. With a gentle nudge, small improvements within systems logic may turn into utopian aspiration for something more. In education, this might mean more than simply preparing students to get good jobs in the new world of work. It might also mean building a social imagination grounded in an ethics of equity that extends beyond the logic of the modern system of paid work with all its inequalities. How, for instance, might a deepening understanding of globalism, difference and the system of working-for-money open out larger questions of our human natures and the ways we inhabit the Earth?

The purpose of education is not just to serve the needs of the economy by creating useful workers. The economic rationale behind much of today's talk of educational change is, on its own, too narrow. Participating in the formation of useful workers is only one of several of the fundamental purposes of education. The following two chapters discuss the role of education in creating fully participating citizens and shaping persons at home in their different identities. In order to be useful and successful in today's work, individuals need to be able to participate, to be good 'corporate citizens'. They also need to be a certain kind of person, comfortable with their identity and able to give something of themselves in their work.

If the educational basics of the traditional classroom produced well-disciplined but compliant persons who relied on the stability of the facts and theories they had been taught, the New Learning will need to open up a space in which individuals can participate in shaping themselves as different kinds of persons; persons with the skills and capacities of adaptability, flexibility, initiative and innovation required by the new workplace. [*See*: It's our responsibility to engage them.[29]]

In responding to the radical changes in working life that are currently underway, we need to tread a careful path that provides students with the opportunity
to develop the knowledge, capacities and sensibilities that will allow them access
to new forms of work. At the same time, our role as educators is not simply to
be technocrats. It is not our job to produce docile, compliant workers who fit
into whatever regime of work happens to be in place or emerging at a particular moment in time. Learners also need to develop the capacity to speak up, to
negotiate and to be able to engage in creating the conditions of their working
lives.

Indeed, the twin goals of access to work and critical engagement need not be
incompatible. The question is: how might we ground our educational work in
the pragmatic needs of today's high-tech, globalised and culturally diverse workplaces, yet at the same time relate these to educational programs that are based
on a broad vision of the good life, creativity, innovation and an equitable society?

The contemporary workplace invests in the creation of new systems for getting people motivated and making them productive. In some moments, these are
exploitative and oppressive. In other moments, we might optimistically conjecture that such systems might be the basis for a kind of democratic pluralism in the
workplace and beyond. In the realm of work, we have called this optimistic vision
productive diversity – or the idea that the multiplicity of cultures, experiences,
ways of making meaning and ways of thinking can be harnessed as an asset.[30]
Paradoxically, perhaps, democratic pluralism is possible in workplaces for the
toughest of business reasons, and economic efficiency may be an ally of social
justice, even though we know from experience that it is not always a staunch or
reliable one.

In building the idea of a New Learning whose goals are transformative, we have
attempted to develop an agenda for education that will work pragmatically for the
'new economy', and for the most ordinarily conservative of reasons. It will help
students to solve problems and get a decent job, and that's particularly important when the dice of opportunity seem to have been loaded against particular
individuals and social groups.

In another reading of today's economy, however, we should be under no illusions about the liberatory potential of the new economy or even, at times, about
how 'new' it actually is. The discourses and practices of today's workplace can
just as easily be interpreted to be a highly sophisticated form of co-option. A lot
of people are left out of the new economy: the service workers in hospitality and
catering who wash dishes and make beds; the illegal immigrants who pick fruit
and clean people's houses; and the people who work in old-style factories in China,
or call centres in India. Patterns of exclusion remain endemic.

From this perspective, we need to take our educational agenda one step further,
to help create conditions of critical understanding of work and power. This will
create a kind of knowing from which more genuinely egalitarian and productive
working conditions might emerge.

Summary

Learning for work	Fordism: The modern past	Post-Fordism: More recent times	Productive diversity: New learning
Dimension 1: *Technology*	Mass production; heavy industry and value in fixed capital, not the skills of workers.	Application of information technologies, small batch production, flexible specialisation, adaptable systems.	More knowledge and culture work, negotiating globalisation and cultural differences, value in the intangibles of the 'knowledge economy'.
Dimension 2: *Management*	Strict hierarchy, work discipline, management by command, centralised sources of knowledge and control.	Teamwork, worker responsibility, management by consent: workers take on corporate culture, shared values, vision and mission.	Negotiating differences, local and global; management through participation and collaboration.
Dimension 3: *Workers' education and skills*	Division of labour, specialisation, machines and the system designed by the skilled few, operated by many unskilled workers. Didactic education: discipline, minimal basic skills for most students, sifting and sorting a small, educated elite from the rest.	Multi-skilling: a broad range of skills that can be flexibly applied. Authentic education: relevant, student-centred inquiry, building motivation and responsibility.	New and constantly changing knowledge requirements of initiative, flexibility, innovation, creativity; premium on interpersonal capacities such as collaboration. The portfolio worker: diverse life experiences and networks valued. Transformative education: central to the economic and social life of knowledge society.
Dimension 4: *Markets and society*	Cheap products for mass markets, mass consumption of uniform, generic products; mass culture, cultural conformity and uniformity.	Differentiated markets; moving the Fordist workplaces to the developing world.	Mass customisation for niche markets, links into diverse local and global markets. Knowledge society: economic and social value in human capacities and knowledge.

Notes

1. Cope and Kalantzis 1997a
2. Jardim 1970, p. 88
3. Ford 1923, pp. 103, 103–104, 105–106, 107–108, 110, 79, 111. See extract at NewLearningOnline.com
4. Ibid p. 79
5. Taylor 1911, pp. 44–46, 59. See extract at NewLearningOnline.com
6. Ford 1923
7. Womack, Jones and Roos 1990, pp. 27–28
8. Jardim 1970, p. 92
9. Marx and Engels 1848 (1973), pp. 73–74, 75–76, 78, 98. See extract at NewLearningOnline.com
10. Foucault 1979, pp. 200–201, 205, 207, 215–216, 218, 211. See extract at NewLearningOnline.com
11. Cope and Kalantzis 1993
12. McCalman 1984, pp. 73–74. See extract at NewLearningOnline.com
13. Quoted in Bernstein 1994, p. 163
14. Burrows, Cope, Kalantzis, Loi, Suominen and Yelland 2006a. See extract at NewLearningOnline.com
15. Cope and Kalantzis 1997a, pp. 54–56
16. Piore and Sabel 1984, p. 17. See extract at NewLearningOnline.com
17. Womack, Jones and Roos 1990, pp. 48–67
18. Peters and Waterman 1984, pp. xx, xxi–xxii, xxv. See extract at NewLearningOnline.com
19. Dewey 1916 (1966), pp. 259–60. See extract at NewLearningOnline.com
20. Sennett 1998, pp. 9–10, 23, 30, 22, 24–25, 10. See extract at NewLearningOnline.com
21. Cope and Kalantzis 1997a.
22. Ibid.
23. Bell 1999, pp. x–xi, xiv, xv–xvii. See extract at NewLearningOnline.com
24. Masuda 1980, pp. vii–viii, 31–33. See extract at NewLearningOnline.com
25. Drucker 1993, pp. 18, 40–41, 51, 53, 88, 97–98, 99. See extract at NewLearningOnline.com
26. For more on 'over the shoulder' learning, see Michael Twidale at http://people.lis.uiuc.edu/~twidale/research/otsl/
27. Schmidt and Varian 2006, pp. 42–46. See extract at NewLearningOnline.com
28. Friedman 2006, pp. 10–12. See extract at NewLearningOnline.com
29. Burrows, Cope, Kalantzis, Loi, Suominen and Yelland. 2006a. See extract at NewLearningOnline.com
30. Cope and Kalantzis 1997a

Chapter 4

Learning civics

Overview

Education is closely interconnected with the public domain of citizenship. The modern state takes considerable responsibility for education, much of which is public or at least partly supported by the state. Education is now almost universally considered to be a right, and for children it is compulsory in most national jurisdictions. Education also plays an important role in shaping certain kinds of citizens.

As the relationship of the state to civil society changes, so does education. Modern, mass, institutionalised schooling emerged in an era characterised by 'nationalism' in the public sphere. Large and strong states established command relationships with their citizens. You did what the state said was good for you. These states also promoted the idea of an homogeneous community with clear borders. Schools played an important role in this process as they became one of the primary places for the socialisation of children – using didactic teaching and taking an exclusionary or assimilationist approach to learners' differences.

Since the last quarter of 20th century, we have entered a phase referred to as 'neoliberalism', during which the size of the state has been shrunk and an ethics of the free market and self-reliance revived from its 19th-century roots. This has translated into a partial withdrawal of the state from education and the privatisation of schooling. Even in public education, there has been a devolution of school management and control of curriculum to the school itself. The practices of authentic education appear to be conducive to the shaping of this kind of citizen.

Our vision of an alternative civic pluralism is based on a strategically optimistic reading of contemporary trends. It describes and prescribes a system of distributed

71

*governance and responsible citizenship – in workplaces, community organisations
and schools, for instance. For this social context, education for civics fosters capacities to participate based on an ethic of self-governance and participation. It also
involves continually negotiating differences and problem solving. In these conditions, we argue that a transformative education is more appropriate.*

On citizenship and education

A citizen is a person who belongs to a political community governed by a state.
The person is a citizen because they have been born there or, if not born into that
nation, has been granted citizenship to live as a full member of that nation. The
citizen obeys the laws of the nation, and enjoys the rights it offers – to vote, to
work and to be supported when they need support.

There are two parties to the pact of citizenship: the state and the members
of civil society. The state makes laws and can legitimately force its citizens to
act and live in the ways it legislates. Civil society consists of ordinary people
going about their everyday lives and associating voluntarily. In a democracy, the
state is designed to be a creature of civil society. The members of civil society
vote for a legislature and the state executive (the president, or prime minister
and ministers). For a defined term they take charge of the civil service, which
administers the affairs of state.

Things have not always been this way, and are not always this way today. Sometimes the relationship between state and civil society is not fully democratic. In the
democracy of ancient Athens, women and slaves could not be citizens. In many
modern states it was not until the 20th century that women and workers without
property were allowed to vote. Even today, democratic principles are distorted
when moneyed interests and lobby groups exert disproportionate influence on
the political system.

The state has an army to fend off external aggression, a police force to ensure
law and order in local communities, a legal system to deal with law-breaking
and disputes, and a legislature to make new laws. The modern state also has
an elaborate administrative infrastructure, which provides services such as pen-
sions, unemployment benefits, roads and hospitals. It creates and sponsors public
institutions, including schools, colleges and universities. All of these services can
be, and sometimes are, provided by private organisations. The state, however, is
the only institution that can be expected to make them available to everybody.
Even when such services are made available privately, the state frequently takes
an interest by legislating practices and regulating standards.

With the rise of mass-institutionalised education, for the first time in human
history the state, through the compulsory schooling system, took on major responsibility for the socialisation of children. Children used to learn what they needed
to know for adult life from the members of their extended family in the clan or

village. Now they learn a lot of what they need to know for adult life from the formal institutions of education. Modern people entrust to the state a large part of the socialisation of their children. Even if parents want to school their children at home, they have to be able to demonstrate that they will be teaching the same things that the school would.

This is roughly how the state has evolved to relate to civil society over the past century or two of modern times. The details of the story, however, are more complicated. Just as we saw large changes in the nature of modern work (that we have characterised as a shift from Fordism to post-Fordism and to emerging forms of work organisation that we have named productive diversity), so too have there been enormous changes in the form of the modern state, and with that changes in the kinds of education that are appropriate to the needs of the state. These different forms we will call 'nationalism', 'neoliberalism' and 'civic pluralism'. This last concept we have developed as a part of our academic work and our work in government, developing 'multicultural' policies.[1]

The changing forms of the state are explored in this chapter according to the following dimensions of the relationship of the state to society and education:
Dimension 1: The way the state exerts power
Dimension 2: The way government services are provided
Dimension 3: Belonging or the dynamics of citizenship
Dimension 4: Character building or learning civility

Nationalism: The modern past

The relation of the state to civil society can be understood in terms of the things that it does: the manner in which it exerts power, the way it provides services, the way in which people are expected to belong in the civic spaces fashioned by the state, and the way in which civility is inculcated, primarily through the education system.

Nationalism was the founding ideology and practice of the modern state.

Dimension 1: State power

Before modern times, societies either did not have a state that was separate from civil society (for example, hunter-and-gatherer societies) or if they had states, they were frequently run on the basis of one form of hierarchical authority or another, such as the feudal relationship between a king or queen and their subjects. Gradually, the idea of a citizen evolved in which the state did not have total and unqualified control over the members of civil society. Citizens had rights that no ruler could simply ignore. Eventually, with the growth of democracy, civil society took ultimate control over the state – or, at least, that's what democratic theory would anticipate. The rule of civil society was a partial achievement of ancient Athenian democracy, the English Magna Carta of 1215, the United States Constitution of 1787 and the French Revolution of 1789. Modern societies are governed on the basis that the state exists for the benefit of citizens and that the citizens ultimately control the state.

However, even in apparently democratic modern societies, the citizens may feel themselves relatively powerless in the face of the power of the state. In fact, many modern states, although they say they are looking after the interests of citizens, have been far from democratic. Imperialism is the impulse of states to conquer and take over the territories of others in order to take the benefits of their resources. Fascism is a form of one-party, authoritarian government that is racist, exclusionary and warlike in its desire to extend the boundaries of its state. Communism in its classical, 20th-century Stalinist form, is one-party dictatorship on behalf of 'workers' and 'peasants', in which the state is the owner of all property and the employer of everybody. The welfare state is a milder form of control in which the state conceives what services are good for citizens and provides that to them, sometimes compulsorily. Citizens don't have much say over the details of the governance of the welfare state. All they can do is vote for a government every few years that will then decide things for them from a centralised position of power.

In one way or another, to different degrees and in different ways, the modern state commands and the modern citizen complies. In the case of the milder, welfare state the citizens have a chance to choose their government periodically, and the officials of the state have to be careful not to overstep the mark if their government is to be re-elected. But citizens still have little direct control over affairs of governance on a daily basis. The balance of agency is weighted in favour of the state at the expense of the citizen. [*See*: George Orwell, *1984*.[2]]

Dimension 2: Public services

Nationalism is the story of the relation of the citizen to the state, in which the state assures citizens of universal and identical rights. Or when this seems implausible (how is it that one person has enormous material resources when another has so few?), citizens are at least assured that the state will provide equal 'opportunity' or 'equity' (any citizen can become rich if they want to and try hard enough, or so the story goes). According to this theory, if the state provides everyone with the same schooling (the same curriculum, the same tests, the same class sizes), everyone will have the same opportunity to succeed.

This theory, however, is rather too simplistic. Because citizens start as unequals – by unequal inheritance of material and cultural capital, by being born as indigenous persons, or by being immigrants, for instance – universal and identical services do not produce equal outcomes. The curriculum of a school in a poor neighbourhood may be formally the same as the one in a more affluent neighbourhood, but the limit on resources available (numbers of teachers, textbooks, computers – at home and at school) will affect the quality of outcomes such that children can never keep pace with their peers in more affluent schools.

The state may try to compensate, to provide at least minimal specialist services to address the most serious injustices – such as remedial school programs and welfare programs. But, no matter how much it tries, inequality persists.

Dimension 3: Belonging and citizenship

The citizen of the modern state is what Gellner calls 'modular man'. Individuals have to be identical in order to be mobile and substitutable. Any worker or soldier has to be replaceable by another. This demands cultural homogeneity and standardisation of the national language.[3] If a child comes to school speaking a foreign language or a dialect, it is the role of education to teach him or her the national language. This is how the nationalist state runs its own institutions and also how it supports the private labour market – by providing workers who speak the same language. [*See*: Gellner on the meaning of nation.[4]]

The modern state also compensates for the unreliability and irregularities of the labour market. In fact, the strongest of modern states are those deliberately created as an antidote to the failure of the market to provide the necessities of life: fascism, communism and the welfare state.[5] The power mechanisms of these states are soaked through with the principles of homogenisation; with services such as mass education and social welfare provided identically to every person and on the basis of universal principles. They were also exclusionary of differences, sometimes viciously or even to the point of genocide in worst-case scenarios for indigenous, ethnic or religious minorities.

As well as this compensatory and redistributive function, nationalist states also serve the function of creating solidarity outside the market in spite of the market and, even at times, as an antidote to the market. The unattractive reality of the market is that isolated individuals can be substituted for each other at any time. Any worker is dispensable because another can be found to take their place.

Nationalism develops a narrative of kinship and national belonging; a story that says there are millions of others who share the same sense of themselves by virtue of experiencing exactly the same things across time and space – from stories of national origins, to the news stories of the day presented through the mass media. Anderson calls these 'imagined communities' because they are real in the imagination, but not in their actual, cultural and spatial proximity.[6] [*See*: Anderson on the nation as 'imaged community'.[7]]

Nationalism is a social and political process which – sometimes more and other times less successfully – attempts to create a veneer of social/cultural sameness. In fact, the fiction of oneness is simply a method for dealing with difference. The modern, nationalist state has two ways of facing differences, either through direct exclusion or by requiring the assimilation of people defined as 'outsiders'. Exclusion may be through codes of restriction of immigration, apartheid, genocide, wars to redefine borders, or refugee movements. To explain these exclusions,

nationalists draw on the ideology of racism, which speaks of the superiority of the
official national 'us' and provides the ostensible reasons it is undesirable to live
with 'those others'. [*See*: Belonging to a 'civilisation': The purpose of history.[8]]

Alternatively, assimilation meets difference by demanding that people become
the same, that they make themselves identical and invisible by taking on the
official language and national identity. Assimilation is, of course, a somewhat
gentler form of racism than outright exclusion. Furthermore, the cultural and
linguistic transformation entailed is supposed to be beneficial to the new citizen.
[*See*: John Dewey on the assimilating role of schools.[9]]

Assimilation can be rationalised for what are apparently the best of reasons;
the inherent virtues of 'our' progress or development in comparison to 'yours';
'our' level of 'civilisation' in comparison to 'yours'. Be it by means of exclusion or
assimilation, however, the intended result of nationalism is always the same: to
create a singular nation. One history plus one geography makes one state.

Dimension 4: Learning civility

Modern nation-states take an interest in building the character of young people.
By learning the stories of the state, they become loyal citizens of that state. When
they go to school, children salute the flag, sing the national anthem, study its
historical narrative and learn to revere its iconic national heroes. Above all, they
learn to be obedient servants of the state. They take oaths of loyalty while a picture
of the head of state, prominently displayed on the classroom wall, watches over
them. This is how civility is inculcated. It is not a coincidence that mass, compulsory, institutionalised education emerges in parallel with the development of the
modern-nation state. [*See*: Eleanor Roosevelt on learning to be a citizen.[10]]

More than any other place in the modern world, schools were the sites in which
Gellner's 'modular man' and modern nationalism were created. For the first time
in history, the nation-state took away a large part of the socialisation of children
from families and communities. Families and communities were diverse; their
lifeworld experiences varied. Schools were to socialise their children into national
'identity'. Education was the key to the creation of a culture of commonality.

In fact, nationalism extended all the way into the depths of the curriculum, in
the teaching of literacy in the official, 'standard' language, the history of national
origins and the geography of borders. Against these measures students were
passed or failed; assimilated or left unassimilated.

Neoliberalism: More recent times

By the last quarter of the 20th century, the growth, consolidation and extension
of the nation-state as a force in the lives of citizens seemed to be slowing down
and even, in places, to be reversed. The change was by no means sudden, more
in the nature of a shift in broad trends than a sudden transformation of the civic

order. One of the key ideologies articulating and advocating for a smaller role in society for the state is called 'neoliberalism'. The 'neo' part of the word indicates that these ideas are not new. Rather, they are a revival of earlier ideas about markets and society that date back to the beginnings of the modern, market economy. Neoliberalism's case is that civil society is better regulated by the market than by state intervention, and that the state should withdraw from any areas of social activity that can be safely left to the market. [*See*: Adam Smith's 'invisible hand'.[11]]

Until this return to classical liberalism, the tendencies of the nationalist state had been to grow the size of government, expand the protective scope of the universal welfare state (often, to counteract the excesses of the market) and to create homogeneous classes of citizenry who consume state-provided services. By contrast, the ideology of neoliberalism advocates a shrinking of the state and the development of an ethics of self-reliance as an alternative to dependence on the welfare of the state. In this respect, neoliberalism also represents a return to older ideas of social hierarchy based on the values of the market and competition. If some people do better than others, the neoliberal argument goes, it is because they have worked harder or smarter in the market. Thus, inequality is attributed to individual differences. In their more recent reincarnations, these ideas are reminiscent in some respects of the 19th-century concept of the 'survival of the fittest'. [*See*: Herbert Spencer on the survival of the fittest.[12]]

Dimension 1: State power

The era of nationalism was the heyday of the big, strong state whose realm of activity started and ended at the borders of the nation. In the era of neoliberalism, the state is made smaller and weaker. In order to achieve this, neoliberal states undertake privatisation; they cut back the welfare state; they 'open' labour markets by restricting the power of trade unions; and they deregulate business, allowing the forces of the market to do their work unimpeded by government legislation. [*See*: Ronald Reagan on small government.[13]]

Neoliberalism is an ideology that mistrusts government and thinks that the market is the best mechanism for providing people with social resources. The market gives people an incentive to work and do well, so the neoliberal theory goes, whereas the 'nanny' or social welfare state is costly, inefficient and protects people to a point where they learn helplessness. [*See*: Margaret Thatcher: There's no such thing as society.[14]]

The turning point in the drift away from the large state and towards neoliberalism was the 1980s, the last years of the Cold War. In the advanced capitalist world, government enterprises – including state-owned utility systems, airlines, railways and banks – were sold as part of the trend to privatisation. Even social welfare and education were partly privatised and if these social services stayed in public ownership, the logic of the market and competition was introduced.

The Berlin Wall fell in 1989, and within a few years the post-communist states of Eastern Europe and the former Soviet Union had taken the neoliberal path. Whereas all industry and farms had been owned by the state in former communist nations, most were now privatised. In effect, this meant that either the managers and other well-placed people took over state industries as their own private property, or foreign firms came in and bought them up, often at bargain prices. In China and Vietnam, the communist parties stayed in control. All production had previously been controlled by the state, but now villagers were allowed a measure of 'personal responsibility' and to produce for the market. Foreign investment was also allowed, state-owned enterprises were increasingly encouraged to run along market lines and private businesses were permitted. [*See*: Deng Xiaoping: Socialism with Chinese characteristics.[15]]

Meanwhile, in almost every country of the world, the welfare state safety net was cut. The key idea behind these cuts was that the market is the best provider of welfare simply because it provides jobs. Better to force people to work than to allow the easy option of living on welfare. State-sponsored welfare removed the incentive for people to take responsibility for their own support. In fact, anything that interfered with the market – trade unions, for instance – was a bad thing. Neoliberals believed that the economy would be stronger if the market was allowed to determine the cost of labour.

Deregulation became another one of neoliberalism's catch-cries. The strong state that had developed in the earlier part of the 20th century created rules for every aspect of social life. It had interfered in areas in which it was not necessarily an expert. The neoliberals argued that all these regulations made it hard for businesses to operate and the market to be truly free – environmental controls, labour controls and controls regulating professions, for instance.

Once freed of these controls, the neoliberal case is that enterprises, industries or professional groups regulate their own behaviour because it is in their own best interests to do this. People do things well and efficiently because the market runs on the principle of competition, rather than rules imposed by government. This, the neoliberals argue, is the best way to produce the social good. [*See*: David Harvey, A brief history of neoliberalism.[16]]

Meanwhile, along with the rise of neoliberalism and the shrinking of the size and dominance of the state, came the larger forces of globalisation. Globalisation also reduced the relevance of the state by blurring its previously neater borders. Free markets – one of the shibboleths of neoliberalism – meant freedom of international finance and trade. Enterprises should be able to invest anywhere; for instance, where labour is cheapest, and trade anywhere without restrictions such as tariffs, quotas or subsidies. Currency exchange rates should be determined by financial markets. Interest rates should be determined by financial markets. Even labour markets are globalised as waves of legal and illegal migrants cross borders in search of work. The result is that, today, we have labour forces of such diversity that the idea of the homogeneous nation-state is becoming an anachronistic impossibility.

Dimension 2: Public services

The period during which the dust settled at the end of the Cold War in the last years of the 20th century represents a turning point in the history of the nation-state and the nature of the relationship of states to citizenries. The welfare state had been the capitalist world's answer to, or defence against, communism. Twentieth-century capitalist governments felt that they had to afford a program of redistributive justice, a large and expensive state that blunted the sharper edges of the market by addressing its worst inequalities.

With the end of the Cold War, milder economic cycles and lower unemployment, states around the world began a conscious program of retreat, shrinking the state and reducing the scale of its welfare programs. The ideology of neoliberalism claims that small states afford citizens greater liberty. According to this theory, society is created through the market, and the state should stay out of social and economic affairs to as great a degree as possible.

Every tax cut, every program cut, is made in the name of this neoliberal inter- pretation of liberty. One side-effect has been to increase inequality. Whilst the affluent have become very much more affluent, the disparities between the afflu- ent and the poor have grown.

In the social service that is education, the drift to neoliberalism has been experi- enced as shrinking state funding, pressure for teaching to become a self-regulating profession, the emergence of self-managing schools that are run like businesses or corporations, the end of geographical catchment areas so schools can compete for students, increasing the numbers of private schools and even privately owned, for-profit schools. Education is conceived more as a market than a service pro- vided to citizens, as it had been during the era of the welfare state. In the context of the shrinking state, public education is reduced to the most basic of basics. Literacy is reduced to phonics and numeracy to elementary mathematical proce- dures, simple to teach and neat enough to be tested easily. The assumption seems to be that the market can do the rest for those who can afford the tuition fees and find value for their money. Neoliberalism in practice reduces the relative quality and status of education for many, particularly those who have no alternative but public schooling.[17]

Dimension 3: Belonging and citizenship

This is when narratives of belonging solely to one people, one land, one nation, start to become less plausible. One reason for this is that, globally, the influence of states as sites of citizenship and focal points for community is waning. Their role in civil society is powerfully supplemented by, indeed perhaps replaced by, transnational corporations (where your work belongs), globalised professional communities, the global media which bring the world closer to home, and geo- graphically dispersed and perpetually shifting diasporas – migrant communities who are more interested in their roots and connections than ever, and with modern transport and communications, able to maintain these connections. People's identities, in other words, are less tied to one neatly defined nation-state – the one in which they live – than they were in the past.

The paradox of globalisation is that, although it seems to lead to cultural uniformity (a McDonald's in every neighbourhood), its universalising spread also produces startling diversification. Neighbourhoods are constantly changing as a consequence of global migration. The local community comes to feel like a micro-cosm of the whole world. And since 1989, global markets are such that there is almost no place in the world where you cannot sell your wares and no place in the world from which people are unable sell their wares into your local market; almost no place in the world to which you cannot journey in a few days; and almost no place in the world that is not instantaneously to be seen or heard at the other end of a telephone line, or the Internet, or a television reporter's camera. Hence, we propose this definition of our contemporary moment of 'total globalisation': for the first time in human history, the globe is the potential domain for any action or representation.

In an era of total globalisation, the racism that often accompanies nationalism is not only bad in principle, it is dysfunctional in practice. It is bad for business. If your neighbourhood or your workplace is diverse as a consequence of global labour flows, you need to get on with your neighbours, your team mates and your customers, or at least quietly accept their differences. If your workplace is part of a global enterprise, you need to be able to get on with parts of the organisation located in different places, and even move to live there if needs be. If your goods can be sold at the other end of the Earth, you need to find out about the kinds of people who might be purchasing them if they are going to sell well. If global tourism is one of the new boom industries, you need to be tolerant of the quirks of visitors from distant places in your midst and respectful of cultures you visit. If the big news is now as much global as it is local and national, you need to become an aware global citizen. As for imperialism, there's no need to take over other people's countries by force in order to access their markets – as the Spanish had done in Central and South America from the 15th to the 18th centuries, and as the British Empire had done from Ireland to the Americas to India to Australia between the 16th and 20th centuries. In fact, if you try it, you'll find that the costs today outweigh the benefits. Besides, why would you? When other peoples' markets are open, your enterprises can do business there without having to fire a single shot.

Meanwhile, the powers that be in former nation-states discover that all is not happily homogeneous amongst their citizens. Civil rights movements, anti-colonial movements, feminists and supporters of multiculturalism all begin to say, loudly and clearly, that exclusion and discrimination on the basis of race, religion, ethnicity, nationality, gender, disability and sexual orientation are not acceptable, in principle and in practice. All manner of social movements vociferously dispute and discredit the idea of the homogeneous nation. The voices of difference become louder and, as Charles Taylor says, their 'denunciations of discrimination and refusals of second class citizenship' become more and more vehement.[18] In place of one-people, one-state nationalism, the early phases of 'multiculturalism' emerge.

One side of this trend is to take pleasure in a new cosmopolitanism – the varied foods and the vibrant neighbourhoods. Another side is a libertarian detachment of the variety 'I don't give a damn, live whatever way you like, as long as I can live my life my way and prosper in the market'. According to the neoliberal argument, the state has no business trying to interfere in culture, or telling people how they should lead their lives beyond the most basic of basics, the market. Create market conditions within which people can pursue their individual material self-interest, so the argument goes, and social welfare and harmony will follow. The market will provide and culture will look after itself. Let the 'invisible hand' of the market do its work, as Adam Smith advised, and society will progress of its own accord.[19] Culture will flourish free of the meddling state. In other words, the state should interfere in society and culture as little as possible. Its main role is to enforce the basic rights and obligations that the workings of the market presuppose, such as contracts and private property. Citizenship carries with it no weight of cultural responsibility beyond allowing people to pursue their own self-interest in the market. In this context, cultural variations may flourish as fashion and fetish and fad, and each according to individual taste and market choice.

People who grew up with the neat assurances of nationalism sometimes find today's bewildering range of in-your-face differences to be disconcerting and dis-orienting. They regret the fragmentation of society and the dissolution of 'tradi-tional' values. In this debate, we hear 'back to the future' reactions in which some people argue for good, old-fashioned civics. Indeed, in many places in the world, the end of the Cold War was accompanied by the virulent ethno-nationalisms speaking for peoples who supposedly wanted their own states to the exclusion of cultural, linguistic and religious diversity. These were belated attempts at the project of creating the modern, ethnically homogeneous nation-state, mostly in places that have been ethnically diverse since time immemorial – in the former lands of Yugoslavia and the Soviet Union, or central and northeast Africa, for instance. This represents a kind of catching up with modernity, and the human cost has been comparable to earlier attempts; attempts such as the creation of a single German Reich under Hitler, or to the policies designed to assist the Indige-nous people to either assimilate or die out in Australia. Fascism and Indigenous 'protection' made a terrible kind of sense in the era of modern nationalism. But states that want to catch up now by going back to the future, neglect another future that is already upon us: the future of global interconnectedness and local diversity.

Dimension 4: Learning civility

Schooling was a significant institutional part of the regime of modern nationalism and compulsory schooling; a creature of the modern nation-state. With the rise of neoliberalism, schooling faces the same crises and transformations that the state does more generally. How do teachers deal with all the differences they face, and that now demand their attention in the classroom? The old citizenship education was easy, but how does one teach for multicultural citizenship? And how do schools and their communities deal with the partial withdrawal of interest of the state in education and, with a reduced tax base, a diminishing capacity to act?

The partial withdrawal of the state from education takes many forms: 'self-managing' public schools with devolved budgets and school councils; the proliferation of private schools offering every kind of cultural promise, from entree to ruling-class networks to fundamentalist religious discipline; parents removing their children and undertaking home schooling; flexibly delivered, distance mode, work relevant training-as-education; and the sponsorships and marketing that reflect the widespread commercialisation of education, a space once sacrosanct and clearly separated from commercial interests. As a consequence, the singularity of purpose within education during the era of nationalism has dissipated, as has its institutional continuity and coherence. [*See*: McLaren on life in schools.[20]]

At points, even the rationale for education changes. From the idea of a common curriculum for all, the new catch-cries are freedom, choice and diversity of educational offerings. In reality, this means one of two things. The first is tokenism when it appears that diversity is honoured – a superficial 'spaghetti and polka' multiculturalism of 'national days' and country studies and community events – but in which nothing much changes in terms of patterns of core curriculum processes and thus educational outcomes. [*See*: Our multicultural society.[21]]

The second is the phenomenon of different social groups parting company. Educational institutions fracture and fragment as they attempt to create self-enclosed communities. Children go to a fundamentalist religious school, run by their religious community, later to be employed in businesses run by their co-religionists. Children of migrant ethnic groups go to a school that teaches bilingually, run by their diasporic community, later to be able to be employed or do their business anywhere in the world within that particular diaspora. Often, this is a sign of a certain kind of politics of disappointment – a retreat that begins with the failed promise of modernity to include everybody on a genuinely fair and equal basis.

In the face of this fragmentation, there is a revival of back-to-the-future educational nostalgias. Hence, the 'culture wars' in which the opponents of multiculturalism loudly articulate their regret for the apparent loss of the virtues of the traditional subject content, the 'Western canon', 'cultural literacy', 'the basics', and a golden era before 'political correctness' became the response to the overwhelming range of differences.[22] These nostalgias are no less anachronistic than the ethno-nationalist backlashes to be found in the broader political arena, reacting to the new realities of local diversity and global connectedness. The fact that education is a significant site of these 'wars' is evidence of its central importance in the project of nationalism, and now neoliberalism and the backlash against neoliberalism.

Civic pluralism: New learning

The ideology of neoliberalism, its critics argue, promotes a relationship of civil society to the state that is far from stable and sustainable in a practical sense and often far from satisfactory in a human and ethical sense. The idea of civic pluralism was developed as a part of our research and policy development work.[23] It is an idea that attempts to be both realistic about what may be possible in the current social and political context and supportive of strategic imagination of a more open, inclusive and just civics. The implications for education are fundamental. The kinds of persons that education creates, right down to the basics of their skills, motivations and dispositions, are vastly different today than what was required for adequate citizenship of the nationalist state. We want to put the case that civic pluralism calls for a New Learning.

Dimension 1: State power

As the state shrinks, disturbingly increased inequalities are created by the unrestricted market. A dog-eat-dog ethic of competition prevails and so much personal responsibility is laid on individuals that it becomes a struggle at times to keep up. Few who had lived under the conditions imposed by ideologically and politically strong states, however, would want to turn back the clock to and return to the kinds of strong states in which people lived for much of the 20th century. Sometimes, in the name of liberty, and sometimes to strengthen their economic and political security, the big 20th-century states deprived people of their liberties – in particular the fascism which ravaged Europe and East Asia at the middle of the 20th century and the Stalinist-style communism which, by the time of the neoliberal turn in the last quarter of that century, encompassed one third of the world's population. Nor would many people want to go back to the barely satisfactory conditions of life offered to less-affluent social groups by the welfare states of the 20th century. The offerings of the welfare state were at best minimal, and delivered by a paternalistic bureaucracy that provided communities with what it thought was best for them – barely basic, one-sizes-fits-all health, schooling and welfare.

Civic pluralism is a way to do things without the restrictions to liberty that so often accompanied the bigger states of the 20th century. Sometimes for the better, the old top-down relationship of state to citizen is being replaced in the era of neoliberalism by multiple layers of self-governing community, from the local to national and global levels. Considering the more positive side of this equation for the moment, this means that there are many more realms of participation than the nation-state. There are many more opportunities for self-governing citizenship in a broader sense: in local communities, in workplaces, in cultural groups, particularly as the new technologies enable people to voice opinions and get a broader hearing than ever before. Recall Henry Ford's workplace. The more innovative of today's workplaces offer expanded space for participation; in fact, they require greater responsibility and self-governance at every level, from the smallest working team to the kind of consensus bosses are supposed to create through their consultation and strategic planning processes. The balance of agency has shifted in such a way that workers have to act more like citizens, as participating members of their team and of their organisation. Even at work, they need to make sure they are good citizens of the broader community, given the ethical responsibilities of enterprises today to be mindful of the consequences of their actions – the safety of their products and services, the appropriateness of their offerings to different niche markets and the environmental consequences of their actions. In these senses, a person at work has to be more of a citizen today than was required or possible in the Fordist workplace.

In the domain of citizenship, the dynamics of belonging and governance now occur at multiple and overlapping levels – from community organisations and workplaces to self-regulating professions, to communities of common knowledge and shared taste, to the increasingly federated layers of local, regional, national and supranational government. We witness the rise of these kinds of self-governing structures in many areas of civil society. The Internet is governed, not by any state or coalition of states, but by the World Wide Web Consortium, a group of interested experts and professionals who cohere around elaborate processes of consensus building and decision making. Professional standards are increasingly developed by the professions themselves – teaching less so than other professions as a consequence of its historic links to the bureaucratic state, but it may be a worthwhile agenda for teachers to take increasing control of their own professional standards. And organisations such as schools, which were formerly the objects of command at the nether reaches of bureaucratic hierarchy, increasingly have to regard themselves as self-managing corporate bodies.

With the decline of the centralising, homogenising, authoritarian nation-state, power and cultural influence are being realigned, to locally diverse communities, as well as to transnational forms of government such as the European Union, and to global webs of influence (business, trade, the media). People increasingly find that they have multiple citizenships, sharing the responsibilities of governance in many different ways in different parts of their lives. This process occurs in self-regulating professions, or sporting associations, or in ethnic diasporas which allow you to vote in elections for places in which you do not live as well as the place where you do live, or in indigenous communities that are insisting that their unique sovereignty over their native lands be recognised. As a consequence, the nation-state is arguably becoming less relevant as a focal point for citizenship or even cultural identity. [*See*: Habermas on globalisation and governance.[24]]

This means that, in a structural sense, in place of centralised bureaucratic control, federalism and subsidiarity are finding a place as guiding principles. Federalism (in this broad sense, not the constitutional in modern states) means multiple and overlapping sites of self-government, whether geographically defined (national, state, local); defined by culture and ethnicity (indigenous self-government, ethnic community groups); defined by expertise (professionals, hobbyists, volunteers); or defined by institution (educational, medical, corporate). Subsidiarity means that certain coordinating, negotiating and mediating roles are delegated from the more particular and localised of these sites of self-governance to the broader and more general. The power of the more general is founded on the commitment to delegation on the part of the more particular. This reverses the logic of delegation inherent in the nationalist state. The result is an apparent paradox: cohesion-through-diversity.[25] [*See*: Handy on federalism and subsidiarity.[26]]

Seemingly intractable problems persist as our civic life remains in the grip of neoliberalism. The disparities between the haves and the have-nots seem to be growing all the time, exacerbated by the unrestrained market. Competition and individualism do not necessarily produce harmonious social relations and comfortable cultural conditions. And, despite its protestations, the neoliberal state is not a reliable friend of democracy. The same politicians who advocate a small state in favour of the market often ignore long-cherished civil liberties when it comes to trying to root out terrorism or stem the flow of undocumented immigrants and refugees. [*See*: Hilton and Barnett on globalisation, democracy and terrorism.[27]]

Dimension 2: Public services

Neoliberals say the removal of the 'nanny' state means that citizens have to take more responsibility in choosing their welfare options in the market, such as pay-for-yourself pension schemes, private health insurance and user-pays education. They also say that competition will temper the complacency and arrogance of bureaucratic monopolies, such as government welfare agencies, public hospitals and public schools. It will force them to improve their offerings and provide better services. It will encourage them to differentiate their offerings from others. Using these quasi-market mechanisms, the neoliberals argue, public and community organisations can prove their mettle, and even attract expanded 'market share'. Their criticisms of the older public offerings of the welfare state may in some cases be justified, but it is far from clear that the market does a reliably better job, particularly for the poor and the disenfranchised.

In fact, to the extent that the self-governing spaces in civil society are opened up by government retreat and tax cuts, formerly important areas of activity for the welfare state may be doomed to penury and failure – for instance, public schools and hospitals whose quality is terrible despite the best intentions of the people who work there and the aspirations of the communities they try to serve. Such failure may begin a dangerous slide into a sometimes not-so-civil society.

The underlying principles of civic pluralism are equivalence, devolution and diversity of service provision. The meaning of social entitlement and fairness changes – to have equivalent access to services does not mean you will be provided with the same services but services whose social outcomes are equivalent. You don't have to be the same to be equal. To achieve this, government supports groups providing services for themselves (such as community support groups or community based, non-government schools), in which they are given a considerable degree of autonomy in creating what works best for them, be that schools, or aged care, or the arts, or media. This is the principle of devolution. The outcome is diversity – of approaches, services, institutions, cultures and communities. There is still an important place for taxpayer funding of services that will never be provided by the market. And any such devolved services need to be supported by regulatory mechanisms in the form of standards, and audit of outcomes in relation to service objectives.

Arguably, too, the welfare state with its mass, generic services often used resources inefficiently. When, for instance, the result of a generic, regimented, one-size-fits-all curriculum was that many learners failed (the ones the curriculum failed to engage), then a lot of public resources were being wasted on bureaucracies, buildings and teachers. Instead of a big state, providing generic services for a mass society, we need a sufficient and efficient state, helping communities to help themselves in their own, particular ways.

Dimension 3: Belonging and citizenship

As citizens, we now simultaneously belong to many more kinds of communities, at the local, the regional and the global levels. Singular citizenship in which a person is exclusively a member of a nation-state and the electoral process is the sum total of their participation, is being replaced by multiple citizenship, in which there are many places of belonging, and thus many overlapping forms of self-governance in a larger and more profound sense. Participation is not just a matter of voting. It is about living actively and contributing in many different spaces. The way you participate in each of these places, and the way you belong, are distinctive and different or special to that place. [*See*: Charles Taylor on the politics of multiculturalism.[28]]

Civic pluralism is a response to the changing shape of the state and its relationship to civil society. In some moments, civic pluralism is limited and pragmatic; in others it is optimistic and utopian. It is a concept that makes space for citizens to create a culture of civility and a sense of belonging, amongst people who live in close local and global proximity but not necessarily of the same kin group, whose values are varied and whose life choices at times may seem at odds with each other.

Differences are honoured by measures of self-government at many levels, from local to supranational. They are honoured aesthetically through the variable iconography of place. The phenomenal growth in tourism is a kitschy version of this honouring of differences. This new sensitivity has had noticeable effects to the extent that the bulldozers of generic development are now halted with increasing frequency by activists who want to preserve environmental heritage values – the fabric of uniqueness and the value of difference in place.

The nation-state certainly does not disappear. Nor do diversity and globalisation force it to become uncommitted in a cultural sense, even though the old story of one people, one nation has become unbelievable and in its more exclusionary forms unacceptable. Rather, the nation-state becomes deeply committed to pluralism and its procedures as a means of getting buy-in and achieving legitimacy. It remains infused with the symbolism and narratives of belonging, but now they are narratives of diversity, inclusion, collaboration and cosmopolitanism. It remains committed to redistributive justice, but recognises that redistributive justice has to work with the raw material of varied life experiences. It strongly commits itself to access to the material resources, social services and symbols of national belonging but without prejudice to the differences between the life experiences of its citizens. Government needs to become a more and more neutral arbiter of differences rather than an advocate of a single cultural vision, as was the case in the era of nationalism. This is particularly the case as we move from more local and specific to more general and federal levels of government – from indigenous community self-government to national government, for instance, or from an ethnic community run school to a regional or national education system. [*See*: The charter of public service in a culturally diverse society, Australian Government.[29]]

Dimension 4: Learning civility

The educational basics of the old citizenship were grounded in what was then considered to be a necessity: to forge national strength by creating cultural homogeneity. Old schooling inculcated loyalty to the nation-state. The moral lesson of its predominantly didactic pedagogy was that the singular image of the nation-state, and the forms of knowledge and power it valued, were to be unquestioningly accepted.

In an era of civic pluralism, by contrast, the New Learning fosters an active, bottom-up citizenship in which people assume self-governing roles in the many divergent communities their lives – in their work teams, their professions, their neighbourhoods, their ethnic associations, their environments, their voluntary organisations, their social networks, their affinity groups. Some of these communities may be local and physically co-located. Others may be virtual and dispersed globally. A pedagogy of transformation is better suited to this world of civic pluralism: developing the skills and sensibilities of active citizenship, forming learners who are capable of contributing their own knowledge and

experiences, and negotiating the differences between one community and the
next. [*See*: New learning is noisy.[30]]

Education is one of the key areas of responsibility for the state of civic pluralism. Unlike the education systems of nationalism, the state of civic pluralism is
agnostic about the lifestyle and values differences it encounters in civil society,
until, that is, these threaten that society's civility. One of the keys to this civility is that the state does have a responsibility to ensure comparable outcomes.
This does not have to mean sameness of outcomes of the exclusionary kind that
characterises one-size-fits-all pedagogy and assessment. Rather, the aim should
be equivalent outcomes, measuring comparabilities and customising the state's
support to the school to ensure that it provides outcomes for its students that
are not the same, but of the same order, as those provided by other schools. [*See*:
Schooling in the world's best Muslim country.[31]]

The cultural agnosticism of education in a state of civic pluralism paradoxically
represents a deep civic and ethical commitment. If the social contract represents
a pledge to create a sense of belonging for all, and if civics is something that
entails deep responsibilities as well as rights, then civic pluralism points us in the
direction of a new commonwealth, a new social contract. In this social contract,
citizens don't have to be the same to be equal.

For this kind of civics, schools must teach new kinds of social competence and
new forms of ethics. They must develop in students an ability to engage in the difficult dialogues that are an inevitable part of negotiating diversity: the morality of
compromise in which parties to negotiations are willing to meet and negotiate on
ground that they do not necessarily share in common; multiple citizenship in both
the literal sense of being a participating member of more than one nation-state
and the metaphorical sense of participating in a range of public and community
forums; an ability to express and represent multilayered identities appropriate to
the different lifeworlds, civic spaces and work contexts that all citizens encounter;
development of cultural repertoires appropriate to the range of contexts in which
differences have to be negotiated; a capacity to engage in collaborative politics
that match differences in relationships of complementarity; and dexterity with
systems devolved according to the principle of federalism, where self-governing
community and work activities are the social core, and more federal forms of
government are subsidiary to these, rather than the other way around. These are
the bases for a new, multicultural citizenship.

What do these generalisations mean in practice? To take the example of literacy
teaching, the nationalist state had never taught literacy as mere skill. Literacy
teaching has always been a civic act. In the case of the nationalist state literacy
was to help students join an homogeneous national community, using official and
standard forms of the language, or to appreciate a literature that captured the
national essence. In this process, there were clear rights and wrongs, standards
and non-standards, literatures and less-than-literatures.

Civic pluralism fundamentally transforms the civic purposes of literacy teaching. Now its purpose is to negotiate the increasing variability of the languages

and discourses one encounters: interacting with other languages through inter-
preters or translations, using context-specific interlanguages, using English as lingua franca, and making sense of the plethora of dialects, accents, discourses and
registers that one inevitably encounters. If the literacy curriculum of the nationalist state taught the rules of grammar as a standard, then the literacy curriculum
of civic pluralism needs to tackle the issue of differences through a kind of equally
rigorous, contrastive linguistics. For example, how can we account for the form
of one text compared to another in terms of the peculiarities of its grammars,
cultural location and the interests of writers and readers? How do we cross the
border of language difference, to make a meaning that works? There are still rules
in the language game and these need to be taught and learnt. These rules, however,
are not located in language fixed to a single, standard, national language. Rather
they are the rules of design, comparison, location and boundary crossing.[32]

Summary

Learning civics	Nationalism: The modern past	Neoliberalism: More recent times	Civic pluralism: New learning
Dimension 1: State power	Modern states command and citizens comply. Some command directly – as was the case in the imperialism, fascism and communism of the 20th century. Others are milder, such as welfare state democracies where citizens periodically get the chance to vote for representatives in government but don't participate much beyond the infrequent electoral process.	Smaller government, allowing the market to rule. Based on values of competition, self-reliance, responsibility. Globalisation reduces the power and significance of the nation-state.	Multiple layers of self-governing community: local communities, workplaces, cultural groups. A shift in the balance of agency that favours citizens. Diffusion and globalisation of the structures of governance. Many levels of civic participation and responsibility: community organisations, corporate, government agencies; local, national, regional, global levels of citizenship.

(cont.)

(cont.)

Learning civics	Nationalism: The modern past	Neoliberalism: More recent times	Civic pluralism: New learning
Dimension 2: Public services	Identical services, unequal outcomes.	Privatisation, deregulation, cuts in the welfare state.	Social entitlement and fairness: equivalence of services with devolution of control and diversity in provision. A sufficient and efficient state.
Dimension 3: Belonging and citizenship	Identical, substitutable individuals. A single national story. Mass culture, mass society. Exclusion or assimilation of outsiders.	Global connections and local diversity become more marked, attempts to homogenise communities are less effective and are considered a violation of rights.	Multiple citizenship.
Dimension 4: Learning civility	Teaching instils loyal belief in the stories of the nation-state. Literacy taught in the standard form of the national language.	Partial retreat of the state: self-managing schools, non-government schools, superficial multiculturalism and uncertainty about what to teach as citizenship.	Learning an active, bottom-up citizenship in which people can take a self-governing role in many divergent communities.

Notes

1. Cope and Kalantzis 1998, pp. 99–110
2. Orwell 1949 (2003), pp. 1–4. See extract at NewLearningOnline.com
3. Gellner 1983; 1994
4. Gellner 1983, pp. 1–2, 3, 34, 57, 3–35, 36, 37, 38. See extract at NewLearningOnline.com
5. Polanyi 1975
6. Anderson 1991
7. Ibid, pp. 7, 26, 35. See extract at NewLearningOnline.com
8. Ward 1952, p. 9. See extract at NewLearningOnline.com
9. Dewey 1916 (1966), pp. 21–22. See extract at NewLearningOnline.com
10. Roosevelt 1930, pp. 4, 94, 97. See extract at NewLearningOnline.com

11. Smith 1776 (1976), pp. 38–40, 26–27, 455–56. See extract at NewLearningOnline.com
12. Spencer 1862, §133. See extract at NewLearningOnline.com
13. Reagan 1989. See extract at NewLearningOnline.com
14. Thatcher 1987. See extract at NewLearningOnline.com
15. Deng 1984. See extract at NewLearningOnline.com
16. Harvey 2005, pp. 1–3, 64, 65–66, 76. See extract at NewLearningOnline.com
17. Apple 2006, pp. 21–26; 2002, pp. 1–23
18. Taylor 1994, p. 39
19. Smith 1776 (1976)
20. McLaren 2003, pp. 22, 55–56, 42, 178, 176. See extract at NewLearningOnline.com
21. New South Wales Department of Education 1983, p. 53. See extract at NewLearningOnline.com
22. Cope and Kalantzis 1997b, pp. 283–329
23. Kalantzis 2001, pp. 110–23
24. Habermas 1998, pp. 317–319. See extract at NewLearningOnline.com
25. Kalantzis 2000, pp. 99–110
26. Handy 1994, pp. 110, 133–35, 143, 146. See extract at NewLearningOnline.com
27. Hilton and Barnett 2005. See extract at NewLearningOnline.com
28. Taylor 1994, pp. 37–38, 51, 44, 51. See extract at NewLearningOnline.com
29. Department of Immigration and Multicultural Affairs 1998. See extract at NewLearningOnline.com
30. Burrows, Cope, Kalantzis, Loi, Suominen and Yelland 2006a. See extract at NewLearningOnline.com
31. Cope 1993, pp. 20–23. See extract at NewLearningOnline.com
32. New London Group 1996, pp. 60–92; Cope and Kalantzis (eds) 2000b

Chapter 5

Learning personalities

Overview

This chapter is about the different places learners come from – their varied backgrounds and attributes: material, corporeal and symbolic. These backgrounds and attributes shape the learner's personality. They also have an enormous impact on their engagement with learning and their educational and social outcomes.

Learner attributes and personalities can be negotiated in a number of different ways. When similarity is expected or differences are regarded as unnecessary and troublesome, societies or social institutions such as schools sometimes use the mechanisms of differential exclusion (allowing in certain kinds of people but not others) or assimilation (allowing different kinds of people in on condition that they fit in by becoming like the people who are already there). Both of these approaches are based on the idea that groups work better when all their members are more or less the same, and that the in-group's way of doing things is the best.

Another way to deal with varied learner attributes is to grant differences some degree of formal recognition. This may include categorisation of groups for the purposes of creating special programs. These programs may be criticised for being limited or because they represent a laissez-faire or 'live and let live' approach that doesn't necessarily deal with inequalities that accompany differences.

In today's conditions of diversity in local communities and sites of human interaction such as schools, and with an increasing global interconnectedness, an inclusive approach to varied learner attributes is a more effective form of engagement and means for improving learner performance. Learner attributes and their differences are subtle, complex and deep. Every person is uniquely formed at the intersection of many lines of influence. We need to negotiate the uniqueness of every learner's life history, and the fluidity of life change. Social groups such as schools work best when everything they do makes all members of the group feel that they can belong and achieve – feel as though they are included – in their difference.

On the significance of learner attributes and the sources of personality

Learners come to school already knowing a lot of things. These things they have learnt in an informal way from their everyday life experiences – from their families, their communities, their cultural environment and the things they have done in their lives.

This realm of everyday life experience is called the 'lifeworld'. The lifeworld consists of the things you end up knowing without having to think how you came to know them. It is the way you end up being without ever having consciously decided to be that way. The lifeworld is not something that is explicit. It is a set of habits, behaviours, values and interests that go without saying in a particular context. The lifeworld goes without saying because it has come without saying. It is made up of things that seem so obvious to insiders that they don't need saying. Nor is the systematic observation and considered reflection of science immediately relevant or particularly needed in the lifeworld. In fact, for much of the time, any such reflection would be odd and out of place. Knowledge of the lifeworld does not have to be taught in a formal way. You learn how to be in the lifeworld just by living in it, and this learning is mostly so unconscious that it is rarely even experienced as learning. [*See*: Edmund Husserl on the lifeworld.[1]]

Formal learning, by contrast, involves conscious teaching (pedagogy); it is explicit about what needs to be learnt (curriculum) and it relies on forms of critical and scientific reflection whose perceptions can penetrate deeply into nature and human experience. By this means, science can see things that are not immediately obvious in everyday, practical life and casual experience. And formal learning can take learners beyond the domain of their everyday lives.

A fundamental challenge for education is to engage with and extend learners' lifeworld experiences. This immediately poses some fundamental 'how to' questions. Just who are these learners? Where do they come from and what do they already know? How does formal school learning connect with, build upon, extend and transform what learners already know from their everyday experience (rather than counter-productively ignore or negate what they know)? What is the role of history, background environment, identity and everyday life experiences in learning? One of the biggest challenges for the educator today is how one juggles the teaching and learning process when learners' lifeworld experiences are so different.

In this chapter, we discuss the dimensions of lifeworld difference: material (access to social resources); corporeal (bodily realities such as age, race, sex and sexuality, and physical and mental characteristics) and symbolic (socially constructed realities of culture, language, gender, family, affinity and persona). We also discuss alternative difference dynamics, or ways in which these differences can be negotiated: exclusion, assimilation, recognition or inclusion – in the broader social domain as well as in schools.

The reason for this discussion is that one of the keys to success or failure in formal learning is the distance between lifeworld experience and the culture and discourse of formal learning (education). Some students come from lifeworlds that are closer to those of formal learning; others come from lifeworlds that are more distant. The language of instruction may not be their mother tongue, the cultural artefacts such as books and computers may be unfamiliar, or the ways of speaking and thinking about the world may seem strange and alienating. If some kinds of students do better than others, more often than not it is mostly because of this lifeworld gap. One of the key challenges of education is to bridge that gap. [*See*: Pierre Bourdieu on cultural capital.[2]]

We explore the range of learner attributes according to the following dimensions:

Dimension 1: Material – or attributes and differences of social class and geographical locale.

Dimension 2: Corporeal – attributes and differences of age, race, sex and sexuality, and physical and mental capacities.

Dimension 3: Symbolic – attributes and differences of culture or ethnicity, language, gender, family, affinity and persona.

From exclusion to assimilation: The modern past

Exclusion and assimilation have been and still are two ways of dealing with lifeworld differences, whether practised by countries, communities, organisations or schools. Both are premised on the idea that the members of a group need to be more or less the same for that group to function well. The exclusionist and assimilationist ways of achieving the goal of sameness, however, are quite different.

Exclusion or separatism is a process by means of which a dominant social group maintains its sameness by refusing to allow in people who are different in defined ways. The segregating school, for instance, does not allow students to attend who are of the 'wrong' race; the single-sex school does not allow in students who are of the other sex; the wealthy school (circumstantially, even when not as a matter of principle) excludes students whose families can't afford to pay the fees. Often, segregation is regarded as discriminatory, and in some circumstances it is made illegal.

Sometimes, however, separatist institutions may be a justifiable way to manage lifeworld differences. Some say that schools designed for specific ethnic or minority communities help learners because they support their languages, cultures and values, thus providing an affirming environment to help them succeed – unlike mainstream schools, where their cultures and languages are marginalised. Others say that schools for girls only give them a chance to succeed without being distracted by, or having to compete with, boys. Clearly, also, separatism works for wealthy schools because it means that learners come to school with the cultural capital of families habituated to social influence and mainstream success – 'good' social standing that later turns into strategically valuable networks with other wealthy and powerful families.

The assimilating social group is just as concerned as the separatist one to make virtue of homogeneous community, but it does not use the same logic or methods. This group says something like, 'we will accept people who are different, so long as they become like us'. The assimilating school, for instance, makes little allowance for the lifeworld differences amongst its learners. It simply immerses everyone in the singular culture and curriculum of the school. If that's what's good for anybody, then that's what everybody is going to get. Whether you feel comfortable or alienated in this environment, or whether you succeed or fail, is up to you, the learner. You may choose to rise to the 'values' and 'standards' of the school and if you don't, you are likely to fail – and then have nobody to blame but yourself.

Sometimes, this approach may be justified, and it may even work. For some learners, it may serve as a kind of crash-course in a new culture (ways of speaking, kinds of thinking, types of people), which opens doors that would never have been opened had they stayed within the comfortable boundaries of their lifeworld origins.

What, then, are bases of separatism or assimilation? What are the differences, real and perceived? Lifeworld differences are complex, overlapping and come across as a spectrum of many hues and shades. Notwithstanding the subtleties, we need categories to describe the differences. For clarity's sake, we group differences into three clusters: material, corporeal and symbolic.

Dimension 1: Material attributes

Social class
Social class is a material or economic measure of wealth, power and status in an unequal and hierarchically ordered social structure. In their historical form before conquest, most first nations or indigenous peoples lived in classless societies. They had other means of social differentiation and hierarchy, for sure, such as age and gender, but they did not have the material difference of social class that has marked the rest of human history.[3] In slave societies (such as ancient Greece and Rome, and also more recently in the southern United States until the Civil War of the 1860s) an underclass of workers was bought and owned and sold by masters.[4] In feudal societies (the pre-modern, peasant–agricultural societies of Asia, Europe, Africa and some parts of the Americas) feudal lords owned the farming land and

peasant vassals gave part of what they produced to the lord in the form of tithes, or a kind of rent.[5] In each case, the wealth of the few was created by the work of the many, and many people of the day considered this to be inevitable and proper. [*See*: Aristotle on inequality.[6]]

Modern capitalist societies create class and inequality in a different way from their predecessors. The key is the modern money economy and the system of paid employment. Unlike slavery and feudalism, people in capitalist societies are politically free to select their workplace and preferred job role; but they are hardly free not to work in the wage labour system. Welfare systems may help the unemployed, the aged, the unwell or the disabled. Even in societies that can afford reasonable welfare arrangements, however, these only provide for minimal support, which keeps welfare recipients near the bottom of the class system. In reality, there is little choice for most people but to work for most of their adult lives, at least if they want to enjoy what is considered to be an acceptable standard of living.

People in paid employment may work hard, but some people's return on their work remains less than others. If you are an owner or a shareholder in a business, you earn more than what you would if you were a worker in that business, without necessarily working any harder than the worker. In fact, as the 19th-century philosopher and political economist Karl Marx pointed out, business owners do well because their workers work hard. They do well because they collect the surplus or profits generated by the hard work of the workers.[7] The system works this way for them just because they were born wealthy or are able progressively to accumulate the capital and property that enabled them to control and profit from other people's labour.

The most obvious sign or measure of social class is wealth in the form of assets (property, shares, accumulated cash) and the income that comes from these assets. If you don't have assets or your assets are few, you have no alternative but to work for a salary or wage. Marx argued that the unequal ownership of social assets creates a self-perpetuating system in which the rich will always get richer and the poor will get poorer. [*See*: On Social Class: Capitalism's Pyramid.[8]]

The German sociologist, Max Weber, added two more measures of class: power and status.[9] Power refers to the degree of control you have over your own life and the lives of others. If you are a wealthy factory owner or a manager, you have much more control over the way you work than do the workers on the factory floor. You give orders rather than take orders; you hire and fire. Economic power also brings with it social power beyond the organisation, including the capacity to influence civil society and the state.

Status refers to the prestige attached to a person's position in society. Social status can be achieved (for example, through education and associated well-paying work) or ascribed (through inherited wealth and social standing). Class and social status are embodied through everyday cultural practices and visible trappings. People of power and status tend to share tastes (for example, in

commodoties, music, literature), cultural interests and styles that require considerable material resources to maintain: a collection of behaviours and demeanours
that are regarded as 'having class'. Such people can afford to buy art to put on the
walls of their houses, purchase tickets to the opera, go on holidays to beautiful
and interesting places, play golf at the most expensive clubs, drink the best wine,
send their children to the best private schools and pay their fees to attend the
most prestigious universities.

Occasionally, someone from a lower class makes good, and when they do, the
status aspect of class immediately sticks out. 'How crass', old money says of new
money or the 'nouveau riche', when they wear gaudy jewellery or drive tastelessly
flashy cars.

Where do schools sit in relation to social class in times and places where differences lead to either exclusion or assimilation? In an exclusionary system –
even when education was provided by the state for all of its citizens – schools
in working-class neighbourhoods mostly have poorer facilities and larger classes.
They lack the resources to provide extra-curricular activities that might compensate for the paucity of available community or family resources. Moreover, students tend to be offered basic literacy and numeracy training rather than a broader
curriculum, and are steered into 'vocational' courses that have them leaving school
early and entering semi-skilled and low-paid jobs. Meanwhile, private schools and
well-endowed public schools in affluent neighbourhoods may have facilities and
expectations that are oriented to further education and extend and deepen networks of power and influence for the ruling class. The more affluent get a better
education because they can afford it. More resources are put into their education.
Greater results are expected, and delivered. This is how, in an institutional sense,
education creates a system of exclusion based on social class.[10]

A milder version of this process of social selection is to assimilate 'bright'
working-class students into the status system. If you do well at school, if you
perform in terms measured by its various disciplines (its subjects and forms of
behaviour), you too may succeed in getting a paid job that may even take you
beyond the class station of your parents. In reality, however, social mobility or
assimilation to a new social class only happens in the case of exceptionally motivated students, such as the children of immigrant parents who are determined
that their offspring should improve their lot in life and at any cost.

By and large, however, even assimilationist systems reproduce social class position across generations. The reasons are material, cultural and institutional. If you
do not grow up in a household full of books and newspapers and where people
read a lot, if your family speaks a language or dialect different to that of the 'standard form' of language used in the curriculum, if your family's way of talking
and thinking about the world is contextual and narrative rather than abstract and
conceptual – to name just a few of the possible gaps between school and home –
school seems to present insurmountable challenges.[11] And when you fail, when

you don't manage to assimilate to its culture, the system tells you (or, even more conveniently, you tell yourself) that you only have yourself to blame. You were not smart enough to succeed even though school gave you the opportunity. [*See:* Bowles and Gintis on schooling in capitalist United States.[12]]

Locale

Locale is another aspect of material difference. Different geographical locations offer different opportunities: the various neighbourhoods in a city; rural or remote versus urban location; different regions in a country; being in a developed or developing country. Locale is a determinant of the quality and depth of material and cultural resources available (education, health, libraries, parks, museums, media access and the like).

Migration is one way to change locale, be that a short distance from the country to the city, or a journey around the world. Many migrants move because they are seeking improved work opportunities, or better schooling and thus social opportunities for their children. However, strict limits are imposed on the flows of migration by receiving countries. And even if one does get the opportunity to migrate, establishing roots in the new locale may be experienced as a process of assimilation, or changing oneself – one's language and culture, for instance – in order to fit in.

Dimension 2: Corporeal attributes

Corporeal or bodily differences have both a physical aspect (the actualities of a person's body) and a cultural or symbolic aspect (the cultural and symbolic meanings ascribed by a person to their own body, or ascribed to their body by others).

Age

Age is a determinant of bodily and mental capacities, and relevant and appropriate forms of learning.

From birth to about the age of two or three, babies are completely dependent on parents and carers. At birth, humans do not have a clear sense of the relations of their bodies to the environment around them, or even a capacity to see objects clearly. In the first months of life, their main activities are simple and reflexive, such as sucking, touching and grasping. Gradually, these develop into more complex, volitional activities – rattling a toy or looking for a hidden object, knowing that it may exist even when it is not visible. The baby comes to understand that there is a distinction between their body and the world outside of their body. Over these years, everything the baby learns is by means of immersion in a context of informal learning. This is how they learn to see, to walk, and to talk. By the end of two years, the baby will have acquired a system for representing the world to themself – using language and other symbols.

From the age of two or three to about five, children develop fine motor skills, begin to relate to their peers in a social context, and learn to express themselves through symbolic processes of communication. Egocentric speech, or talking to oneself in a kind of monologue, reflects a way of thinking about and understanding the world. The child may believe that the natural world has been made by people and that the whole world shares the same feelings, desires and perceptions as he or she. For example, when covering their eyes, the child believes nobody can see them. Nor is the child able to make a distinction between symbol and symbolised, or word and thing. In terms of visual representations, children start representing meaning in this period without making a distinction between writing and drawing, and gradually separate the two modes as they begin in the formal educational setting of early childhood education.

From about age six to 12 years, children in modern societies attend primary or elementary school. Fine motor skills are refined. Cognitive capacities progressively grow and develop. Children acquire a capacity to classify and order, coming to the realisation that something with the same properties may appear in different manifestations. These are the beginnings of logical thought processes, problem solving and the capacity to create and apply abstract concepts – generalising thoughts that cross varied sites and instances, and naming these thoughts with concepts. They also develop a capacity to see something from another person's perspective and to realise that their own perspectives are just that, not necessarily the final truth.[13] Same-sex friendships predominate, with some children (particularly girls) reaching puberty or adolescence towards the end of this period.

From ages 12 to 17 years, most young people are in secondary school, and in a transitionary period as they move from child to adult behaviour and take on greater social responsibility. They find themselves in an ambivalent and contradictory middle-ground of dependence, with growing expectations of maturity. Adding to the pressure is puberty and the development of adult sexuality. Peer group pressures arise – the need to belong, and to form an identity that accords with that sense of belonging. Cognitively, young people in this age bracket develop capacities for formal logic (such as induction and deduction), to conceive abstractly, to evaluate interests and perspectives critically, and to act in ways that have a wider impact on the world and take responsibility for these actions. [*See*: Piaget's stages of child development.[14]]

Between about 15 and 21 years, young adults go through a number of rites of passage that eventually mark them as adults. They leave school; they vote; they get a driver's licence; they can purchase alcohol or cigarettes. From then until about age 40, they typically go through a period of early adulthood in which they may complete their education (such as vocational or higher education), start work and begin family life.

From about 40 to 60 years, these adults continue to work, now freer of responsibilities for children. Formal learning may continue through adulthood, but when it does, its sites and dynamics are quite different to child learning.

From about age 60, people may begin to retire from full-time work, independently at first, and as they get older and more dependent in increasingly supported, quasi-medical environments.

These age transitions are characteristic of modernity. In earlier societies, more people were involved in taking care of young children than a stay-at-home mum or a child-care specialist. Learning was in a social context that involved many adults, rather than in a specialised institution – the child-care centre and after that the school – designed exclusively to look after children. Children had to make more adult-like contributions and to make them earlier. In fact, the culture of childhood in its current form (from its toys to its patterns of dependency) is a relatively recent invention.

For the first time in human history, from about the 18th century, modern societies began to make a number of clear distinctions of age that locate people of different ages in institutions specially designed for that age group at that particular stage in their life-course. Formal educational institutions clearly make these age separations. Babies are typically the responsibility of non-working mothers in the nuclear family, or crèches. Three to five-year-olds are frequently sent to early childhood education settings or preschool. By the age of five, almost all children are sent to kindergarten. Six to 12-year-olds go to primary or elementary school, or middle school. Thirteen to 17-year-olds go to secondary or high school. The United Nations Convention on the Rights of the Child defines childhood as a period lasting until the age of 18.[15]

Race

'Race' refers to phenotypical differences, or differences in physical appearance, between one human population and another: skin colour, facial features, hair colour and texture, height and physique. The roots of the word in English are to be found in old Italian and French words for breed or lineage, where the term was initially used to describe subspecies right across the natural world. The modern obsession with classification led 19th and early 20th-century scientists to divide humans into distinct racial groups, such as 'Negroid', 'Australoid', 'Caucasoid' and 'Mongoloid'. [*See*: The races of man.[16]]

Neat categorisation like this is regarded with suspicion today, and 'race' has become a controversial term.[17] Biologists and anthropologists dispute how useful the term can be to describe groups of humans. Racial grouping is based on certain kinds of genetic difference, which may appear obvious but do not reflect many important underlying genetic differences. Indeed, on most biological measures of difference, there is greater inherited biological variation within populations (such as blood types, range of body shapes, heights and the like) than the average variation between populations.

Amongst those who wish to use race as a biological category, there has been considerable controversy about how many races there are, and where one race begins and the next ends. Indeed, one of the factors that confounds the concept of race is the extraordinary range of global movement of the species and the extent of interbreeding over the quite brief span of existence of modern humans as a species.[18] No human populations have been separated for more than a few thousand generations – not long enough for significant biological variations to emerge through processes of natural selection. In fact, if one considers one's biological ancestry as two intersecting pyramids, one at which you are at the peak of the pyramid (with two parents, four grandparents, eight great-grandparents) and another where an ancestral 'Eve' was a member of a tiny population from which the species emerged (who had however many children, and grandchildren and great-grandchildren), the human family is so closely related over the few thousand generations of its existence that nobody today can be further removed than 50th cousin.[19]

Even though race is not a particularly helpful biological category, the recognisable differences it describes have figured large in our social imaginations. These differences have been associated with different states and stages of civilisation and progress, with different human capacities and with different levels of acquired intelligence. They have been used to justify imperialism as the 'white man's burden' to bring the coloured races to a higher level of civilisation. They have been used to rationalise the unequal results of schooling – if blacks do not do well at school as a statistically measurable population, it must be the result of innate intelligence, so the argument goes, and this means that the problem cannot be solved by changing educational or social conditions.[20]

In these senses, 'race' is very real. It is a historic and cultural construction that has real effects. Indeed, it often becomes the basis for an interpretative framework or worldview that is today called 'racism'. Racism is an ideology that ascribes causal social, cultural and historical significance to biological differences between groups. It can be explicit in the form of pejorative or negative statements, or implicit in worldviews and social structures that have the effect of reproducing patterns of exclusion and inequality for populations marked by their visible difference.

In modern times, racist ideology has been used to justify apartheid (in South Africa, for instance), slavery (such as in the United States before the Civil War), segregation (in the United States after the Civil War), mission settlements for the isolation of supposedly dying races in the initial phases of colonisation (such as Indigenous peoples of Australia[21] and the indigenous peoples of the Americas) and genocide (the Nazi project to exterminate the Jewish 'race' in Europe, or the 'black line' in Tasmania, Australia, which set out to eliminate the Indigenous Tasmanians[22]). Each of these exclusionary policies was based on race classification. [*See*: Apartheid education.[23]]

Sometimes, also, assimilationist race agendas have been practised, such as the removal from their families of Australian Indigenous children of 'half-caste' parentage (or some other fraction of 'blood'), who were placed in white foster families on the assumption that it was possible to 'breed out' their Indigenous characteristics – that their racial characteristics would progressively disappear as future generations intermarried with whites.[24]

Sex and sexuality
Sex is the biologically inherited difference between females and males. In the animal kingdom, creatures of the female sex typically produce the larger of the two reproductive cells. The smaller cell is contributed by the male. The female also bears offspring. In humans, females have two 'x' chromosomes; a reproductive system consisting of a vagina, clitoris, uterus and fallopian tubes; a predominance of the hormones oestrogen and progesterone; and after puberty a menstrual cycle, breasts, a smaller physique than men and a distinctive overall body shape. Males have one 'x' and one 'y' chromosome; a reproductive system consisting of penis and testes; a predominance of the hormone testosterone; and after puberty, facial and body hair, a lowered voice, a larger physique than women with less fat and a distinctive body shape. Girls reach puberty several years before boys, and women's reproductive capacities end before men's, at menopause.[25]

There are behavioural differences between men and women, too, but it is hard to determine the extent to which they may be the result of biological inheritance (sex) or cultural acquisition (gender). The wide variation in human propensities and social attributes within each sex, across and between different societies, suggests that cultural factors outweigh or can override biological factors.

Until recently, modern societies were reluctant to take sex differences into account beyond the simple female–male dichotomy. For instance, when a person had a combination of male and female sexual organs, this seemed to require a one-way-or-the-other approach in which one sex or the other was ascribed.[26]

The bipolarity of earlier modern gender roles also excluded permutations of sexuality and gender roles that have become more public in recent times. In the past, heterosexuality was considered the norm and continues to be considered so in many communities today, based on the premise that female–male attraction and partnering is natural. People who felt they did not fit the prevailing gender mould found they had no alternative but to lead 'normal' lives, repressing their sexual orientation or practising their sexuality in secluded places – having to hide homosexual or bisexual inclinations, 'in the closet'.[27]

Physical and mental characteristics
What is it to be tall or short? What is it to be 'fat' or 'thin'? What is it to have physical characteristics that may be conventionally classified as 'beauty' or 'ugliness'? And what is it to have a 'disability' of some form or another? All of these bodily attributes powerfully frame identity. One aspect of the framing is cultural ascription, in which a person's identity is developed in relation to prevailing views of what is 'normal' or ideal. Another aspect is physical, or what a person's body, including their brain, can or cannot do.

In earlier modern times, views of the 'normal' or ideal were more clearly defined than they are today. People whose bodily or mental capacities were too far removed from the norm of the able-bodied and mentally fit norm were frequently labelled in categories that had, or came to have, pejorative connotations. Such people were labelled as 'crippled', 'lame', 'spastic', 'deaf', 'dumb', 'blind', 'insane', 'mad', 'feeble-minded', an 'idiot' or a 'moron'. Clear institutional separations were established. Bodily and mentally 'subnormal' people were not expected to go to 'normal' schools or work in regular workplaces. They were confined to home if a full-time carer was available. Or they were sent to special institutions – schools for the blind, deaf and disabled, asylums for the insane and 'sheltered workshops' for the physically disabled.[28]

Dimension 3: Symbolic attributes and differences

Symbolic differences arise from the human propensity to make meaning. Humans make sense of their encounters with the world in creatively varied ways.

Culture

Uniquely in the natural world, humans are symbol-making creatures.[29] They have the capacity to envision the world, and use these visions to drive their actions to refashion the world. Making symbols is at the heart of culture. Humans are cultural beings by nature. On this definition, all symbolic activities could be called 'culture', including language, gender, family, affinity and persona. For the moment, however, we define culture more narrowly, as nationality, ethnicity or ancestry.

The modern world is geopolitically divided into nations. Nationalism is an ideology and a set of political and cultural practices that attempts to create more-or-less homogeneous peoples to fit within the boundaries of nation-states, or the geographical territories covered by state sovereignty. Typically, the majority or most powerful cultural group stamps its cultural mark on the nation. Their language or dialect becomes official. Their story becomes that of the nation. Their members benefit by gaining privileged access to political power, material resources and symbolic kudos.

The term 'ethnic group' typically refers to minorities, although the distinctive attributes of majority national cultures could just as easily be called 'ethnic'. It suits majorities to regard their culture as the norm and other people's cultures as exotic or different. Sometimes, ethnic groups are historic minorities, people who may have lived in a place for a long time alongside today's majority group, but who found themselves to be in the minority at some point in the past when the borders of the modern nation were drawn. Other times, ethnic minority groups have formed as a result of migration.

Indigenous peoples, or first nations, are not usually considered to be ethnic groups because of their unique historical status as original landowners and their social position in the modern nation-state. Indigenous peoples have typically become minorities at some point in the past, when imperial conquest and migration of new settlers brought an end to their exclusive sovereignty over their lands. On this basis they make justifiable claims to ongoing ownership of wild lands and compensation for their loss of lands now inhabited by settler communities and their descendants. They also tend to have had vastly different lifeways to the invaders and new settlers, and suffer severe social dislocation and enduring injustice as a consequence of the encounter.

The modern nation-state has two approaches to ethnic groups and indigenous peoples. One is exclusion or separatism – to ban immigration of certain groups, or to remove indigenous peoples to reserves and homelands without the right to citizenship in the nation.

The other approach is to insist on their assimilation. A condition of joining the nation is that the ethnic or indigenous group must take on the cultural attributes of the dominant group – learn to speak its language and imbibe its values. If there are to be any traces of ethnic or indigenous identity, these have to be confined to the home or to private life. [*See*: A missionary school for the Huaorani of Ecuador.[30]]

Language

Modernity brings with it decreasing language diversity. Of the world's approximately 6000 ancestral languages, many have disappeared over the past half-millennium, and the majority of those that remain are threatened by the dominance of the major imperial languages in the most powerful domains of knowledge, society and economy.[31]

The story of language diversity tells of innumerable differences of dialect (the accent, or word choices or manner of speaking of a particular group), register (a variety of language used in a particular setting, such as in informal, formal or professional setting), social language (a mode of communicating within a particular group, such as the social language of football or computing) and discourse (language peculiar to a domain of activity).[32]

Modern societies privilege certain dialects, registers, social languages and discourses. Some of these are more or less powerful in the public realm. Some carry more or less powerful forms of knowledge. Some bear the symbolic burden of representing more or less marginalised cultural and social groups. [*See*: Speaking properly.[33]]

In schools, children may be disadvantaged when they don't speak the language of instruction as their mother tongue. Or, given the enormous significance accorded to written language in modern societies, children may be disadvantaged if they come from speech communities that don't provide substantial access to, and afford significant value to, books and writing. Typically, those who are disadvantaged are speakers of minority immigrant or indigenous languages, who speak the national language as a second language, or those who are poor and who speak in a working-class register that is more distant from the language of writing than middle or upper-class speech.[34] [*See*: William Labov on African-American English vernacular.[35]]

One possible 'solution' to this problem is to advocate assimilation, to learn the language of the mainstream in order to succeed. Whether this can work, or is even meant to work, is a matter of contention. [*See*: Assimilating migrants.[36]]

Gender

Connected to the biology of sex, gender roles are socio-cultural, or symbolic. They are the result mostly of processes of informal learning or socialisation. Babies, whose only manifest differences are biological, style themselves as boys and girls, prefiguring the archetypical adult roles assumed by men and women. Girls amuse themselves with dolls, dress daintily and play house. Women become homemakers or join professions of caring and nurturing such as nursing, teaching or secretarial work. Boys interact with toy vehicles and weapons, and play rougher sports than girls. Men become workers who venture out into the robust public worlds of the professions and trades. From the moment a baby develops a human consciousness, pervasive cues and influences prompt them to develop subtly and deeply gendered habits, interests, demeanours, stances and dispositions. It becomes hard to disentangle what is learnt or socialised and what is sex-related biological inheritance.

In an earlier modernity, gender-role differentiation seemed to be more straightforward than it often appears today. Learning typical or 'normal' gender roles was such a pervasive and subtle 'fact' of the lifeworld that these differences appeared to be natural.[37] To the extent that gender roles were more clearly defined in an earlier modernity and continue to be defined in traditional ways today, girls and women feel emotions more keenly and are more able and likely to express affect. They are more sensitive to social and interpersonal realities. Boys and men tend to dominate in social settings and act more aggressively more often; they are more likely to take risks; their actions are based more on instrumental or means-ends rationality; and they have a closer relationship to machines and technology than girls and women. These kinds of attributes become the stuff of feminine and masculine personae, behaviours, dispositions and social aspirations. [*See*: Jean-Jacques Rousseau on Sophy's education.[38]]

In an earlier modernity, the adult world of gender roles took clearly differentiated structural and institutional forms. Women and men had a different legal status. It was not until the 20th century that women could vote. Women would mostly join the workforce only if they were poor or until they were married or had children. Men, meantime, would build lifetime careers. Women's jobs were paid less than men's.

Schools were frequently gender-segregated, particularly secondary schools, teaching subjects appropriate to boys and girls' social destinies – trade skills in boys' schools and domestic science or home economics in girls' schools, for instance. It was to be expected that an elite group of boys would go on to higher education in order to join one of the male professions. Girls might go on to train to be nurses or secretarial assistants. Teaching was primarily a low-status, female profession. [*See*: Catharine Beecher on the role of women as teachers.[39]]

Gender roles in the modern household came to be defined around the nuclear family, with dad working on the labour market, mum doing unpaid domestic work and looking after the two-point-however-many children. Never before had the private realm of the home and women been so dramatically separated from the public realm. Women were placed in isolation with their immediate biological children, staying in separate household spaces, often undertaking their domestic work with scarce or no help from their husbands and with little or none of the community engagement with the wider world that their husbands experienced at work.

When the husband came home, he clearly asserted his dominance as head of the nuclear family. The often-authoritarian tone of the traditional nuclear family was not so unlike that found in the public realms of work and citizenship. Most husbands were expected to comply in these public spaces. When they came home, however, these same husbands became the head of the household, assuming an authoritarian position there. Wives and children were expected to take orders from their husbands. Family life, in other words, was conducted through another one of those relationships of command and compliance typical of the times. The man, who had been compliant in his public persona, was transfigured into a command personality when he came home.

The cultural and institutional processes of exclusion in modern gender relations are called 'sexism'. Sexism is an ideology and set of practices that ascribe naturalness and inevitability to the gender-role differences that are associated with sex differences. Its effect is to justify and perpetuate the inequality of males and females. Sexism conveniently starts with the bodily realities of sex differences, and then naturalises the cultural practices of gender roles and their unequal outcomes. It is as though the inequalities are inevitable because they are natural. The effect is the exclusion of women from the public realm and realms of power that are the traditional preserve of men. However, when we separate the underlying bodily realities from the cultural construction of gender roles in the lifeworld, the inequalities that have historically been associated with gender roles are neither natural nor inevitable. There can be no biological justification for the patterns of exclusion. [*See*: Mary Wollstonecraft on the rights of woman. [40]]

Sometimes gender roles present themselves as so powerfully ingrained that the inequality which comes with these roles appears almost insurmountable. The only way for a woman to succeed in a man's world, it seems, is to become like a man – to focus on her career at the expense of domesticity or to act like a man by taking risks and focusing on means-ends rationality. In other words, the only alternative to separatism is assimilation. If she is not to be excluded from the world dominated by masculine gender roles, a woman needs to assimilate to at least some of the attributes of the male gender role. [*See*: Simone de Beauvoir, *The Second Sex*.[41]]

Alternative frameworks for sexuality beyond the bipolar male–female norm throw traditional gender roles into question. Sometimes homosexual men and women, for instance, take on aspects of male and female gender roles typical of their sex. Sometimes they don't. However, homosexual people living outside the conventional male–female gender bipolarity of earlier modern times were pressured by processes of exclusion and assimilation to take on conventional gender roles. If they did not conform, they faced a prevailing culture of homophobia or fear and dislike of homosexuality.

Family

Family type is closely related to gender and culture. In an earlier modernity, the ideal and typical form of family was the nuclear family – mum, dad and a few kids. Other types of family were frowned upon or practically hard to manage. Extended families, such as those of immigrant or indigenous groups, were not easy to maintain because the physical forms of housing and dispersed work opportunities made them difficult to sustain. Single-parent families were the result of the death of a parent, or what was regarded to be the immorality of extramarital sex (and unmarried mothers were encouraged to adopt out their children), or the then-stigmatised and relatively rare phenomenon of divorce. Serial monogamy was frowned upon because marriage was meant to be for life. Parallel sexual relationships were clandestine and condemned as adulterous. De facto marriages were rare. Blended families in which siblings had parents from different marriages were regarded as anomalous and dysfunctional. Polygamy, as practised by some fundamentalist Christian and Muslim groups, was so remote from public consciousness as to be almost unimaginable. Same-sex marriages and parenting were unheard of.

The realities of family life were always more complex than the nuclear ideal. The differences, however, were handled through processes of social exclusion and cultural assimilation. Persistent pressure was applied to conform to the symbolic norm. Children from families not conforming to the norm could at times suffer in public contexts, for example, when they were taunted at school. They could also be disadvantaged by the peculiar culture of their family life – whether the national language or the language of instruction was spoken at home, or whether they had access to resources in the home (toys, books or trips that gave them a wider experience of the world), or whether their family could provide the cultural capital at home (the ways of thinking, the ways of speaking and the aspirations and expectations) that meshed with the culture of the school and its curriculum. [*See*: What Sissy Juppe didn't know about horses.[42]]

Affinity and persona

You are who and what you associate yourself with. You are the person you envision and style yourself to be. Despite the pressures to homogeneity of the earlier modernity, differences of affinity and persona have always abounded. There have always been variations in religious belief, from one major religion to another, from one denomination to another, and from people who believe there is a God or are gods, to people who don't know or care about the presence of a god (agnostics) and people who are clear in their own minds that there is no god (atheists). There have also been large differences in political viewpoint, expressed implicitly through a person's ideological framing of the world, or explicitly through political advocacy or membership of a political organisation. There have been enormous variations between the kinds of people who belong to different types of organisations (football team members compared to members of a golf club, for instance), or whose interests and enthusiasms are different, such as their hobbies or their preferred leisure activities. There have been differences in peer culture within and between age groups. And there have been different personality types, such as introverts or extroverts.

The way the earlier modernity dealt with these kinds of differences was to regard affinity or persona as an essentially private affair. What you think is your own business, and is better not expressed in public. ('Never talk about religion or politics', the old adage went.) What you did with your free time was your own affair. This kind of difference, it was thought, was best kept at home rather than taken to work or school.

Recognition: More recent times

Since the mid-20th century in particular, ideologies and practices of separatism and assimilation have been thrown into question and, with this, their shared assumption that the members of a well-functioning social group should be more or less the same. Many of the most distinct forms of strict institutional separation have been challenged – racial segregation or apartheid, the strict delineation of men's and women's jobs and roles, and the institutional separation of disabled people from able-bodied people, for instance. The discourses and practices of sexism, racism, homophobia and discrimination have come to be regarded as unacceptable. Universal covenants have been developed that create a conceptual and international legal basis for human rights. These changes are the result in part of political contestation and institutional change. They are also a consequence of changing social conditions and shifts in values.

At first, the shift away from separatism and assimilation is a cautious one, a step in the direction of the recognition of differences. Instead of pretending the differences don't exist, or hoping they will go away, or trying to make them go away, differences are recognised and at least minimal measures taken to try to produce more equitable outcomes.

Sometimes, the process of recognition is no more than that. People come to recognise publicly that there are big differences in the ways people live and speak and think in their everyday lifeworlds. But they may go a little further than this and say, as French speakers would, 'laissez-faire', or let things be. There's nothing much we need to do. If differences have a life of their own, they are best left alone. 'I'm happy with my way of life,' a proponent of laissez-faire might say, 'and I'm happy that you seem to be happy with yours. So let's leave things they way they are. I won't interfere in your lifeworld if you don't interfere in mine. If I have a private opinion about your way of life, I'm going to keep it to myself.'

This approach to difference often fits the shift from what we have called didactic to authentic education. Authentic teaching tries to connect the curriculum to learner experiences, without necessarily challenging these experiences or attempting to make any significant change to people's conditions of life. How then do different learner attributes present themselves in the initial stages of their recognition? And what do schools and teachers do about these differences?

Dimension 1: Material attributes

Social class

In the era of post-Fordism and neoliberalism, complex changes occur in the dynamics of social class. In the developing world, many of the poorest remain grindingly poor. Some move to cities, find work and become somewhat less poor. Or they become poor in different ways, perhaps earning a greater cash income than they did as peasant farmers. But now they might find themselves living in slum settlements rather than in villages in which, in the past, they had been able to grow some of their own food and live more healthily. In the developed world, many of the poor get slightly less poor and acquire some of the inventions of the consumer society – mobile phones, televisions and the like. Meanwhile, the already affluent get much more affluent, and the gap between the affluent and the poor becomes greater.[43]

The waters of social class become muddied as more and more subtle distinctions of status are created, between 'new economy' jobs and old, for instance. In many 'new economy' jobs, the ethic of post-Fordism gives everybody a degree of responsibility for their own work. The distinct, class-differentiated neighbourhoods of the modern city become more mixed. Working-class suburbs of the inner city become gentrified even though pockets of the former poor may remain. The working poor move to more distant suburbs where their poverty is not so obvious. Poverty then manifests itself in the daily pressure of transport costs and meeting mortgage payments. Throughout the city and on its fringes, relative poverty and comparative wealth are increasingly juxtaposed, cheek by jowl. Material advantage and disadvantage are increasingly recognised to be, not only functions of social class, but the intersection or overlay of social class and race, culture, disability, gender and the other now more widely recognised markers of difference.

As the welfare state is dismantled, a more laissez-faire approach is taken to differences of social class. If poverty is going to be fixed, the poor are supposed to fix it for themselves by taking greater responsibility for their own welfare. It becomes harder and harder to get income support from the state if you are not in regular employment. This puts pressure on people to go back to work. The pay may be low and working conditions tough, but the poverty of this new 'working poor' is less visible than older forms of poverty.

The 'class struggle' of earlier modern times abates, too. The communist revolutions from the Russian Revolution of 1917 through to the 1970s come to an end as the classical communist states collapsed or reinvented themselves by grafting market mechanisms onto their one-party states. In the capitalist world, trade union membership declined and strikes became fewer. Yet, the tensions of class inequality were never far below the surface of society, even if the mark of poverty was expressed tangentially through high rates of criminality, violence and substance abuse.

The political quiescence of the less well-off may be a consequence of consumerism. Advertising promises that clothes or cosmetics or electronic goods or cars will be life-enhancing, even though the products the poor can afford tend to be cheap and shoddy. The social differentiations of class are more subtly cultural than they had been in the past – those who can afford to consume prestige-conferring products and brands, and those who cannot. The poor in developed countries spend more of their time shopping for the products they might consume, or purchasing the entertainment that fills their free time. They do not seem to focus as they did in the 20th century upon actions to contest the structures of class inequality – the classical union struggles or communist revolutions in which the workers take over the state and the state takes control of workplaces.

The new inequality does not require an authoritarian state to impose order and maintain the status quo. The less well-paid workers and the poor stay quiet because they have bought into the dreams of consumerism. The heavy hand of the Fordist boss and the nationalist state is replaced by the soft power of advertising hype, lifestyle brands, trashy entertainment, sporting team identifications and junk media.

This state of affairs creates new complexities for schools. Are they segregating along class lines more or less than they did before? One answer is 'more segregating', as the affluent send their children to expensive schools. Another answer is 'less segregating' when the social class of people within geographical reach of a school may be more varied than in the past, or when the children of poorer people are coming to a school because it offers greater opportunities, or when the school deliberately aims to serve a broader social constituency in a more equitable way.

Despite these changes, there does not seem to be any evidence that schools are bridging lifeworld gaps any more effectively than they have in the past, despite the attempt to apply progressivist or authentic approaches to teaching. Maybe it is hard, impossible even at times, for schools to make up for the patterns of disadvantage and advantage that are the consequences of social class. Clearly, however, the gap is getting larger. As 'knowledge' is an increasingly important factor in securing economic opportunity, this failure on the part of schools is no longer justifiable or sustainable. [*See*: Basil Bernstein on restricted and elaborated codes.[44]]

Locale

Over the course of the 20th century, rural and remote locales remain relatively disadvantaged in comparison with cities because people by and large have reduced access to public and cultural goods – quality schools, public libraries, museums, galleries and a comprehensive range of media, for instance. However, new pockets of disadvantage emerge as the sheer geographical expanse of many cities becomes so much greater. Those living on the distant suburban fringe who don't have a motor car, for instance, may find they are as disadvantaged in their access to social resources as anyone in a regional or rural area.

Dimension 2: Corporeal attributes

Age

Over the course of the 20th century, a more finely differentiated recognition of age differences emerges. These differences come to be more clearly delineated and rigidly institutionalised. Age groups also begin to behave in newly distinct ways.

Some of this is a consequence of changing gender relations. The stay-at-home mums of the traditional nuclear family relied on complementary sibling differences – for instance, older children's level of maturity and thus responsibility for themselves and their younger siblings. Working parents today send their children to age-differentiated crèches and childcare facilities. Children spend more time with peers than with children of different ages. Even at home, families of the recent past were characteristically larger and more age-differentiated than they are today. In all parts of the world, one or, at most, two-child families are becoming more common, and in China today the one-child family is law.

Children's culture also becomes more finely graduated – toys, books and other media are targeted at narrower and narrower age bands. Some of these activities for children, such as video games, lead them to forms of abstraction and cognition that at times surprise child psychologists and push down what were thought to be the lowest thresholds for certain kinds of thinking and identity. For these children, doing school in the traditional way seems boring, and when it's boring they may become disengaged or present a 'discipline problem'.

Moving on through the age levels, puberty happens earlier now. Pre-teens or 'tweens' are more like what teenagers used to be. However, at the other end of adolescence, young people are staying at school longer, and so taking longer to make an adult-like contribution to society. It might take until their mid- or even late 20s, after the completion of their second, professionally oriented degree, before a young person gets full-time employment. In the meantime, they remain dependent on their parents. Given the cost of housing, sometimes they continue to live at home even after they get a job. Nor are adolescents and young adults the relatively homogeneous cultural group that they were in the past. As an age-bracket, these young people are increasingly fractured by diverging styles, interests and personae.

These ambiguities of dependence, responsibility and diverging values create intense crises of identity – around family and institutional authority, substance abuse, depression and suicide, to name just a few of the most vexing flashpoints. New rites of passage become the subject of contestation between generations and opposing value orientations – the appropriate time and form of sexual experience, or whether, when and how to use cigarettes, alcohol and drugs, for instance. The stages of development from child to adult are more than ever the result of culture and values rather than predictable and general stages marked by age level alone.[45]

Race

In the second half of the 20th century, social institutions and ideologies that had once used the concept of 'race' to justify and perpetuate inequality came under increasing attack. Anti-colonial movements successfully secured independence for countries still subject to imperial rule. Civil rights movements protested apartheid and racial segregation, which had given one racially defined group rights and privileges at the expense of another. By these means, racism in its most explicit institutional and ideological forms comes to be eliminated. Institutional and attitudinal racism are also progressively proscribed, at least in name and in law. It is no longer regarded as natural and inevitable that groups of people suffering from the historical legacies of slavery or conquest, for instance, should remain socially marginalised and materially impoverished.

Racism, however, persists in the subtly exclusionary attitudes of those in privileged positions and the institutional realities of those racially distinguishable groups who 'happen' to be poorer and have less access to high-quality education.

Rightly and sometimes wrongly, 'race' categories continue to be used, themselves legacies of the era of racism. The historical application of the category of 'race' still needs to be negotiated, and the enduring cultures of prejudice associated with visible differences. In this context, various social agencies still use race classification to make sure that employment access or school results are improving for racially defined minorities, or indigenous peoples, or immigrant groups. 'Affirmative action', 'equal opportunity', 'desegregation' or 'equity programs' all use these categories.[46]

However, the case is often made by both the supporters and opponents of the civil rights movement that these categories are at times used in less than helpful ways. They are overly simplistic, not accounting for the variety of social experience and privilege within racially distinguishable groups. They are a heavy handed way to ensure equity, to the extent that they sometimes create a counter-productive anxiety and anger on the part of individuals who don't feel they are getting favoured or even fair treatment from redressing the hand of social justice. They create separate programs that, in the name of cultural identity, intensify historical consciousness of separateness. And they use the flawed category of 'race' as though the appearances mattered, or could be allowed to matter still. The real problem, the more sympathetic of these critics argue, is not race, but the legacies of racism. Buy the old category and you buy into the old argument.[47]

Sex and sexuality

Sex and sexuality by the second half of the 20th century became less centred around the male–female dichotomy and its bipolar pattern of supposedly 'natural' attractions.

Traditional sexual relations were radically destabilised by the widespread acceptance of homosexuality. One permutation of sexual relations, male–female, was replaced by three when male–male and female–female were added, and more if you added permutations of bisexuality, or attraction to both sexes. New sexual alternatives came out of the closet. They are increasingly public – in neighbourhoods, in popular culture and in everyday life. The prevailing view of homosexual people is that their sexuality is a matter of biology – of sex more than gender, a truly corporeal rather than a principally symbolic thing. The way they feel is in their natures, they say, and not a matter of cultural choice or something that could have been any other way.[48] Meanwhile, public institutions increasingly came to recognise homosexuality. Homophobia became unacceptable in a wider range of social settings.

However, despite the growing recognition of alternative patterns of sex and sexuality, the new communities spawned by these social changes tend to remain relatively separate in the first instance.

Physical and mental characteristics

Views of body form that measure deficits against a norm – height, weight and certain kinds of physical ability – have become less acceptable in recent times. There is an increasing recognition of the range of body forms. Programs of action have been designed to enable better access for people with certain kinds of disabilities – be that the capacity to walk, or to see, or to hear, for instance. Terminology or attitudes that label a person's bodily features in a prejudicial way are regarded as less acceptable.

There is also recognition of a wider range of disabilities and the relativity of these to specific tasks. Rather than focusing solely on a lack of physical or mental ability in some area people with specific disabilities need to focus on alternative abilities that might be marshalled to support a task. A disabled person is often able to do a range of things in different ways. Rather than classify and then marginalise a person as disabled, the social conditions around them need to provide the conditions for their enablement. Despite this recognition, it is not the case that public buildings such as schools and their teaching programs enable optimal learning experiences for learners with a diverse range of bodily abilities; and to this extent social institutions themselves remain the source of disability rather than an individual's bodily capacities. A view also emerges of disability as something that can be both inherited or acquired (with accident or age, for instance), and that counterbalancing abilities are things that can be learnt.[49]

Notwithstanding this progress, people with specific disabilities are still frequently regarded as separate groups. They are often classified in overly simplistic ways. And, in relation to body forms more generally, there is a subtler and more widespread view of the ideal body image, sometimes reaching the point of being extreme and unrealistic. Such a view can be found pervasively in a 'beauty myth'[50] promoted in fashion and advertising, and the lionisation of the 'sporting type'.

Dimension 3: Symbolic attributes

Culture
Cultural assimilation never did work very well, and certainly not consistently or reliably. Granted, assimilation was a somewhat more open approach than outright segregation. However, for every individual success story where immigrant children, for instance, did well in school, evidence pointed to the less-than-happy fact of more general patterns of educational disadvantage amongst 'minority' students.[51] Despite the assimilationist rhetoric, the outcome in these cases continued to be exclusion.

Cultural diversity is not something that could be so simply erased. Despite the public rhetoric of assimilation, cultural heritage remained a cornerstone of the domestic life of both immigrants and the indigenous peoples. 'Ethnic' organisations and lobby groups were emerging. In countries in which significant numbers of 'minorities' had the vote, they came to constitute an important electoral pressure group. It may well be, however, that one of the reasons assimilation didn't work was that its proponents were never entirely serious about it. The way things conveniently happened to turn out could be described as a structural racism in which assimilation may well have been the theory (the promised 'opportunity'), but rarely what actually happened. The hurdles proved just too great. Few in minority groups actually assimilated to the extent of achieving socio-economic parity.

What followed from about the third quarter of the 20th century were social policies and practices that might be loosely called 'multiculturalism'. On the one hand, the strong national identities and clear state sovereignty characteristic of the era of nationalism have been weakened by the forces of globalisation. On the other hand, the laissez-faire ideology of neoliberalism allows social groups any forms of self-reliance they may choose. Ethnic and religious groups are, for instance, encouraged to run their own self-managed child-care centres, schools or aged-care facilities.[52]

Meanwhile, global diasporas become more closely interconnected. Today, you can watch cable or satellite TV from your country of emigration. You can stay closely engaged with its politics, to the extent, in some cases, of being able to vote in national elections and maintain active citizenship of two states, the state of one's ethnic origins as well as the destination state of migration. Such migrants can set up businesses and other networks that capitalise upon these diasporic connections.[53]

The story for indigenous peoples is somewhat different in its details, though similar in its underlying narrative. Indigenous peoples and their sympathisers fight for land rights and some degree of sovereignty over their ancestral lands. In response, the neoliberal state is sometimes willing to hand over a degree of self-determination or self-management to indigenous peoples. Better that they sort out their problems for themselves, the rationale seems to run, than the state try to sort it out for them. So, the state grants limited land rights to indigenous people, mainly over areas that have not yet been settled by non-indigenous people. Sometimes this comes with economic concessions that allow these communities to be self-supporting, such as rights to mining royalties from the land or the right to run casinos.[54]

Multiculturalism and indigenous self-determination come with their limitations.[55] They often come with an 'authentic' approach to education that allows learners to express who they are in their learning, and undertake activities that reflect the realities of their lifeworld. This approach affirms differences instead of seeking to exclude or erase them. In the case of cultural differences, students might do country studies of the diasporic communities represented in the classroom. They might bring in their families for national days – and samples of their food, national costumes, dances and artefacts. However, as important as this might be as a mark of acknowledgement and a strategy to make students and families feel they belong, it does not necessarily tackle the question of access, or how education might provide minority students with more open avenues to social power and material resources. At times, this kind of recognition of difference feels tokenistic, or patronising even. Other times it creates stereotypes, whereby a child has to go searching for the school's vision of what is sufficiently exotic to be classified as interestingly different. At still other times, it creates categories that are all-too-neat and that oversimplify the more complex realities of identity in ways that are less than helpful.

Meanwhile, access programs for demographically defined groups may overcome the limitations of tokenistic affirmation – such as English as a Second Language (ESL), or bilingual education programs, or special mathematics or science programs for girls. Such programs can be valuable when they assist the group for whom they were intended, either to gain access to 'mainstream' educational and social goods, or to flourish in their diversity. However, they may be not so good a thing when they divide groups and create barriers to wider interaction, set their sights lower to achieve 'realistic' outcomes for disadvantaged students, or trigger counter-productive reactions in the 'culture wars' from those who think they are being left out of special programs.

Such programs also attract noisy critics who still support the assimilationist view, even though rarely these days the explicitly exclusionist view. Teach our national culture, the Western canon, mainstream disciplines, they say, because that's how you will help students to get on in life. That's also how we will prevent social disintegration and tribalism and create a common, shared national culture.[56]

Language

The forces of globalisation have had two, seemingly contradictory, effects on language diversity. On the one hand, multilingualism is a more evident and necessary phenomenon. On the other hand, English has become the dominant global language, at the expense of the visibility and importance of other smaller and even quite large languages.

The world today is a seeming Babel of multilingualism – as we pass through the world's airports, as we read the instructions that come with products and in the streets of our neighbourhoods as locals talk to each other in the languages in which they happen to be most proficient.[57] Classrooms in schools are made up of students who speak any number of languages at home – a fact that teachers can only ignore to the detriment of students' learning. Learning a second language is not the same as learning to read and write in a first language. Students are disadvantaged who come to school without the national language, if that's the medium of instruction. They don't learn to read and write as easily as students who have spoken the language of instruction at home. They often don't do as well in regular subjects such as science and mathematics if they are not native speakers of the language in which these subjects are being taught. So, special second-language learning programs are devised such as ESL in English-speaking countries.

Schools also often teach the first language of minority language groups. Alternatively, parents send their children to community based schools, be these full-day schools, after-school or weekend community language schools. Whichever way, the objectives of such teaching are mostly mixed: maintaining their language and cultural heritage, keeping up the learning that had been started in a first language rather than having to start again, and creating opportunities for children to participate in the local and global work and life possibilities that are offered by diasporic communities.[58] If you are a native speaker of a Chinese language or Arabic, for instance, learning the language formally may open up all kinds of opportunities in a globalising world.

Bilingual education programs are another approach to language diversity in which part of the curriculum is taught in the home language of the learner even when this is not the main language of the society or the language of instruction of the school. The purpose of bilingual programs is to ensure that students' learning is not disrupted, when, for instance, they enter school mid-way after migrating from a country where they had been taught in another language. Their transition to the main language of instruction can then be at a pace that meets their needs. Or bilingual programs may be offered for the whole of school as a way of maintaining the group's language to levels that are useable in professional and formal knowledge contexts.[59]

As is the case with multiculturalism, there is often a vociferous backlash against multilingualism. It slows down the assimilation or integration process, its critics say. To be sure that everybody is unequivocally in the same civic space, all public signs and communications should be in the main national language. Such are the claims of the 'English Only' movement in the United States, one example of this kind of movement. English Only lobbyists have gone so far as to insist on legislating that English be the official language of all public places, including schools.[60]

One would hardly have thought this necessary, in one sense, because of the overwhelming global dominance of the English language. Spoken by only a million people in a little country off the coast of Europe just 350 years ago, it is now spoken by about one person in five across the world, the majority of whom now speak it as a second language. English dominates the Internet, popular music, film, the news media, science and academic knowledge. Students flood into universities in English-language countries so they can get closer to the inside of this global language of power.

The price of this is the inescapable fact that small, indigenous languages are disappearing faster than ever. Even large, European languages are considered to be under threat.[61] The French-language experts of the *Academie Francaise*, for example, go out of their way to create new French words rather than take on English words for new things like 'email'. This is why they invented the word *'courriel'* from the words *'courrier electronique'*, or 'electronic mail'. The French Ministry of Culture then announced a ban on the use of the word 'email' in all government documents and publications.

Gender

Gender roles have changed enormously, particularly over the course of the past half-century. Civil limitations on women's rights, such as the right to vote, have been removed in most countries of the world. There are more women in the workforce. And traditionally male and female professions have become less exclusively so. There are more male kindergarten teachers and nurses than in the past, and more female police officers and lawyers. From being highly unequal, the highest levels of education attained by girls and women compared to boys and men have come closer to a balance. There is less gender-segregated schooling and when there is, a full range of subjects is offered to girls in single-sex schools. More girls are doing traditional boys' subjects such as mathematics and science, and are encouraged to do so.

In both schools and the wider society, sexist practices are sometimes illegal (for instance, discrimination or sexual harassment). Sexism in its attitudinal or discursive forms, such as sexist language, is regarded as unacceptable. Men are expected to rectify those aspects of stereotypical male behaviour that impact badly on others and limit their own social effectiveness, such as taking an aggressive stance, or dominating a conversation and not listening, or exhibiting poor interpersonal skills and lacking 'emotional intelligence'.

These changes are a testament to the feminist movement and the struggle for equal rights for women, which first came to widespread public consciousness with the fight for female suffrage. These changes also happen to mesh well with the general direction of the post-Fordist, neoliberal world. It's good for the economy to have more women in the workforce and integrated more fully into the market economy. Not only are they more readily available for the labour market; it is also possible to enlist them as consumers of things that were once produced in the unpaid domestic economy of the nuclear family, outside of the direct reach of the market. It is better for business and the market economy if busy mothers have to purchase already prepared or fast foods for their families, rather than cook it themselves. It is better they pay for child care rather than do it themselves. The change, in other words, is part of a larger development project in which the market and consumerism penetrate every corner of the world that they have not yet commodified. [*See*: Simone de Beauvoir on emancipating women.[62]]

Parallel to this, masculine and feminine gender identities become less clearly aligned to male and female sex. Typical behaviours for boys and girls are less clearly defined, and broader in the range of possibilities. There are butch girls and effeminate boys. Some of this is connected to the growing acceptance of homosexuality; however, gender identity is not necessarily a predictor of sexuality – hence the 'metrosexual' men and the determinedly and publicly ambitious, tough women who are nevertheless heterosexual. [*See*: Connell on gender roles and masculinity.[63]]

Family

Differences between family types have come to be much more accepted and recognised than they were during the era when the nuclear family was dominant. There is less pressure to conform to the nuclear family norm. In fact, amongst households, the nuclear family has become a minority form. Alongside it there are single-parent families, extended families and, with increasing rates of divorce and remarriage, blended families.

Changing gender relations also transform the family, even nuclear families. As more women work and sexism is regarded as unacceptable, men are increasingly expected to share the burden of childrearing and domestic work. The rule of the husband in the household is replaced by shared decision making between men and women as equal partners. Meanwhile, the traditionally authoritarian parent, and particularly the father figure, is displaced by increasingly 'permissive' childrearing practices, allowing children more autonomy to make up their minds about things for themselves. The hard power of corporal punishment is replaced by softer forms of persuasive discipline. [*See*: Dr Spock on permissive child rearing.[64]]

To traditionalists, these changes are distressing. Rather than affirming family environments for children or the liberation of women, they see disintegrating values, unruly children and dysfunctional families. They yearn nostalgically for the days when there were straightforward norms of parental authority and clearly differentiated gender roles.

Affinity and persona

Patterns of personal association change, too. For instance, there are many more shades of religious and non-religious identity, seemingly less able to tolerate each other's doctrines. These appear in the widely varied religions of diasporic communities; the more and more polarised views of religious liberals and religious fundamentalists, at times even within the one religion or denomination; the panoply of 'new age' belief systems; and the proliferation of quasi-faiths of self-improvement.

In the realm of political identity, traditional left–right politics around access to material resources was centred on the role of the state in economic activity, from the politics of the welfare state and the demands of trade unions, to communism in which the state controlled all economic activity. With the end of the Cold War, the demise of communism and the triumph of neoliberalism, the focus of politics began to shift. The subject of political discussion moved from traditional political parties and into social movements based on group identity and moral concern. Different kinds of people found themselves supporting or opposed to movements supporting environmental protection, women's rights, justice for ethnic and racial minorities, and the right to abortion or same-sex marriage. These movements and the people who belong to them take more of a public stand on matters that would, at one time, have been regarded as a matter of private opinion. Nor do they sit on a neatly definable political spectrum.

Nostalgic for an earlier politics, some people regret the eclipse of those straightforward claims for economic justice that were the basis of traditional left–right politics. Others warn of social fragmentation as different kinds of people make loud and insistent moral claims and establish agendas for action that are antithetical to each other.[65] Still others think this 'postmodern' politics is a good thing, opening up issues that have been ignored in the past, and addressing injustices that would otherwise have been perpetuated.[66]

Inclusion: New learning

Our case for an inclusive approach that aligns to our propositions about a New Learning does more than simply recognise or acknowledge differences. It is grounded in an active, engaged understanding of the fundamental social dynamics of diversity. Differences never remain still. They are not states that are simply to be found, classified and dealt with. They are always moving. Differences, more-over, are invariably relational. Groups cannot be neatly categorised and described as though that were the end of the story; rather, they are constituted in relation-ships in which one group or type of person is defined in relation to another. They exist in dynamic, and never stable, tension – class to class, gender to gender, cul-ture to culture. They are also internally differentiated. In fact, a rough general metric would be that the internal differences in attitude, attribute and behaviour within any demographically defined group are greater than the average difference between groups. This means that the demographic groupings, whilst helpful to our understanding of the historical and experiential basis for certain moral agen-das and social claims, are oversimplified and sometimes counter-productively so. Finally, the differences intersect. There are not just a dozen or so key categories of difference. For any individual the chance of any one particular combination (class, gender, race, sexuality, body form, affinity and the like) is so low that they can only ever belong to the tiniest of minorities. This means that throwing a per-son into one of the larger demographic categories may do disservice to their more precisely defined needs and interests.[67] [*See*: My students.[68]]

Moving from 'recognition' to 'inclusion' means to shift emphasis from static 'diversity' to dynamic 'divergence'. No longer can we remain content to leave dif-ferences more or less the way they are. In fact, we may want to move them along. This can be either from the perspective of an insider – a woman who wants to change the role of women, or an indigenous activist struggling to improve the conditions of life of their people, for instance. Or it can be from an outsider's perspective, in cases where educators assist learners in their self-transformation or growth, helping them to achieve dreams and aspirations that may have seemed beyond the scope of possibility within their lifeworlds.

Authentic education reflects diversity in the world as it is found. Our case for an inclusive, transformative view of education, by contrast, works on agendas for action. It works with learners to invent and reinvent themselves and their worlds – as high-performing workers, citizens, learners and confident social beings. Such an approach may be driven by a range of social and self-transformative agendas, from establishing and building a career, to entrepreneurial innovation, to ethical concern for social justice or a practical concern for the future of the environment. Our New Learning proposal, in other words, supports a full spectrum of potential individual and social objectives, from the pragmatics of self-advancement to the social–ethical agendas of emancipation and sustainability.

Dimension 1: Material attributes

Social class
With the exception of one or two small, remnant, communist states, the world entered the 21st century with societies based on a market-based logic of material

resource distribution. Workers work for business owners; they are paid less than the full value of their labour; and owners with the good fortune to have been born to ownership or the good luck to have acquired it, make a profit and become wealthy. In the 19th century, Karl Marx thought the workers in this kind of market–capitalist system would get poorer while the owners got richer, and that this disparity would eventually bring the system down.[69] In fact the capitalist system did come down for one third of the world's population from Russia to Vietnam over the course of the first three quarters of the 20th century.

Marx did not envisage, however, that many of the workers in capitalist societies would gradually become better off, at least to the extent that they would be satisfied enough with their jobs, what they earned and what they could afford to buy. Indeed, although greatly reducing disparities in wealth, communism failed to provide the mass of the population with the consumer goods and freedom that capitalism offered. Nevertheless, the gap between the less and the more affluent has grown, and continues to grow in ways that are still explicable in terms of the underlying logic of the capitalist system.

Since the collapse of classical communism and the end of the Cold War, there has been little incentive to change the capitalist system in any fundamental ways. Nor has there been a realistic possibility of achieving fundamental change. Other major changes can be and have been more readily made; for instance, to establish gender relations on a more equal footing, or to eliminate the worst excesses of explicit ideological and institutional racism.

Though material inequality seems for the moment an intractable problem, some aspects of it are intolerable and unsustainable. Even the most enthusiastic supporters of the capitalist system would agree that there are great dangers when poverty is experienced as perpetual hopelessness. Such poverty is a breeding ground for violence, criminality, war and terrorism.

Education seems helpless to address the deep structural sources of material inequality, even though educators must deal with the consequences on a daily basis. Despite the neoliberal retreat from the large-scale, redistributive project that had been taken on by communist and welfare states alike, states around the world continue to assume some responsibility for redistributive justice, domestically through the taxation and welfare systems and internationally through aid programs. This remains a challenge for broader social and political movements to address; movements aimed at the inclusion of the disadvantaged through the allocation of material resources.

Some things, however, education can do. Education is a key variable in the nexus between work and material resources, most obviously in building knowledge and capacities that will provide entry into forms of work that pay more. The education–work–material resources connection is one of the great 'opportunity' or mobility promises of an unashamedly unequal society. If you don't inherit material resources or chance upon them, education is almost the only path to mobility. Without education, the promise of opportunity at the heart of democratic capitalist societies would ring extremely hollow. If education can't do redistributive justice by reallocating material resources, it can do it by providing symbolic or knowledge resources to individuals and groups.

As it happens, knowledge resources are becoming more pivotal to the new capitalism, and this opens new potentials and creates new responsibilities for educators. Politicians and captains of industry tell us that knowledge is now a key factor of production, a fundamental basis of competitiveness – at the personal, enterprise and national levels.[70] And as knowledge is a product of learning, education is more important than ever. This is why education has become such a prominent topic in the public discourse of social promise. The expectations of education have been ratcheted up. More than ever before, our political leaders are saying that education is pivotal to social and economic progress. This does not necessarily translate immediately into greater public investment in education (a businesslike approach, one would think). But today's rhetoric about the importance of education does give educators greater leverage in the public discourse than we had until recently. Stated simply, in a knowledge economy in which more and more jobs require greater depths of knowledge, schools must do what they can to bridge the knowledge gaps. If they can do this, they are at least doing something to ameliorate the worst systemic material inequalities. Schools, in other words, have a new opportunity, a new responsibility and a new challenge to build societies that are more inclusive of social classes whose access to material resources was historically limited.

Locale

The dynamics of locale are changing, too, as cities sprawl into their hinterlands and as regions themselves turn into semi-urbanised sprawls. These create more complex human geographies, where wider differences of wealth, culture and affinity find themselves more closely juxtaposed.

Paradoxically, the magnetic attraction of the city is no longer so powerful as it once was. The Internet, satellite TV and next-day delivery can connect almost any place in the world to any other. As the world's big cities become more expensive, businesses are moving to less-expensive regional places. The poor are moving to get jobs and live in places where they can enjoy a better standard of living, even though their wages may be low. Welfare recipients are moving to regional areas too, so their meagre payments can be stretched further. Meanwhile, people of the middle class are moving to places where they can purchase a better lifestyle for what they earn – a bigger house for the same money, and cheaper products and services. The rich are establishing at least part-time, but also sometimes full-time, places of retreat, commuting and telecommuting to their places of work or business. All these fractions and fragments of social class find themselves uneasily juxtaposed in newly growing regional cities, towns and semi-rural 'sprawl'.[71]

If suburbia was the characteristically new urban form of the 20th century, the growth centres of the near future and the sites of our next wave of social transformation are in a distributed 'extra-urbia'. This new extra-urbia consists of the semi-rural hinterlands of big cities, small regional or remote urban communities and rural or remote households that nevertheless can now subsist in a pseudo-urban or virtually urban domestic economy. No matter where they are, extra-urban households have a relation to information, culture, work and commodities equal to any urban household and at a fraction of the cost – as a consequence of cheap freight and online shopping, e-learning at every level of education, telecommuting or geographically agnostic knowledge work (the call centres, for instance), and the fact that any book or piece of music or film in the world is now within reach of an Internet download, or satellite TV, or next-day delivery. The new economy is producing completely new geographies to the urbanisation that characterised an earlier modernity.

For these reasons, education outside of the big cities becomes an increasing matter for concern. The composition of extra-urban communities is changing rapidly, representing extremes of poverty and wealth, and diversity of identities as great as any. Equitable access to the full range of quality education becomes a challenge for designers of e-learning environments.

Meanwhile, on a world scale, the global becomes the domain of the local – the rapid communications connections that bring people so close, the products that can come here or go there by overnight dispatch, the streets in which one household connects into one global diaspora and the next household another. Global movements of people are picking up the pace, particularly as more of the productive population retires, and as the population in the reproductive age range has fewer children. The consequences are both orderly and disorderly global movements of people.

Dimension 2: Corporeal attributes

Age
Today, the traditional separations of chronological age seem to be breaking down. Or, at least, they seem in need of a social transformation that will actively break them down.

How early should formal education begin? And who should do it – professional institutions of early childhood education, or parents with the assistance of educational toys, video and television? Age-related measures of learners' capacities also seem less relevant, as the range at any one age level, of emotional maturity, conceptual capacity, forms of responsibility, seems greater today. Finer grading into more homogeneous groups does not seem to be the answer. Rather, an inclusive approach may involve having a wider range of ages in a group, and teaching strategies targeted to the dynamics of difference – reciprocal learning, peer mentoring, collaborative activities, learners pursuing varied interests and tasks, and the like. These all challenge the conventional communication architecture of the classroom and its everyone-on-the-same-page approach. A reinvention of peda-gogy may be necessary to meet the demands of the pluralistic divergence in today's classrooms.

As young people mature earlier and stay dependent longer, new kinds of frame-works of responsibility may be required, whereby their learning is connected with or supplemented by responsibilities in the community, on a voluntary basis or involving a nominal payment. The neat institutional separation between school and work may no longer be sensible or viable, particularly as the proportion of the population within the age range of the traditional labour force declines. This blur-ring of age boundaries will continue throughout life. Education will no longer be straightforwardly provided by a geographically located institution and attached to a particular time of life. It will necessarily be lifelong and life-wide. People may also be able to, and want to, work longer, be that in paid or voluntary work, and to do this they will need to constantly update their skills. Once retired, people will need to learn new things if they are to maintain their capacity to participate in a rapidly changing world.

The overall effect of the blurring of the traditional boundaries of age, and age-related learning institutions, is to create new opportunities and challenges for education. An inclusive education will allow you to learn a wider range of things in a wider range of ways at a wider range of sites, at any and every age.

Race
It has lately become possible to return to the question of race, aided conceptually by the findings of recent genetic research. For a long time, the biology of race had been discredited because it was linked to an older science of physical anthropol-ogy, which measured differences in skull capacity and drew spurious conclusions about intelligence. The new research examines human genetic divergence from DNA samples. This research has demonstrated that human beings are all very closely related genetically. There is also such a degree of genetic mixing that it is almost impossible to delineate one group from another in biological terms. The geographical departure from the original source of humans in Africa is so recent in generational terms – perhaps 500 generations for the peoples of the Ameri-cas and 1 000 for the peoples of Europe – that the differences are immeasurably insignificant.[72]

The result is that race is no longer justified as a meaningful category for dif-ferentiating the intelligence or educability of human groups. It is now widely recognised that there is no scientific basis upon which to argue that different edu-cational outcomes for racially defined groups at school are based in the inherited, biological differences in the brain. Changes in attitude to racial difference have led to a widespread recognition that such differences are, and have always been, the product of political, economic and cultural conditions.

Racism, however, remains an important category, even if its forms have become more subtle and thus harder to address. Institutional racism is an affront to international human rights covenants and is illegal in most places. The discourse of explicit racism is unacceptable in public contexts. But the legacies of racism persist: in the patterns of inequality that reproduce themselves; in the 'invisibility' of some groups in the public culture; and in the 'choice' of groups to live in separate and unequal communities based on locality, employment and affinity. Racism is so entrenched and pervasive that outcomes do not necessarily improve even when desegregation is enforced, such as when children are 'bussed' from the area in which they live to a desegregated school in another area. The challenge of social and educational inclusion today is to address these harder-to-identify and harder-to-remedy forms of racism.[73] [*See*: Brown v. Board of Education US Supreme Court Judgment[74]; *also see*: Martin Luther King, 'I have a dream'.[75]] The neoliberalism of recent times and the backlash against political correctness, however, have made the discourses and social policies around race more, not less, complex, than in earlier periods of overt racism. The global dialogue about human rights does offer a way to address social inclusivity in a way that allows people to be different without being unequal.

Sex and sexuality
Sex is no longer regarded as inevitable and definitive. People have a greater capacity than ever in the past to remake their bodies – with surgery, with medication and with diet and exercise. This could be in order to conform more closely to an idealised sexual norm (breast or penis enlargement, for instance). Alternatively, people can choose to sculpt their bodies surgically and with medication in order to change sex from the one assigned to them at birth. People who make this choice are called transsexual. Transsmen are people who have been born female and who have changed to be men; transwomen are people who have been born male and who have changed to be women. Transsexual people may have a range of sexual orientations.[76] An intersex person is born with genitalia and other sex characteristics that mix male and female characteristics or are ambiguous. They may choose to remain intersex, or move in the direction of one or other sex. In the past, this decision was often made at birth by doctors or parents. Medical procedures were performed that sometimes took people in the direction that they would not have chosen for themselves.[77] In an earlier era, it wasn't possible to choose one's sex so easily and to transform one's sex so thoroughly. Now, sex and sexuality are a matter of personal decision and a commitment to be true to what the person considers to be their natural self.[78]

Sexual orientation is considered by many today to be an aspect of a person's nature, or corporeal inheritance.[79] This is manifested psychologically (a person's erotic desires) and in practice (the sex partner or partners one chooses). The principal categories of sexual orientation are homosexual (gay and lesbian), heterosexual and bisexual. Other forms of sexual orientation include celibacy or a deliberate choice to refrain from sex irrespective of desire; asexuality when people are not sexually attracted to others; and auto-sexuality or a preference for auto-arousal. People may opt for one of these forms of sexuality, or a combination – for instance the celibate lesbian, or the transwoman whose sexuality is exclusively autoerotic, or the person who is a heterosexual male who also cross-dresses and gains autoerotic pleasure from this. The range of sex and sexualities today encompasses a widely variable range of body forms, sexual identities and sexual practices.

What do schools do? Identities grounded in sex and sexuality are profoundly the concern of an institution whose purpose is the development of children and young people into adults. Vexing questions arise such as the age at which sexual orientation can be recognised and sex reassignment considered. There is the question, too, of the role of the school in negotiating these complexities, in so many areas, from counselling to curriculum. The situation is further complicated by divisions in the community, particularly when some people condemn the range of sex and sexual orientation options available today and others support what they consider to be a personal liberty. The consequences of practices that are prejudicial or exclusionary are dire, even when pressures are subtle, as evidenced in the levels of depression and rates of suicide amongst young people struggling with their sex and sexuality.[80]

Physical and mental characteristics

Stereotypical views of the normal body are disrupted by the growing acceptance of a wider range of body forms. Normality, ironically, is destabilised by images of unrealistic hypernormality – from the tall, dangerously thin female models to the overdeveloped body builders. Ideas of the normal body are also thrown into question by a wider range of interventions on the body: dieting and anorexia; body building practices and drugs; and tattoos, body piercing and hair designs.

The range of disabilities that are recognised also expands, and the classifications become more finely grained as we become better informed by the research of educators, social workers and medical scientists: a range of hearing impairments from various forms of restricted hearing to deafness[81]; sight restrictions of different kinds, such as myopia and colour blindness through to full blindness[82]; speech impairments of many varieties and with differing impacts on speech[83]; orthopaedic conditions that limit motor functions including cerebral palsy, spina bifida, muscular dystrophy, clubfoot, amputation, paralysis, stroke, arthritis; developmental disorders such as Down Syndrome and small stature[84]; mental disorders including schizophrenia, depression, bipolar disorder, phobias of various kinds, anxiety disorder, neurosis and obsessive-compulsive disorder; emotional, social and behavioural difficulties such as autism, Asperger's Syndrome, attention deficit disorder and attention deficit hyperactivity disorder[85]; learning disabilities including visual discrimination, auditory discrimination, spatial or temporal perception, dysphasia (language ability), aphasia (language loss), dyslexia (reading difficulties), dyspraxia (difficulties in coordination and movement); and chronic disease.

These and other disabilities may be inherited, or acquired by accident or with age. In the past, these disabilities were identified exclusively through a clinical lens. Today, disability is regarded as a social construction as well as a clinically identifiable condition of the body or brain. The social construction may take the form of the stairs that prevent wheelchair access, or the websites that do not meet accessibility standards for the visually impaired, or other people's generalised expectations of 'normality'. It may be the image and self-image of disabled people that limits their access to some social domains. Disability activists throw into question the ability 'norm'. They also insist on the right to assistive technologies and to education and training that does not focus on the lack, but positively nurtures parallel and compensatory abilities. Disabled people can do many of the things able-bodied people can, albeit in different ways. And the distinction between able-bodied and disabled is never so clear. Perhaps the able-bodied are only ever temporarily so. They are always vulnerable to the possibility of accident or disease, and the aged usually face one form of disability or another.[86]

The question for institutions such as schools is how does one create a genuinely inclusive environment for people whose body forms and abilities are so manifestly various? As the range of disabilities comes to be more adequately recognised and as the variety of meaningful educational responses becomes better known, disability presents itself as a bigger and more pressing issue for educators. Taking into account the enormous range of permutations of abilities and disabilities, and the overlay of other material, corporeal and symbolic dimensions of difference, there can be no simple classification of challenges and solutions.

In the past, differences of body form were ignored, or the people most deviant from the norm were sent to special institutions. Today, 'mainstreaming' and integration are often attempted. A danger here, however, is that communities of similar experience are broken up (for instance, sign-language communities). Teachers end up dealing with so many differences, each requiring such specific educational responses, that they sometimes find themselves dealing with specific situations outside of the scope of their competence. The solution, in part, is to work collaboratively with experts outside of the classroom, and also to create an open learning environment in which the experience of learning can vary according each learner's needs and interests – from each according their ability, and to each according to their need. [*See*: Bowe on barriers to disabled people.[87]]

Culture
A paradoxical thing happens to culture in the era of total globalisation. The whole world becomes the domain of representation and action – products, media, communications, travel. In one moment this appears to be a process of homogenisation – the consumer products that look much the same wherever they are, the media and entertainment giants that make their presence felt everywhere, and English as the lingua franca of the new, digital media. In another moment, these very processes of universalisation prompt people to go out of their way to make poignant differentiations – the products whose special quality is that they were made in a distinctive place; the media that tell stories that shock and awe, of differences in culture and circumstance at the ends of the Earth; the flourishing of many small as well as large languages using the new media; and the travel and

tourism whose very rationale is the fact that the destination is different. The cultural logic of globalisation, in other words, is as much one of cultural divergence as cultural homogenisation. For every cultural thing that seems to be becoming pragmatically – or distressingly – standardised, there is something else that people are actively trying to differentiate.[88]

In the case of ethnic and indigenous cultures, today's paradoxical forces of globalisation provide new openings for cultural self-differentiation, local community self-governance and more powerfully interconnected diasporic communities. And another paradox: you might be concerned that the way in which your neighbours live is off on a worryingly diverging tangent to yourself (and where do their loyalties really lie?). However, people who feel they genuinely belong, in their difference, develop a more powerful and effective sense of inclusion than they would if homogeneity were forced upon them.

From territories as expansive as the nation-state and as localised as the classroom, the most powerfully inclusive senses of belonging are created when differences are recognised, productively used, and seen to be to everybody's advantage. For the nation, or the enterprise, having a diverse membership creates links into diasporic networks and markets and provides the benefits of a broad variety of experiences and perspectives. In the classroom, students can learn from each other's differences – of perspective, experience, content, knowledge and ways of thinking. Their differences become a learning resource. And if all the learners in a classroom feel they belong in their difference – that the learning environment values and uses their different knowledge and perspectives – then this learning will be so much more powerful. Try to ignore the differences, and many learners will feel less comfortable about their relation to what is being taught and other learners.

The paradox of belonging is that if you are to live more comfortably in the mainstream, that mainstream must recognise your difference and regard that difference as one of the mainstream's strengths and resources. But by this time, the mainstream, from the narrative of the nation to the lesson in a classroom, has transformed itself into something that is open and pluralistic in character. Then, when the story of the nation finds its way into the classroom, it may have become the stories in the plural – of different cultural groups and their fruitful collaborations, and of struggles for rights and democracy including, at times, heroic acts of inclusion.

Language

The paradoxical cultural dynamics of globalisation offer new hope to small languages. The possibility arises, for instance, of recording and making accessible through the World Wide Web language instruction, oral histories and literature. The digital communications revolution makes this cheaper and logistically easier than at any time in the past. At the same time, the educational reasons to do this become more insistent. Mother-tongue language learning affirms and builds upon a child's home language and cultural background. Education also plays a significant role in language maintenance. Strategies to cater for small and dispersed languages include online learning and after-school or weekend schools run by language communities themselves. The spread of English as the global lingua franca does not have to mean reduction in language diversity.

Even the dominant global language, English, changes. On the one hand, for the majority of its speakers, English becomes a pragmatic language of global interchange and communication of knowledge rather than a language of identity. On the other hand, English becomes fragmented into hybrid and unstable forms that are less mutually intelligible, including the creoles of post-colonial societies, the dialects of urban ghettoes, the arcane vernaculars of divergent youth cultures, the specialist discourses of experts and the technicalese of sports and hobbies. More than diversity – differences as found objects that are to be preserved for their inherent value – language is in a dynamic state of divergence.

The social response to multilingualism, moreover, includes the use of graphemes rather than phonemes (the male or female symbol which is pro-nounced 'toilet' by Australians and 'rest room' by Americans); the multilingual interfaces (the ATM where you can choose your own language); improved tech-nologies of machine translation that make any website or electronic document roughly intelligible regardless of the source language; and the multilingual call centres (which means that if you are a Greek speaker and you have lost your credit card in the backwoods of Argentina, you can still speak to a bank officer on the phone in Greek).[89]

How do we address the tendency to divergence within a language like English? In public life, we need to switch quickly and often between one social language in one discourse community and another.[90] In each of these places we need to speak like (and act like and feel like) that community. When we don't quite get what is being said, or the other person does not quite get us, the old literacy of correct usage and rules leaves us stranded. There is no point in suggesting to the other person that they speak properly because there is no single 'properly' any more – there is only aptness to situation. So, instead of teaching language learn-ers the rules, we need to teach them the 'multiliteracy' techniques of contrastive linguistics: how do we make sense of the differences in meanings we encounter, and how do we create reader- and listener-aware communications?[91]

Gender

Now we find the unequal gender relations of earlier modern times in a process of re-ordering. This is, in part, a consequence of the activism of the feminist movement. A first wave of feminists struggled for formal legal rights, notably female suffrage, or the right to vote. The next wave fought for economic equality (the right to work and earn equal pay to men in comparable jobs) and equality at home, so the biology of reproduction did not so closely tie women to childrearing. Domestic work was to be shared by men and women. More recent feminists have criticised the idea of the 'liberated woman' as too closely aligned to a middle-class, white, professional ideal. They have wanted to acknowledge the many and varied experiences of women – in the developed world and the developing, amongst diverse cultural groups, or according to women's sexuality, for instance. According to the proponents of this wave of feminism, there can be no single model or ideal for gender relations.

There is also today more social disagreement about gender roles than ever before. Religious fundamentalists stridently argue that traditional differences in roles are ordained by God and nature. Activists, meantime, argue that there is no single path to redressing the inequalities created by sexism. In fact, a clear separation of gender roles and identities is at times justified as a means to empowerment or as a social ideal. Feminist groups and women's career networks at times exclude men in order to build a strategy for access into domains in which men still dominate. Arguments for all-girl secondary schools are frequently mounted, the case being that adolescent girls do better in environments in which they do not have to compete with boys.[92] Some Muslim women argue that gender-role differentiation creates space for a flourishing community of women, and that modest women's clothing reduces women's exposure as sexual objects.

The variety and range of expressions of gender identity linked to sexuality have also expanded greatly in recent times. Although the case is widely made that sexuality is a matter of corporeal or biological inheritance, there is no one-to-one relationship between sexuality and gender identities. There are heterosexual as well as homosexual men who do body building to accentuate their masculinity, and 'metrosexuals' who are heterosexual but assume what might be considered a characteristically effeminate or gay persona. Lesbians may be butch or femme. Transgender people may retain their original sex but cross-dress and take on the persona of the opposite sex. This need not be connected with their sexual orientation, which may be heterosexual or homosexual or bisexual. Intergender people may not want to define their gender clearly, or want to be able to express themselves through different gender symbolism at different times. There is also widespread androgyny, or ambiguity created by the mixing of gender characteristics.

Sex, sexuality and gender identities are clearly closely interrelated, to the extent that the separation of corporeal and symbolic realities that is suggested by the sex/gender distinction seems far too simplistic today. We propose the word 'gendre' to describe the complex range of differences that manifest themselves today in the close interplay of sex, sexuality and gender – often to the point where it is hard to make an analytical distinction between sex and gender. We use this word from Middle English because, although it is the root of the modern word gender, it has a wider meaning derived from its Latin source, *genus* and Old French source, *gendre*. In these original languages and uses, 'gendre' means 'kind' or 'type' – a meaning that continues today in another derivative word, 'genre'. However, we want to give the word 'gendre' a particular meaning, using it to describe a person's kind of corporeal and symbolic being created in the intersection of sex, sexuality and gender.

The enormous variety and subtle complexity that is 'gendre' may suggest social chaos, fragmentation and uncertainty about the relationships of sex to sexuality to gender, which once seemed so clear. Adolescents emerging to sexual maturity and having to define adult gender roles for themselves may experience this as an emotional roller-coaster. Parents and peers are often ill-prepared to deal with gendre diversity and change, now so pervasive in the lifeworlds of young people. How do parents and educators address the personal choices now so readily available to young people, a world of identity and lifestyle alternatives in which there are no longer unequivocal models of normality? This is the case as much as anything for those who vehemently choose traditional roles of sex, sexuality and gender. The sheer range of symbols and practices referred to by the concept gendre expands daily, it seems, and the alternatives are ever more visible. The insistent public expression of gendre difference, diversity and divergence is one of the key characteristics of today's youth scenes. Schools have to deal with all of this today, particularly secondary schools. [*See*: Connell on changing gender roles.[93]]

Family
Family types are more varied, and the variations are regarded as less aberrant, as a smaller proportion of households reflect the older norm of the nuclear family. Fewer people get married, or they get married later; divorce rates increase; fewer families are founded on lifelong monogamy. Polygamy is more visible and acceptable, in all its varied forms, from fundamentalist religious communities to the de facto polygamy of 'extra marital' relationships. Reproductive alternatives have also expanded, raising for many children the question of the identity of a biological parent. In the case of same-sex couples, children may or may not be biologically related to one of their parents, and this creates yet another dynamic of family and identity.

Families are also affected by broader social transformations. The neat separation between the domestic and public economies becomes blurred, not just in terms of the gender locations of men and women, many of whom now have to perform competently in both sites, but also in terms of the old institutional separations. 'Family friendly' working conditions are created to encourage the lifestyle choices of 'new men' and 'new women'. The possibility of working at home or telecommuting arises with the help of the new technologies, a consequence of which may be that family and work do not have to be physically separated.

Specific family circumstances also create increasing concerns for social institutions such as schools. Emotional relations between parents and children, neglect, violence, sexual abuse, substance abuse – these are all factors that can have a profound effect on children's wellbeing and their propensities to learn.

The child's 'cultural capital', the advantages or disadvantages they bring to the school setting from their families, also plays an increasingly recognised role. Some kinds of families provide children with forms of cultural capital that advantage them – ways of speaking, thinking and seeing the world. Others do not seem to have the cultural capital they need in order to do well at school. The key to success and failure at school is the degree of distance between a child's lifeworld experience and the culture of schooling.

Given the range of family forms and circumstances today, coupled with the growing significance of education as a path to social enablement, patterns of educational inequality present themselves as unconscionable insofar as they limit learners' opportunities and prove counter-productive to the needs of contemporary society. Schooling must become more inclusive, developing strategies that engage with the identity of every student, no matter what their lifeworld or family circumstances. The gap between the child's lifeworld experience and the culture of the school should not disadvantage the child. The school cannot change the child's lifeworld experience; it can, however, build an inclusive culture and curriculum that removes or at least reduces lifeworld distance as a variable that affects learner outcomes.

Affinity and persona

The range of lifeworld experiences today is broader than was ever the case in an earlier modernity – differences in life history, interest, affinity, group membership, peer culture and sub-culture, to name just a few variables. Two instances of this dynamic will suffice: the influence of media and markets.

With its handful of newspapers, radio stations and TV channels, the mass media of earlier modernity created common culture for national audiences, even if perhaps artificially and against the grain of different lived experiences and actual histories. In recent times, things have become complex. The new media consist of a myriad of newspapers and magazines that are airfreighted to their final points of sale, or available on the Internet; thousands of satellite cable TV channels, tens of thousands of radio stations available through satellite or the Internet, and billions of websites. The less-regulated, multi-channel media systems of today undermine the concept of collective audience and common culture; instead, promoting the opposite: an increasing range of accessible, sub-cultural options supporting increasingly divergent specialist and sub-cultural discourses. This spells the definitive end of 'the public' – that homogeneous imagined community of the nationalist state.

Some of this change is the result of new technological possibilities; 'narrowcasting' to finely targeted audiences, or 'pointcasting' to Internet browsers who have customised their syndication feeds. These changes, however, are by no means solely a fiat of technological change. Some of the new, fragmented media also use older communications technologies, hence the proliferation of specialist magazines, niche radio stations and carefully targeted direct mail. Cultural divergence is at the root of these changes, and the customisation of communication according to ethnic and language group, indigenous origins, sexual orientation, gender politics, ethical concern, domain of expertise, hobbyist fetish, or proclivities for consumption, fashion, fad, taste or personal style. Each speaks to its audiences and constituencies in distinctive ways. With the collapse of the homogenising cultural processes of earlier modernity, discourses of sub-cultures progressively become more divergent, and thus less mutually intelligible and harder for outsiders to get into. Yet, at the same time as this fragmentation is occurring, divergent sub-cultures find themselves juxtaposed in more intimate ways within workplaces, neighbourhoods and the media.

A second area of profound impact on affinity and persona is the market. In an earlier capitalism, people consumed generic commodities, mass-produced products deemed by the entrepreneurs and their designers to be what the consumer needed. The new consumerism tangles deeply with people's divergent identities – the family markets, the single-women's market, the gay men's market, various ethnic markets, generational markets or markets based on occupational profile. Anyone who works in the advertising industry today is able to slice and dice potential markets according to any number of demographics. More deeply than ever before, this is a cultural play that engages identities in the poignantly and emphatically plural.

Reversing the older logic of mass consumption, markets today are undergoing a process of increasing sub-cultural fragmentation around divergent 'niches'. From the affluent end of the spectrum of consumption towards its middle and even its cheaper end, we find a proliferation of 'boutique' products and services, drenched in an identity differentiating, commodity aesthetics. At the cheapest end of the spectrum, the working poor and welfare recipients may find at times that they have no alternative but to consume generic products. Or they may have to buy second-hand cast-offs. However, even the less affluent at times find themselves close enough to the nether regions of niche identity consumerism to be seduced by its promises.

Today we live in more and more narrowly defined communities, but also in many more of them – media-defined, consumerist, workplace, ethnic, sporting, sexual-preference, religious, hobby-interest – and the sum-total extent of these many communities for any one person is often enormous. The paradox is that, despite the seeming descent into social fragmentation, we end up being more connected than ever. We are simultaneously members of multiple lifeworlds. Our identities have multiple layers that are in complex relation to each other. No person is a member of a singular community. Rather, they are a member of multiple and overlapping communities. In each of these communities, you find you are a different kind of person, interacting in a different kind of way. And because, over the course of a week, or a day or even an hour, you belong to many communities, your identity becomes multilayered, your personality multiple. Your self has many sources.

Language, discourse and register are one of the many markers of these lifeworld differences – ways of speaking that reflect ways of thinking and acting. As lifeworlds become more divergent and their boundaries more blurred, the central characteristic of our meaning-making becomes the multiplicity of these meanings and their continual intersection. A teacher speaks professional teacher-talk to another teacher, but translates this into teacher–parent talk in a parent–teacher interview. Their way of speaking in this context is very different to what it would be in the many other social and cultural contexts in which they circulate. Just as there are multiple layers to everyone's identity, there are multiple discourses of identity and multiple discourses of recognition to be negotiated. We have to be proficient as we negotiate the many lifeworlds each of us inhabits, and the many lifeworlds we encounter in our everyday lives.

The paradox in all this is that the more society appears to be breaking up into communities-unto-themselves, the more sociable we seem to become, the greater number of these communities that each of us belongs to, and the greater the extent of their reach, from the highly localised to the global. You can meet somebody and find many things unfamiliar and distant about who this person is; then you find surprising points of common experience, interest or aspiration. This, increasingly, is one of the common and familiar aspects of our everyday social experience in the era of civic pluralism and total globalisation.

What, then, do we do to bring the New Learning? Here are seven ways in which we propose that an inclusive education can address lifeworld differences:

Know your learners

Be able to identify the differences amongst your learners: material, corporeal and symbolic. What are your learners' demographics? Then, don't trust first appearances, don't think that knowing the obvious demographics is sufficient. What are the particularities of each learner's lifeworld experiences? How do the different dimensions of their difference intersect? Watch out for the unpredictable and the dangers of group stereotyping, based on what you may have considered predictable. Then consider how you would design for equality. What would it take to meet the needs of each learner – physical infrastructure, organisational structures, curriculum and pastoral care? How do you go beyond formal recognition and affirmation to an active program of inclusion?

Create open learning pathways

One response to diversity is to try to do everything but to succeed at nothing – the crowded curriculum or the shopping-mall curriculum. Another is the 'anything goes' approach, in which inequality ends up being rationalised as diversity. And still another response is to butt out – education can't deal with issues of identity because they've simply become too big and too hard; it should just stick to core business. Key questions and challenges in the development of an inclusive approach include: How do you develop a flexible approach to delivery that does not require every learner to be on the same page at the same time? How does one negotiate learning pathways that are appropriate to students' interests and dispositions, without short-changing the disadvantaged by shunting them aside into the 'Mickey Mouse' curriculum?

Connect with diverse lifeworlds

Make points of contact with learners' lifeworlds. Create avenues for learners to say who they are, and to be who they are. Value what they already know by frequently asking what that is. Ask them to connect new experiences and knowledge with what they already know, think and feel. Not to second-guess the dimensions of difference, open out the curriculum to embrace what learners bring to the learning experience, surprisingly perhaps. Open a window onto their identities and figure out what makes them 'tick'. By honouring their lifeworlds as places of valid and useful knowledge, a teacher creates the sense of belonging that is central to inclusive education. The paradox of belonging today – to the nation, to the workplace, to the classroom – is that this belonging has to be in your difference and rather than by trying to take on the found attributes of each new place.

Connect with different ways of seeing, feeling, thinking about and knowing the world
Students need to be able to express themselves in the ways they feel most comfortable. They need to be able to create new knowledge in different kinds of ways, depending on what works best for them. Effective teaching and learning in the context of deep social diversity needs to involve multiple and varied pedagogical approaches. This entails different emphases and mixes of 'knowledge processes' to suit different 'learning orientations'. [*See:* Helen Verran observes a mathematics classroom in Africa.[94]]

Create space for learner agency
All too often, our institutions and practices of schooling still reflect the knowledge transmission and personality frames of the command society, such as the communication patterns of classroom discourse, the information architectures of curriculum or the rigid expectations of 'right' and 'wrong' answers in testing regimes. These were all oriented to uniformity, or one-size-fits-all education.

The more we take agency into account, however, the more multifarious its manifestations become – material, corporeal and symbolic – and the more complex the matrices and intersections. And to face all these agencies in one classroom! The solution of the command society was one teacher talking at the middle of the class, one textbook telling one narrative, one chapter at a time, one test telling of one way of knowing. The result was assimilation to the middle way, or failure.

A more inclusive approach will recruit learner agency, subjectivity and identity as an energy for learning. This means that the classroom must be very different to those to which we have become accustomed. It must allow alternative starting points for learning (what the learner perceives to be worth learning, what engages the particularities of their identity). It must allow for alternative forms of engagement (the varied experiences that need to be brought to bear on the learning, the different conceptual bents of learners, the different analytical perspectives the learner may have on the nature of cause, effect and human interest, and the different settings in which they may apply or enact their knowledge). It must allow for different learning orientations (preferences, for instance, for particular emphases in knowledge making and patterns of engagement – experiential, conceptual, analytical or applied). It must allow for different modalities in

meaning-making, embracing alternative expressive potentials for different learners. And it must allow for alternative pathways and destination points in learning.

If we could allow this much scope to learner agency, we would allow a thousand
differences to flourish at the same time as creating a more powerful sense of
inclusion and belonging. This would also mean that learners would have more
opportunities to jump out of the rut of narrow lifeworld destiny, opening their
horizons of possibility and their potentials for self-transformation. [*See*: Designing
for diversity.[95]]

Create a knowledge ecology of productive diversity

Centring educational energies on learner agency in all its variety will also create
a new dynamics, sociability and ethics of knowledge creation. Inclusive education changes the direction of knowledge flows so learners and teachers are more
actively involved in the construction of knowledge. Learning is a matter of engagement, moving backward and forward between the lifeworld formally developed
or scientific knowledge. When learner–knower lifeworlds are so varied, diversity
of perspective becomes a resource. Learning–knowing is most powerful when
collaborative and diverse perspectives are brought to bear. Knowledge construction and learning, in other words, are all the more potent for their productive
engagement with diversity. This is the basis for learning and knowledge ecologies that are very different from traditional transmission models of pedagogy and
broadcast models for communicating knowledge. The educational outcome is not
content knowledge, or at least not that primarily. It is the development of kinds
of persons who have the capacity to learn and act in particular ways. They can
navigate change, negotiate deep diversity and make and lead change rather than
be knocked about by it. They can engage in sometimes difficult dialogues; they
can compromise and create shared understandings; and they can comfortably
extend their cultural and knowledge repertoires into new areas. They are tolerant, responsible and resilient in their differences. The key questions for educators,
then, are how do these new 'types of people' learn to be themselves, learn to relate
with others and learn how to get things done in today's knowledge ecologies? [*See*:
Jeannie Herbert on Aboriginal pedagogy.[96]]

Know what your learners have learnt

Learner transformation is a central mission for education. This occurs through
the extension of one's repertoire of knowledge and capacities. It involves boundary crossing and expanding one's horizons in a world of differences. This does not
mean having to leave one's old self behind as was the case in the days of assimilation. Nor is it just a matter of recognising differences and leaving them more or
less the way they are. New Learning is about the learner transforming themself
and their world. The starting point for this has to be lifeworld differences, from
the most pragmatic of points of view. This and only this will work, particularly
in our times. The end point will be diversity, too, though a diversity that ideally

would be more equitable, not only promising opportunities but actually delivering on the promise.

How, then, do we create forms of assessment and evaluation that enable learners to meet high standards and can tell us in meaningful ways how learners have grown through their learning experiences? How do you measure progress in achieving education's most basic promises, for individuals and the groups to which they belong? The answer is only in part in conventional terms – test results that get you into certain educational sites and that open up certain employment and life alternatives. It also means using innovative assessment and evaluation practices that provide meaningful feedback such as portfolio evaluation, peer review and the personal testimonies of learners.[97]

Summary

Learner backgrounds and attributes	From separatism to assimilation: The modern past	Recognition: More recent times	Pluralism: New learning
Dimension 1: Material attributes	Social class and geographical locale have the effect of excluding people from access to material resources; if access is to be gained, the excluded group needs to assimilate to the ideas and norms of the more powerful and affluent group.	Recognising the differences in material access and locale, but without doing anything that noticeably redresses these differences.	Realising the democratic promise: the newly significant role of schools in a 'knowledge economy'.
Dimension 2: Corporeal attributes	Excluding people or isolating them into separate institutions or groups on the basis of age, race, sex and sexuality or body form; or allowing minimal mobility on condition of assimilation to a 'norm'.	Recognising differences in a 'laissez-faire' kind of way, without making significant impact on social outcomes.	Developing strategies for inclusion in which corporeal differences do not create disadvantage.
Dimension 3 Symbolic attributes and differences	Excluding people on the basis of culture, language, gender, family, affinity and persona, or forcing them to assimilate.	A sense of cultural dissolution and fragmentation as symbolic differences proliferate.	Living productively with symbolic differences that are becoming more different – diverging – whilst people are becoming more expansively sociable and their identities multilayered.

Notes

1. Husserl 1954 (1970), pp. 109, 121, 127–28, 132, 133, 139, 142, 343. See extract at NewLearningOnline.com
2. Bourdieu 1973, pp. 71, 73, 78, 80–81, 84, 85–86. See extract at NewLearningOnline.com
3. Sahllins 1974
4. Anderson 1974b
5. Anderson 1974a
6. Aristotle 350 BCE-b, Bk3 Pt 6, Bk1 Pt 5, Bk 1 Pt 12, Bk1 Pt 13. See extract at NewLearningOnline.com
7. Marx 1976
8. http://en.wikipedia.org/wiki/Industrial Worker
9. Weber 1922 (1968)
10. Bowles and Gintis 1976
11. Bernstein 1971
12. Bowles and Gintis 1976, pp. 131–32, 147. See extract at NewLearningOnline.com
13. Piaget 1929 (1973); 1971; 1996
14. Piaget 1976, pp. 2–11. See extract at NewLearningOnline.com
15. Evans 1998
16. Bean 1932, pp. 86, 94–95. See extract at NewLearningOnline.com
17. Miles 1989
18. Cavalli-Sforza and Cavalli-Sforza 1995; Sykes 2001
19. Shoumatoff 1985
20. Eysenck 1971; Herrnstein and Murray 1995; Fraser 1995
21. Reynolds 1996
22. Reynolds 1995
23. Gilmore, Soudien and Donald 1999, pp. 341–50. See extract at NewLearningOnline.com
24. Neville 1947
25. Suggs and Miracle 1999
26. Dreger 1999
27. Sedgwick 1990
28. Bowe 1978
29. Deacon 1997
30. Rival 1996, pp. 153–67. See extract at NewLearningOnline.com
31. Phillipson 1992; Kalantzis and Cope 2004a, pp. 2245–50
32. Cope and Kalantzis 2000b; Gee 1996
33. Swan 1844, pp. 3–5. See extract at NewLearningOnline.com
34. Kalantzis and Cope 1993, pp. 38–62
35. Labov 1972, pp. 4–5, 36, 201–202. See extract at NewLearningOnline.com
36. New South Wales Department of Education 1951, pp. 317–20; 350–52. See extract at NewLearningOnline.com
37. de Beauvoir 1952 (1993); Mitchell 1971
38. Rousseau 1762 (1914), pp. 321, 327–28, 330–31, 336. See extract at NewLearningOnline.com
39. Beecher 1829, pp. 7–8, 10–11, 15. See extract at NewLearningOnline.com
40. Wollstonecraft 1792, pp. 8, 33, 37–38, 53, 55–56, 99–100, 103, 174, 178. See extract at NewLearningOnline.com
41. de Beauvoir 1952 (1993), pp. xliii, xlix–l, 629, 636, 635. See extract at NewLearningOnline.com
42. Dickens 1854 (1945), pp. 16–18. See extract at NewLearningOnline.com
43. Harvey 1996

44. Bernstein 1971, pp. 125–26, 127, 151, 143, 151–52. See extract at NewLearningOnline.com
45. Mortimer and Larson 2002
46. Post and Rogin 1991
47. Miles 1989; Cope and Kalantzis 1997b, pp. 283–329
48. Carroll and Wolpe 1996
49. Bowe 1978
50. Wolf 1991
51. Kalantzis and Cope 1988, 39–57
52. Kalantzis and Cope 1999, pp. 245–76
53. Kalantzis 2001, pp. 110–23
54. Battiste and Henderson 2000
55. Castles, Cope, Kalantzis and Morrissey 1992
56. For instance, Sheehan 1998
57. Lo Bianco 2000, pp. 92–105
58. Kalantzis, Slade and Cope 1990, pp. 196–213
59. Kalantzis, Cope, Noble and Poynting 1991; Cummins, Jim 1986; Cummins and Swain 1986
60. Crawford 1992
61. Crystal 2000; Skutnabb-Kangas 1997
62. de Beauvoir 1952 (1993), pp. li, lii, xlix, 713, 731, 733, 735, 753, 752, 754, 767. See extract at NewLearningOnline.com
63. Connell 2005, pp. 26, 233, 37, 40, 218, 219. See extract at NewLearningOnline.com
64. Spock 1958, pp. 57–60. See extract at NewLearningOnline.com
65. Nolan 1996
66. Bauman 1992
67. Cope and Kalantzis 1997a
68. Burrows, Cope, Kalantzis, Morgan, Suominen and Yelland 2006b. See extract at NewLearningOnline.com
69. Marx and Engels 1848 (1973), pp. 62–98
70. Kalantzis 2004, pp. 1827–33
71. Bruegmann 2005
72. Cavalli-Sforza 2000; Sykes 2001
73. Tatum 2007
74. 'Brown v. Board of Education' 1954, p. 483, US Supreme Court. See extract at NewLearningOnline.com
75. http://usinfo.state.gov/infousa/life/people/mlk/excerpts.htm#15
76. Hausman 2006
77. Preves 2003
78. Herdt 1994; Vetterling-Braggin 1982
79. d'Augelli and Patterson 2001
80. Rasmussen, Rofes and Talburt 2004
81. Roeser and Downs 2004
82. Barraga 1983
83. Bishop and Leonard 2000
84. McGuinness 1985
85. Halasz, Anaf, Ellingsen, Manne and Thomson Salo 2002
86. Bowe 1978
87. Bowe 1978, pp. 25–26, 137–38, 159–61. See extract at NewLearningOnline.com
88. Kalantzis and Cope 2006b, pp. 402–411
89. Cope and Kalantzis 2004, pp. 198–282; Cope 2001, pp. 1–15
90. Gee 1996

91. Cope and Kalantzis 2000b
92. Datnow and Hubbard 2002
93. Connell 2005, pp. 227, 246–48. See extract at NewLearningOnline.com
94. Verran 2001 *Science and an African Logic*, pp. 2–3. See extract at NewLearningOnline.com
95. Burrows, Cope, Kalantzis, Morgan, Suominen and Yelland 2006b. See extract at NewLearningOnline.com
96. Herbert 1998. See extract at NewLearningOnline.com
97. Kalantzis, Cope and Harvey 2003

Part C

Responses – Ways of Learning and Teaching

Chapter 6

The nature of learning

Overview

In this chapter we investigate the nature of learning and explore alternative understandings of how learning occurs.

Behaviourism is one of the earliest schools of thought in the modern discipline of psychology. Behaviourists argue that we cannot know much about the human mind and consciousness – these subjects are too difficult and, given the illusive subject matter, too liable to bias from alternative perspectives and interpretations created in the mind itself. All we can reliably know is what we can see by observing behaviours. By studying animals and humans, behaviourists conclude that the most basic and universal learning mechanism is stimulus–response–reinforcement.

A number of newer approaches to learning can be grouped under the category brain developmentalism. These include developmental psychology, which describes stages of cognitive readiness that indicate levels of brain development; the study of language to interpret the general shape of the 'language instinct' in all humans; and neuroscientific studies of the working brain.

Recent social–cognitivist approaches to learning benefit from the growing body of research into the workings of the brain, but add a social and cultural dimension. The brain provides an extraordinary range of affordances, and these translate into very different potentialities depending on social and cultural context. Intelligence is not just in the brain; its sources are social.

On learning

Learning is the process of getting to know new things. These new things can be a consequence of learning *about* (experiences, facts, theories or perspectives, for instance), and learning *how to* (do certain things, behave in particular circumstances or think in certain ways, for instance).

Compared to other animal species, humans are born with very little of what they need to know and to be able to do in order to be fully functioning members of their species. They have to learn an extraordinary amount. And they learn this in a remarkably short period of time. By the age of about three, they have acquired the unique thinking apparatus that is language. They have developed a perceptual field that is not present at birth. These are just two of the extraordinary learning achievements of infants, achievements that are entirely unschooled. They happen without pedagogy, without education in the formal sense of a consciously designed program of learning.

Humans, though helpless at birth, have an innate and unusually open capacity to learn. The stuff they encounter in their environment – objects, people and language – teach them a lot. The lifeworld provides a remarkable informal teaching environment for infants. The child may have a natural inclination to learn, but they are also immersed in enormously rich surroundings, full of things that are begging to be learnt. And the child is born into a social environment in which peers, older children and adults have a natural knack for teaching.

These are some of the basics of learning with which nobody could disagree. Beyond that, however, there are many different perspectives on how learning occurs, and these perspectives support alternative approaches to the formal learning processes of pedagogy and education. We examine three perspectives in this chapter, roughly in the order in which these ideas entered the discipline and practice of education: Behaviourism (capitalised because it is a distinct school of thought), brain developmentalism and social cognitivism. There are points of perceptive value in all three, and all three are used by contemporary educators at various times and in various places. Although paying its respects to the traditions of Behaviourism and brain developmentalism, the New Learning draws greater inspiration from more recent social–cognitivist thinking.

We investigate each perspective according to the following dimensions:
Dimension 1: The processes of learning
Dimension 2: The sources of ability
Dimension 3: Infrastructure for learning
Dimension 4: Measuring learning

Behaviourism: The modern past

'Behaviourism' is a school of thought within the discipline of psychology that was founded in the first half of the 20th century. Most famous amongst its initiators were John B. Watson, Edward Thorndike and B. F. Skinner. They argued that the only thing we can know with any degree of certainty in the science of psychology is what we can see in the form of observable behaviours. There is no point in thinking about thinking, or using the mind to figure out the nature of consciousness. Such 'introspective' endeavours, using the mind to reflect upon the mind, the Behaviourists thought, were too vague and unreliable to be scientific. [*See*: John B. Watson on the science of psychology.[1]]

These are the dimensions of Behaviourism as an approach to the study of learning and the science of education:

Dimension 1: The processes of learning

Once we leave out the peculiarly human question of consciousness, the Behaviourists argued, there is no real difference between the learning processes of animals and humans. We might as well study animal learning to find out some of the key aspects of how humans learn. In fact, it is better to use animals to study the processes of learning because there are things you can do to animals in a laboratory situation that you couldn't ethically do to humans.

So, in an attempt to understand the basics of learning, the Behaviourists set about studying rats, chickens, pigeons, dogs and cats. The founder of this kind of experimentation was the Russian psychologist, Ivan Pavlov. In one of his most famous laboratory experiments, dogs were fed each time a buzzer sounded. After a while, they started to salivate – a sign that they were anticipating food – as soon as the buzzer was rung, and even before they had been given the food. They had learned to associate the buzzer with food. This learnt association Pavlov called a 'conditioned response'. [*See*: Pavlov's dog.[2]]

Dimension 2: The sources of ability

Having dismissed the question of consciousness and simplified learning to observable behaviours, the Behaviourists believed they could prove empirically that both humans and animals learned in this way: an observable stimulus produces an observable response. Learning is 'conditioned' by external stimuli. These stimuli may take the form of negative reinforcement (pain, punishment) or positive reinforcement (pleasure, reward). For any individual creature – animal or human – these processes of stimulus and reinforcement are the primary sources of learning.

The difference between informal learning, which occurs naturally, and for-mal education is the conscious work a teacher does to create an environ-ment of optimal conditioning: stimulus in the form of curriculum content, fol-lowed by response in the form of reward or punishment. [*See*: B. F. Skinner's behaviourism.[3]]

Dimension 3: Infrastructure for learning

Once the laws of behaviour are established, we can design systems for controlling behaviour. The lesson in the classroom is one such system. In learning based on Behaviourist principles, appropriate stimuli produce educational responses. These should be followed up with positive reinforcement in the form of rewards ('good girl', 'A+') or negative reinforcement in the form of punishments ('bad girl', 'F').

Education is conceived as a process of behaviour modification. Pedagogy, in this conception, is a process of stimulus (for instance, introduce new content), followed by response (the student is asked a question in class or takes a test), followed by reinforcement (confirmation by the teacher of right or wrong answer, or getting good or bad marks).

Rather like the Fordist production line, learning according to the Behavourist model could then be broken up into little bits, with a stimulus–response–reinforcement sequence driving each step in the produc-tion of learned behaviours. The approach to education implied by this kind of Behaviourism tended to be didactic – a stimulus initiated by the teacher leads to a response on the part of the student, which in turn prompts positive or negative reinforcement on the basis of preordained answers.

Dimension 4: Measuring learning

In the Behaviourists' view, not everybody's capacities for behaviour modification are the same. Some people, they argue, are naturally more intelligent than others. They are able to learn more from their experiences – to pick up on the stimuli, respond more intelligently, learn better from positive and negative reinforcement. Such differences in intelligence they attribute to differences in innate mental capacity between one individual and the next. Some people will never be very smart, no matter how much knowledge we try to give them, because their natural stimulus–response mechanisms don't work so well.

Within this frame of reference, psychologists in the 20th century set out to mea-sure intelligence, or people's mental capacities. They devised intelligence tests in which a person's mental behaviours could be systematically observed and mea-sured against peers of the same age. The assumption underlying such tests is that intelligence can be measured separately from what a person has been taught and what they had learnt or their particular life experiences. Facts, experience and things that have been taught are mere knowledge. You can know a lot of things without being intelligent.

Intelligence, by contrast, is the underlying capacity to think, learn and thus acquire knowledge. Intelligence can and should be measured, the proponents of the tests argued, because there are natural differences between people. Some people are innately more intelligent than others, and nobody can ever improve upon or exceed their inherited intelligence. [*See*: Binet's intelligence test; Henry Goddard on IQ.[4]]

In reality, it is difficult – some would even say impossible – to separate natural or innate intelligence from what you have learnt: the language you speak, your cultural context and the social and educational experiences you happen to have had. Although many Behaviourists spent much of their energy analysing how learning occurs, as the same new discipline – psychology – they also studied behaviours in order to discern what were considered to be innate differences in mental capacity between individuals.

For all their experiments and 'scientific' investigation, much of the Behaviourist psychology is conceptually flawed. The numbers may have added up in the laboratory or the test taken by children in school. The Behaviourists may have been very committed to their methods and convinced that they were scientific because they were being so careful and rigorous. However, the basic concepts they used (such as the distinction between knowledge and intelligence) were fundamentally flawed. Despite the mountains of tests taken and all the observations made in calculating the 'Intelligence Quotient' (IQ), it may well be that the science of intelligence has failed to uncover the facts of intelligence, either for individuals or groups. [*See*: Yerkes' army intelligence tests.[5]]

Brain developmentalism: More recent times

Research into the workings of the human brain began to make headway during the 20th century. There is still a lot that we don't understand about the brain, but thanks to the research disciplines that are today called 'cognitive science' and 'neuroscience', we are beginning to understand more.

The focus of brain research is on the workings of the developing brain. What conclusions can be drawn from knowledge of the brain for theories of learning and education? Some research into the brain examines its physiology. Other strands in what we call the 'brain-developmental' approach make inferences about the growth and workings of the brain from our developing ways of thinking and use of language.

In contrast to the Behaviourists, brain developmentalists regard the human brain to be uniquely different from other animal brains. In some respects – its capacities for language, consciousness and culture, for instance – it is so different that comparisons with other animals may not even be meaningful.

Although the methodologies used in the various strands of brain developmentalism are at times quite different, they share a basic assumption: that we can find out about learning by investigating the working of the brain (not just behaviour), and that when we do observe behaviour, we can make meaningful inferences about the nature of the brain and the character of human consciousness. We discuss several examples of this work here: Piaget's developmentalism, Chomsky's linguistics and recent work in the cognitive sciences.

Dimension 1: The processes of learning

Jean Piaget was a leading exponent of a theory of brain developmentalism that is often called 'constructivism'. Piaget's stages of child development were discussed in Chapter 5. Children's mental capacities grow through four major stages: from sensorimotor or pre-language, to pre-operational language and thought, to concrete operations or logical thought and multiple perspectives, and finally, by mid-adolescence, to the formal or propositional operations embodied in abstract reasoning. These stages occur at certain ages, before which learners are not ready to learn certain things. Learning occurs through processes of assimilation, in which things perceived in the external or social world fit into the existing conceptual framework of the internal mental world, and through accommodation, by means of which the internal or mental world transforms itself in response to things perceived.[6]

The constructivist aspect of this theory claims that, once a learner's brain has developed to a certain stage of 'readiness', the learner themself needs to build the capacities to think in the ways characteristic of that stage. This the learner does by figuring things out for themself. The learner's mind will only achieve that stage of development if they construct that particular understanding of the world on the basis of their developing mental capacities. Learning does not simply 'come naturally'. Mental capacities are no more than that – potentiality – which the child has to turn into cognitive reality by doing the mental work required to conduct a particular 'operation'. Although children may live in vastly different social conditions in different parts of the world, Piaget believed that the stages of self-development of human potentiality on the part of the child were fundamentally common. [*See*: Piaget on child development.[7]]

Linguist Noam Chomsky also focuses on common human factors, but in his case on the nature and origins of language. He was one of the most devastatingly effective critics of Behaviourism, contributing in a significant way to its eclipse as a theory of learning.[8] Chomsky argus that language is so profoundly complex that it cannot be learnt in a few short years and from stimulus and response or environmental experience alone. There could never be enough behavioural sequences in those years to explain the fullness and subtleties of language. The basic structures of language, Chomsky concludes, must be already present in the brain in a kind of 'language organ'. These are then filled out with the specifics of

he language or languages to which an infant happens to be exposed.[9] A student
of Chomsky, Stephen Pinker, calls this innate capacity 'the language instinct'. [*See:*
Pinker on the language instinct.[10]]

More recently, cognitive scientists and neuroscientists have begun to develop a
detailed understanding of the workings of the brain, and the differences in brain
physiology and learning for infants whose brains are rapidly developing, compared to children and adults.[11] [*See:* Bransford *et al.* on How the brain learns.[12]]

Dimension 2: The sources of ability

There is an ongoing debate in education about the relative roles of 'nature' versus
'nurture' in the sources of ability. To what extent is our intelligence innate and
inherited, or to what extent is it a cultural product and learnt? The Behaviourists
professed not to be able to know much about consciousness and mind. So, they
focused exclusively on behaviour, from which they attempted to draw conclusions
about an individual's level of intelligence.

The brain developmentalists also draw conclusions about an individual's
nature, literally – the stuff in their brain. Their conclusions, however, are rather
more egalitarian and socially optimistic insofar as everyone (except people
with physiologically grounded disabilities) goes through the same developmental stages (Piaget); or has the same language instinct (Chomsky and Pinker); and
has the same basic learning capacities written into their brain physiology (the
cognitive scientists).

Dimension 3: Infrastructure for learning

For Piaget, students will only learn what they are developmentally ready to learn;
and some of this learning will happen sooner or later, with or without education.
The 'language instinct' theorists happen to be not very concerned about how language is learnt, because they regard its basic structures to be innate and thus
unteachable. Similarly, the cognitive scientists tend to tell stories of nature more
than nurture when they are discussing the brain. One of the occupational hazards
of brain developmentalism in its various forms is to focus more on the nature side
of the learning equation. As much as we need to understand their insights on the
natural or physiological grounding of learning, the discipline of education needs
to pay more attention to the nurture side of that equation.

The naturalistic inclinations of these approaches suit them to what we have
earlier in this book called 'authentic education'. In Piagetian developmentalism,
the learner will only learn what and when they are 'ready'. Then, the learner
is an active player in the world, actively constructing their mental conceptions
of the world. Teaching, then, should be true to this readiness. It should create
conditions in which learners can construct understandings at levels appropriate
to their stage of developmental readiness. In Chomskian linguistics, immersion in

a particular language fills the learner with the symbolism of a specific language, from universal potentialities already structured into the brain. Cognitive science is interested in processes of brain maturation and what works best for particular persons in particular places at particular times of their lives.

A teacher working on the basis of these learning theories may tend to be less interventionist, and less didactic, than the teacher operating off behaviourist learning theory. Rather, they may set out to create learning experiences in which students can self-activate or construct mental operations and knowledge on the basis of their natural capacities at a certain age or stage in their development.

Dimension 4: Measuring learning

Modern educational science has thoroughly discredited theories about differential intelligence, and certainly those claiming that class and racial inequality are the result of inherited differences in intelligence. [*See*: Chomsky on IQ and inequality.[13]]

However, the measures of learning implied by brain developmentalism have been criticised for their at-times monocultural perspective and for their individualistic bias. Again, the perspectives of the brain developmentalists are not necessarily deficient – they just need to be balanced with an analysis of sociocultural factors. To take the point about culture, for instance, the examples of the mental games Piaget provides feel very school-ish and academic – a peculiar developmental trajectory that may have been very different to that of peasant/subsistence farmers, or hunters and gatherers of earlier times, and peoples of different cultural and intellectual persuasions in various parts of the world today. If you regard Piaget's stages as a universal, quasi-natural sequence, there can't be much space for cultural variety. If, however, you regard these stages as something peculiar to particular modern societies, then their biological basis is thrown into question.

Similarly, Chomsky is often criticised from the point of view of a comparative and contrastive linguistics.[14] Some languages speak about the world in such different ways that they imply quite different ways of thinking on the part of their speakers.[15] Indeed, there is so much variation between languages, and such profound subtle variations in meaning from language to language, that it is hard to imagine a hard-wired, universal language instinct.[16] Cognitive science also often speaks in general human terms, without sufficiently recognising social and cultural differences.[17]

Finally, a focus on what's happening in the brain tends to be individual. In the case of the idea of constructivism, the individual child makes their own understandings of the world by interacting in the world, based on their developmental stage. Learning, in constructivist theories, is driven by the motivated ego. In the case of the 'language instinct', that instinct is something that is to be found in a person's head, less than it is in, and of, and from, their social and cultural surroundings. So, too, cognitive science studies the brain as a singular physiological object. To counter-balance this individualistic emphasis, we also need to take social and cultural factors into account.

Social cognitivism: New Learning

A social–cognitivist approach to the question of learning attempts to balance social and cultural factors against the potentialities written into the brain. Social cognitivists want to develop a fuller account of the 'nurture' side of the nature-plus-nurture mix. Of course, theorists on both sides of the nature–nurture debate agree that an enormous amount is learnt in a social context by means of the processes of socialisation. The main point of disagreement is the mix – how much learning is social, and how much is biologically based.

Dimension 1: The processes of learning

Human learning is social, in ways that are different from any other animal learning. More than any other creature, humans are what they have learnt. Babies are immersed in oral language. They learn the words for things, and languages that put these words together into frameworks for meaning. They come to understand the world through the way in which language means the world. Language is not just the stuff of communication with others. It is a conceptual tool with which one represents the world to oneself, as though one were to understand things at least in part by talking to oneself. Babies are also immersed in sights, images, scenes. They learn to make sense of this perceptual field, to see the world in ways characteristic of the images and sights of their lives, to develop a kind of mind's eye in which the world can be visualised in meaningful ways. They learn to make sense of the sounds of their environment, to hear things in meaningful ways – noises, music, alerts and the like. They learn the bodily meanings of touch, smell and taste. They learn to gesture. And they learn how to read and make sense in and of space – interpersonal, architectural and environmental. In each case, we acquire from our cultures the means of meaning, the raw materials with which we make sense of the world. Unlike any other creature, these means form into a system of symbols.

The Russian psychologist Lev Vygotsky describes children's transition from what he calls 'complex' to 'conceptual' thinking through the social process of language acquisition. Children's developing capacity to think is embodied in the structures of language. Through language learning, children undergo a parallel and complementary process of social and cognitive development. Children learn in a social context, in which meanings are first framed interpersonally in social interaction. Only later is the full depth of these meanings realised intrapersonally or within the individual mind. [*See*: Vygotsky on language and thought.[18]]

This process is integrally connected with the human language inheritance, and other complementary and uniquely human and related modes of symbolic representation – image, sound, gesture, touch and space. Animals communicate, and presumably represent the world to themselves, by creating relationships between sound or gesture and events or emotional states such as fear and satisfaction. These are one-to-one resemblances, a kind of 'pointing at' some thing or event, which is sometimes called 'indexical' representation or communication. [*See*: Kanzi learns language.[19]]

Human symbol systems, by contrast, connect signs with each other to form structures of meaning that have a life of their own. Babies may start with words whose meanings are not unlike the indexical type of meaning (the word 'points at' something) of which some animals are also capable. But they soon pick up the enormous flexibility and generativity of the human symbol-making systems of language, image, sound, touch, gesture and space. In these systems, symbols do not just relate to the thing they are pointing at; they also relate to each other, forming structures or systems of symbol-to-symbol relationships.

As these systems develop in the growing young human, the meanings become more and more profound, as for instance, in the transition Vygotsky describes from words whose relationship to meaning is what he calls a 'complex' to words which, in the older child, have become the basis for 'conceptual' thinking.[20] Children may use words when they are young, but not 'get' their full meaning until they are older and their thinking has developed. [*See*: Terrence Deacon on the symbolic species.[21]]

Dimension 2: The sources of ability

All animals learn, even animals that have cognitive power as limited as that of a fruit fly. But humans learn more than any other animal. In fact, they have to learn so much to become fully contributing adults in the species, that their inherited biology provides less of a guide than any other creature. It is humans' learning capacity – in fact, the sheer breadth and depth of the necessity that they learn – that distinguishes them so dramatically from every other creature in the natural world. Human babies have so little to go by when they are born that they are helpless and dependent in a way no other animal is. [*See*: David Christian explains the uniqueness of the learning species.[22]]

The key question, then, is how much of what we know is innate and how much is learnt? Certainly, many involuntary reactions and emotions are innate. But is language innate? Some theorists, such as Chomsky and Pinker, argue that language is so complex and learnt so quickly that its underlying structures (as distinct from the particular language we happen to speak) must have become part of humans' biological inheritance.[23] Other theorists, such as Vygotsky, Donald, Deacon and Gee, argue that language is learnt and that the baby's brain has a remarkable capacity to learn modes of symbolic representation.[24] The meaning underlying these modes of representation is essentially a cultural inheritance, something that is learnt. In this view, the fully functioning human brain is co-constructed by the baby, using resources for meaning supplied from the surrounding culture. In fact, we now know that learning even transforms the biological structure of the developing person's brain. [*See*: Merlin Donald on the evolution of human consciousness.[25]]

How, then, does one account for the sources of human ability? In the social–cognitivist view, nature provides humans with a range of 'affordances'. Nature does not provide a blueprint, but a series of potentialities that are filled to a substantial degree by the socio-cultural cognition that is our cultural inheritance. Being external to the individual brain, this is necessarily acquired through learning. This is how nurture allows us to fill out the potentialities provided by our human-physiological nature.

Dimension 3: Infrastructure for learning

You are as smart as your surroundings – what you have learned from your environment, the knowledge sources you can draw upon, the physical and cognitive tools you can draw upon, and the other people with knowledge whom you can rely upon when you need them.

By choosing to regard our human nature as an affordance, our focus accounts for the ways in which nurture gives substance to nature's offerings. We need to know about nature, to be sure, because that helps us explain the fertile physiological ground in which nurture grows our humanity. But the really hard and important questions for educators are about nurture. This is a place where we can reliably explain human differences. It is also a space in which we can act or intervene to improve or change the conditions of learning. Biology, on the other hand, is much more determined and determining, be that a measure of 'innate intelligence', a 'stage of development' or a 'language instinct'. When we choose to attribute biological sources to a human characteristic, there is less we can do, or even perhaps even less we should try to do, than when we interpret the sources of that characteristic to be socio-cultural. Sometimes it may be practically hard to achieve, but you can always do something to improve socio-cultural conditions.

So, when we take as the basis for our analysis the open capacities or affordances of the human brain, our focus shifts to the cultural conditions that provide different opportunities to learn and explain differential educational and social outcomes. This approach also makes sense in terms of the limited extent of contemporary knowledge of the brain. Until neuroscience can tell more about the physiological functioning of consciousness and learning, the social cognitivists will at the very least give educability the benefit of the doubt. As we can always do something to improve the social conditions of learning, let's assume that socio-cultural intervention could have an impact, and let's try to do what we can to improve opportunities. [*See*: Ted Honderich, on consciousness.[26]]

If cognition is social, then the most powerful learning is social rather than individual. It exercises an individual's capacity to learn in and with the people and the knowledge resources that are around them. 'Situated learning' in a 'community of practice' is a conception of learning, which is not an individualised, psychological-cognitive thing, rather a relationship with others in a knowledge or learning community.[27] [*See*: Wenger on learning in communities of practice,[28] and Lave and Wenger on situated learning.[29]]

This learning, however, is far from incidental or accidental. The offspring of other animals do learn things from more experienced members of the group into which they are born. No creature other than humans, however, teaches its young via a process of conscious pedagogy. Other creatures may learn from adults, but only by being with and observing adults – not because the adults have set out to teach them. The parents of young children, teachers in schools, mentors in workplaces and the authors of help menus teach the novices they encounter in a premeditated way not to be found in any other species. They push the learners they encounter beyond what they already know, but within the bounds of what they as the teacher know is knowable for them, based on their pre-existing knowledge. Vygotsky calls this their Zone of Proximal Development.[30]

The result is that the knowledge in a person's head is much more than that. It is a social cognition, the very shape of which is given by shared cultural inheritance. Our cognitive capacities are social, not individual. We also rely on knowledge we can't know but nevertheless need – the experts we depend upon either implicitly or explicitly when we ask for help (mothers, teachers, doctors, engineers), the tools we use that we could not have created for ourselves (physical, conceptual), and the symbolic legacy or knowledge of things we always know we can 'look up' when needed.

This, then, provides the foundation for an educational agenda for New Learning. Development, in the social–cognitivist view, is not a product of brain development. Brain development would not happen without learning. Intelligence does not come from the brain. Intelligence is in the genius of our socio-cultural inheritance and our brains happen to have been open to that inheritance. Cognition is outside of the brain. It finds fertile ground in the open potentialities of the brain, and so shapes the brain. The transformative task of education is to support this learning process.

Dimension 4: Measuring learning

The social–cognitivist approach to learning leaves more scope for differences, and thus broadens the range of measures of learning. One consequence of the deep sociability of learning is the sheer diversity of alternative ways of being, a range of alternatives that is not available for creatures without symbol systems or social processes of conscious pedagogy. You are what you learn to mean and, as the learning context varies, so do you. Take as an extreme case the rare times when developing humans who have survived outside of society show the extraordinary range of human potential. Particularly revealing are the bizarre stories of 'feral children', such as children who became quite like wolves in some respects because they lived with wolves for a time.[31] [*See*: The 'wolf children' of Godamuri.[32]]

Cultural and linguistic differences also cross a broad range. Learning will vary enormously according to social needs and interests. The aims and institutions of education need to vary just as much. [*See*: Marika and Christie on Yolngu ways of knowing and learning.[33]]

Even within a particular social setting, teachers will encounter many different kinds of intelligences or 'learning styles'. Monocultural, didactic approaches to education historically favoured certain learning styles over others. Certain ways of thinking, speaking and points of view were adjudged 'successful', whilst others were condemned to 'failure'. Educators have attempted to develop alternative ways of conceiving intelligence and learning in order to alleviate the exclusionary effects of this kind of approach to education. For instance, Howard Gardner argues that there is not one intelligence, but many and varied forms of intelligence, some of which we may become better at than others in different circumstances of learning.[34] [*See*: Gardner's multiple intelligences.[35]]

In a social–cognitivist view, learning is a product of social circumstances rather than a biological code written into an individual's brain. As these circumstances vary, so do the nature and substance of human ability. Social cognitivists speak of the affordances of the brain, and the multiple and varied abilities that happen to be nurtured by the intelligence that is around the learner. For this, multiple and varied measures of learning are required.

Summary

The nature of learning	Behaviourism: The modern past	Brain developmentalism: More recent times	Social cognitivism: New Learning
Dimension 1: Processes of learning	Learning can be understood by studying behaviours; there are no fundamental differences between learning in humans and animals.	Stages of biological development and 'constructivism' in which the child builds their understanding based on 'readiness'; the 'language instinct'; and the intrinsic learning capacities of the brain.	The cultural bases of learning and the acquisition of social systems of meaning; the social shaping of the individual mind.

(cont.)

(cont.)

The nature of learning	Behaviourism: The modern past	Brain developmentalism: More recent times	Social cognitivism: New Learning
Dimension 2: *Sources of* *ability*	'Conditioning': stimulus– response– reinforcement (positive = reward; negative = punishment).	A focus on nature and biology; universal and invariant sequences; inherited differences in ability.	A focus on nurture, grounded in the broad scope of the affordances of nature.
Dimension 3: *Infrastruc- ture for learning*	Developing conditioned learning sequences; didactic teaching.	Authentic education based on naturalistic understanding of brain and readiness.	The transformative task of education is to work with learners in the acquisition of a socio-cognitive inheritance.
Dimension 4: *Measuring learning*	Measuring 'natural' differences in intelligence.	A tendency to monocultural and individualistic understandings of cognition and learning.	A social perspective which recognises that, as so much of what is learnt is sourced from outside an individual's brain, there can be enormous variety in knowledge and learning.

Notes

1. Watson 1914, pp. 1–2, 7, 11, 27. See extract at NewLearningOnline.com
2. Pavlov 1941, p. 166–85. See extract at NewLearningOnline.com
3. Skinner 1968, pp. 61–62, 64–65, 155–58, 167–68. See extract at NewLearningOnline.com
4. Binet 1905 (1916), pp. 37, 39, 40, 42–43, 64. See extract at NewLearningOnline.com
5. Gould 1981, pp. 194, 196–97, 207, 211, 230–32. See extract at NewLearningOnline.com
6. Piaget 1929 (1973); 1971; 1976
7. Piaget 1971. See extract at NewLearningOnline.com
8. Chomsky 1959, pp. 26–58
9. Chomsky 2000; 2002, pp. 64–65
10. Pinker 1995, pp. 125, 409. See extract at NewLearningOnline.com
11. Pinker 1997; 2002; Searle 2004; Koch 2004; Rose 2005
12. Bransford, Brown and Cocking 2000, pp. 116–117. See extract at NewLearningOnline.com

13. Chomsky 1972, pp. 26, 27, 28, 30. See extract at NewLearningOnline.com
14. Searle 2002
15. Sapir 1921; Whorf 1956
16. Kalantzis and Cope 2004a, pp. 2245–50
17. Gee 1992
18. Vygotsky 1934 (1986) , pp. 110–111, 112–113, 127, 126, 135, 136, 142, 149–50, 171, 173, 166–67, 150. See extract at NewLearningOnline.com
19. Donald 2001, pp. 120–21, 144. See extract at NewLearningOnline.com
20. Vygotsky 1934 (1986)
21. Deacon 1997, pp. 21–23, 66, 79–82, 321–22, 334–36. See extract at NewLearningOnline.com
22. Christian 2004, pp. 139, 142–43, 144, 145–46. See extract at NewLearningOnline.com
23. Chomsky 2002, pp. 64–65; Pinker 1995; 1997; 2002
24. Vygotsky 1934 (1986); 1978; Donald 1991; 2001; Deacon 1997; Gee 1992
25. Donald 2001, pp. 10–12. See extract at NewLearningOnline.com
26. Honderich 2004, pp. 155–57, 183, 184, 187–88, 198. See extract at NewLearningOnline.com
27. Wenger 1998; Lave and Wenger 1991
28. Wenger 1998, pp. 4, 6, 86, 102, 134, 136–37. See extract at NewLearningOnline.com
29. Lave and Wenger 1991, pp. 33, 29, 40. See extract at NewLearningOnline.com
30. Vygotsky 1978
31. Candland 1993
32. Ibid, pp. 56–61. See extract at NewLearningOnline.com
33. Marika-Mununggiritj and Christie 1995, pp. 59–62. See extract at NewLearningOnline.com
34. Gardner 2006
35. Gardner 1993, pp. 6, 8–9, 12. See extract at NewLearningOnline.com

Chapter 7

Knowledge and learning

Overview

Learning is the way in which a person comes to know. Science is the work put into knowing that produces more reliable and trustworthy knowledge. The science of education is about the more focused ways of coming to know, and the ways these can be translated into effective teaching.

In this chapter we explore the nature of knowledge. We introduce a number of different ways of knowing and discuss the kinds of learning and education that typically come with these ways of knowing.

One cluster of ways of knowing we call 'committed knowledge'. These ways of knowing operate as though they are the best way of knowing, at least for a particular purpose. The knowledge you have or create in these ways, its knowledge-makers believe, is as close to the 'truth' as you can get. Religious truths, for instance, are based on the idea that ultimate and absolute knowledge comes from a divine creator of the universe. Empirical truths derive from experimentation and observation, which produce hard-to-dispute 'facts'. Rationalist truths are the product of the capacity of human reason to make sense of the world. Canonical truths base themselves in bodies of knowledge and important writings.

Another set of ways of knowing we call 'knowledge relativism'. Epistemological or cultural relativism is the view that no way of knowing should claim itself to be superior to any other. Such relativism views knowledge as a matter of perspective in a cultural context, such that no culture can claim superiority over any other. Postmodernism has aimed to unsettle the convictions of modern knowledge – the pretensions to truth of factual science, the conceit of Western rationality, and the one-sidedness of the Western canon. It seeks to value previously marginalised perspectives and ways of knowing, and also popular or media cultures that may have been regarded with disdain by powerful or elite knowledge makers.

We want to suggest an approach to the question of knowing and learning that draws on the best of committed knowledge frameworks and knowledge relativism, and also goes one step further. People doing science, as well as learners who are more flexible and effective in their learning, draw on a variety of purposeful ways to know, or what we are calling 'knowledge processes'. These ways of knowing can be used to respond appropriately to particular circumstances, problems and challenges, and can be put together purposefully to form a carefully designed comprehensive and balanced knowledge repertoire.

On the connections between knowing and learning

A widely held view of knowledge is that it is stuff that is made and kept in your head; that is, knowledge is a thing of the mind. In this chapter, we put the case that knowledge is more than that. The connections between what's inside your head (memories and thinking processes) and what's outside (your body sensing the world and the social knowledge on which you depend) are so intimately connected that it is only possible to conclude that knowledge is everywhere, always and at once inside and outside of an individual's mental and corporeal space.

The knowledge that is made in your head consists of memories of things you have sensed and done, the sum total of your experiences. You can only recall a tiny fraction of these experiences at any one time. Some you will have forgotten. But the experiences that you have remembered are still there in your mind, ready to be recalled if and when you need to or want to recall them. The mind consists of impressions that have been made upon you while growing up and living in the world. It also consists of your mental capacity to figure things out – to put things into categories, to name individual things or categories of things, to make logical connections and to draw conclusions. The mind, moreover, contains social capacities – to communicate, to persuade, to negotiate, to collaborate, to mislead and to deceive.

The stuff that's inside your head, however, would be nothing without a lot of 'knowledge stuff' on the outside. One kind of 'outside' is our bodily presence in the world. Knowledge, in this sense, is much more than what is in your head. We connect with the world, which we cannot help believing exists outside of our heads, by noting things that we have perceived through our senses of sight, hearing, touch, taste and smell. We have a sensuous bodily presence in the world. Our brain is itself only a physical presence in the world, and the mind only exists because we physically exist in the world.[1]

Another kind of 'outside' is the intrinsically social character of knowledge – the things you know because you have been told, things that you rely on other people to know and things that you can find out when you need to. When we make knowledge, we rely heavily on these outside resources. We connect with outside knowledge resources in the form of knowledge handed on to us by other humans from their accumulated experiences – their ways of categorising things, their ways of making logical connections and the conclusions they have come to about the nature of the world. These are given to us in the form of already constructed and always-ready-to-be-shared meanings: in language, patterns of gesture, imagery and spatial and tactile environments. These meanings are the raw materials of human society and culture. They are the stuff of beliefs, values, rules, ideologies and identities.

Learning is the process of coming to know, not just in the conventional sense of getting knowledge into your head, but also in the sense of learning to do and learning to be in the world. Individuals learn, and so do groups. Individual learning is how the knowledge around a person comes to connect with the knowledge in their head and their enacted behaviours. Social learning is how groups of people make knowledge that can be shared, and this, of course, is far greater in sum than what could ever be kept in one person's head.

The status and effectiveness of knowledge vary. Some knowledge may consist of casual impressions that are fleeting; observations that are superficial; perceptions that turn out to be illusions; conclusions that prove to be erroneous; emotions that cloud sound judgement; intuitions that are ill-informed; opinions based on personal prejudice; ideologies representing narrow self-interest; statements that can be shown to be illogical; perspectives that are based on limited experience and are inappropriately applied beyond their parochial source; lore or rule that has been handed down from authorities and has been accepted unquestioningly but which may not be more broadly true; or wishful thinking when you really want something to be true but come to the realisation that it is not. The less-than-knowledge of everyday lifeworld experience is often like this.

Some kinds of knowledge are regarded as more reliable than the casual forms of knowledge of the lifeworld. In order to become critically knowledgeable about phenomena of the embodied lifeworld, and in ways of knowing beyond taken-for-granted experience, systematic observation is required, as are the application of strategies for checking, questioning and verification, immersion in the culture of the way of knowing under examination and the use of multiple sources of information. Knowledge-making strategies include: corroborating perceptions with others who have seen the same thing and that can be further tested and verified by others; applying to emotions and feelings insight and awareness tempered by broad experience; justifying opinions and beliefs to oneself and others, including others whose judgements are to be respected based on their expertise; taking into account ideologies that represent interests broader than one's own and which take a longer view than immediate gratification; making statements whose logical consistency can be demonstrated; developing perspectives based on long, deep and broad experience and that are broadly applicable; grounding principles in critical reflection by oneself and others; and forming intelligence in the light of wary scepticism and an honest recognition of one's own motives. The knowledge that is founded on these kinds of knowledge-making practices forms a person who may be regarded as knowledgeable, a person who puts a special kind of focused effort into some aspects of their knowing.

Modern science requires that we employ certain knowledge-making practices, and by so doing to produce deeper and broader understandings that do justice to the knowledge ideal. If learning is the process of coming to know, the science of learning is the science of how one comes to know, and know more deeply and broadly than is possible in everyday, commonsense or casual lifeworld experience.

How do we achieve deeper and more reliable forms of knowledge? Are some ways of making knowledge more productive and trustworthy than others? There are several kinds of answers to this question. In this chapter we sample some ways of making knowledge, the theories of learning that come with them and the places in which these kinds of learning typically occur. These ways of knowing we place into three groups: committed knowledge (clear assertions of an ideal way of knowing and learning, which at least implicitly considers itself to be more powerful than others), knowledge relativism (in which the knower concedes that there are many ways of knowing, and no one can ever be able to claim legitimately or definitively prove that theirs is superior to others) and knowledge repertoires (or the idea that you can do a variety of things to know, and the wider the range of things you do, and the more appropriate this mix to the kind of knowledge you are creating at any particular time, then the more solidly grounded the knowledge will be). In describing these ways of knowing, we examine several dimensions of the knowledge-making process:

Dimension 1: The nature of each way of knowing.
Dimension 2: What this means for the process of learning.
Dimension 3: The sites where this kind of learning typically takes place.

Committed knowledge: The modern past

Some kinds of knowledge come with a strong commitment to what is regarded as the intrinsic superiority of one particular way of making that knowledge. This is expressed as a sense of certainty that this particular way of knowing the world is best, or at least clearly better than other ways of knowing the world. Whether by implication or explicitly, the proponents of committed knowledge frameworks tend to say, 'I am right and you are wrong about this or that, because my way of knowing the world is more powerful than yours'. The origins of some committed ways of knowing can be traced back for millennia. However, in earlier modern times, these consolidated into the forms of knowledge we discuss below. Again, to repeat an early word of caution about the way this book is organised: the knowledge paradigms we outline in this chapter should not be regarded as a neat chronology. At most, they represent a general drift along the lines we suggest here. Meanwhile, the older paradigms remain resilient, and indeed periodically reinvent themselves to serve changing social conditions.

Dimension 1: Ways of knowing

Here are a few examples of committed knowledge frameworks.

Religious truths
Religion is knowledge that is built around the idea that there is a supreme power – a God or group of gods – who created the world and invisibly governs its course. Religions claim to provide definitive answers to fundamental questions of existence, such as those regarding the source of life and what happens to a person after death. They also offer moral rules for good and right behaviour. Religions are based on a strong idea of truth: there is one truth; this truth has been handed down to the community of believers by a higher being; this truth is absolute; and its laws are to be obeyed by all followers.

Since the invention of writing, religious knowledge has been recorded in sacred texts such as the *Torah*, *The Holy Bible*, the *Koran*, various Buddhist texts, Hindu texts and the writings of many other prophets, old and new. The truths of each religion are revealed through its holy texts. These texts are authoritative – to be learnt, believed without question and obeyed. Religious truths are absolute and non-negotiable. There can be no errors or contradictions in religious texts. [*See*: The Buddha on enlightenment[2]; Al-Ghazzali on the Sources of Knowledge.[3]]

Sacred texts tell stories of godly people or prophets, some of whom may be historical and others who may be mythical. Religious knowledge requires an acceptance of the truths told in the text even when they describe things beyond ordinary experience and stretching everyday belief. Before mass literacy, people who were not able to read sacred texts relied on priests or religious people as divine intermediaries and teachers. When mass literacy came, the sacred texts were often still not in the vernacular languages of believers (the *Koran* was in classical Arabic and *The Holy Bible* in Latin for Roman Catholics). Even when translated, the texts are at times obscure, difficult and seemingly inconsistent, requiring interpretative exegesis by experts. As interlocutors between God and humans on fundamental matters of life and death, priests and religious hierarchies assume a powerful social position and perform an important educational role as purveyors of knowledge or truth.

Consistent with an absolutist notion of truth, most religious believers regard non-religious points of view as fundamentally flawed, and so it is the mission of believers to convince non-believers of the errors of their ways. This commitment to their own way of knowing may also extend to holding the view that other religions, or even other denominations within the same religion, are fundamentally flawed.

[*See*: 9/11 at Eternal Grace School.[4]]

Empirical truths

Empiricism is a way of knowing that sets out to understand the world through systematic observation and scientific experimentation. In their most committed moments, empiricists reject religious revelation as an invalid source of knowledge and also the rationalists' idea that people figure the world from ideas innately generated in the mind – the latter position is discussed in the next part of this chapter.

Empiricists claim that there is a world 'out there', which we learn about through our senses. When we are born, our minds are blank and we learn all that we eventually come to know by absorbing the outside world through experience. In the lifeworld, this learning happens in a natural kind of way, in the form of the experiences a baby or a person happens to encounter as a part of their growing up and then living an adult life.

Empirical social and natural sciences try to systematise the observation process in order to make sure that our senses are not deceiving us. The 'scientific method' goes something like this: first, we develop an hypothesis, a proposition or question about something which we could be right about already but which we don't know for certain. Then we observe that something very carefully, collecting data from extended, intensive or repeated observation. This allows us to isolate facts (things that have been proven or shown to be repeatedly or inarguably true) from mere conjectures or opinions. We draw conclusions from these facts by a process of inductive reasoning, or using our minds to infer the general meaning of what we have learned from experiencing one, or better still, a number of particulars. Once we have observed the same thing closely enough or a sufficient number of times, we might then come to the conclusion that it happens generally. Then we put these conclusions together into a theory or generalisation which, unless exceptions are found or until it is disproved, is considered to be true knowledge.

For instance, climate scientists may carefully measure glaciers around the world and find that many of them are shrinking. They make careful measurements today. They compare old measurements. They do this at a good number of glaciers. On the basis of this evidence, they might then come to the conclusion that the world's climate is getting warmer. Each of us may not be able to come to reliable conclusions about climate change from the perspectives of our daily lifeworld experiences of the weather, but by systematic observation, testing of facts and drawing conclusions, scientists can provide deeper knowledge than what is available to us from everyday, casual experience.

Empirical science does not rely on conventional wisdom. Indeed, it constantly questions conventional wisdom. Nor does it rely on divine revelation. Most natural scientists would claim, for instance, that the Jewish, Christian and Muslim account of the world being created by God in seven days about 4 000 years ago has been definitively disproved by science. On the question of the place of humans in life on Earth, the facts, they argue, overwhelmingly support the theory of evolution.

Different areas of knowledge creation may use different empirical methods, as appropriate to their subject matter, and the use of different methods is reflected in the division of academic research into disciplines and school learning into subjects. Biological science proceeds via laboratory experimentation, history by looking at original source documents, archaeology by examining evidence dug up, economics by calculating what happens in markets, literature by reading texts very closely and education by looking at student results after different kinds of curriculum intervention.

Whatever the variations in empirical method from one discipline to the next, strict empiricists become highly committed to their method and consider other ways of knowing the world to be inferior. They believe that the knowledge they form using their method is about as true as true can get, or at least until further empirical investigation can be undertaken. Their conclusions may be proved wrong later on, but only by providing new, more thorough and more convincing empirical evidence. [*See*: John Locke on human understanding.[5] *See also*: Ibn Tufayl on knowledge from experience and the discovery of the creator.[6]]

The critics of empiricism, however, argue that it is too narrow in its understanding of knowledge and truth. Caught up in detailed observation and careful calculation, empiricists sometimes lose sight of the bigger picture. They might have lots of facts, but have they been asking the right questions and looking for the right things? Do the questions they ask beg certain answers, so the 'facts' end up coloured by the perspectives of the questioner? Empiricists can also tend to form a new 'priestly class' of experts who control knowledge because they have access to special methods and bodies of knowledge that ordinary people do not. They may hide their opinions and beliefs in a bewildering fog of facts, complex theories supposedly founded in evidence, and a 'trust me, I really know' approach to non-experts.

Rationalist truths

Rationalism is a way of knowing that places reason and the human mind's capacity to make sense of the world at the centre of knowledge. The early modern philosopher René Descartes argued that you can never really trust your senses. Whatever you think you see might always be subsequently proven untrue – it may have been a dream, or an optical illusion. The only thing you can know for sure is the existence of your doubting self. In fact, you only ever know about something as close to you as your body and its sensations because your mind tells you about your body. The mind, then, is something separate though connected to the body, and is the final source of all knowledge. 'I think therefore I am', was Descartes' famous conclusion about the ultimate source of knowledge. [*See*: Descartes: 'I think therefore I am'.[7]]

Several centuries later, another modern philosopher, Immanuel Kant, argued that the concepts or categories we use to understand the world are the products of the reasoning mind. Time and space, for instance, are 'prior' concepts, or basic concepts of the mind, rather than things that can ever be proven to exist 'out there', in the world. The knowledge-making work of reason uses the human mind to figure things out. Scientists, for example, never simply observe the world. They use their reason to decide the right questions to ask, to make logical connections, to come to conclusions and to create theories. This is the creative activity of the human mind, and not simply a reflection of what has been absorbed from the outside world. Kant's focus on the reasoning mind has implications for learning. Empirical knowledge suggests that you describe what you have carefully observed, or trusts the facts that others have reported to you and put together into theories. But rationalist knowledge entails a deeper understanding in which you are able to figure things out for yourself, and know how to arrive at the answer. [*See*: Immanuel Kant on reason's role in understanding.[8]]

Reasoning involves rigorous logical thinking, famously described by the ancient Greek philosopher, Aristotle. Here is an example of his formal, logical reasoning: 'If all humans are mortal, and all Greeks are humans, then all Greeks are mortal.' This kind of reasoning may be connected with experience, where the facts are known or assumed (Aristotle assumes we already know about mortality) and logical connections or likely consequences are figured out from these by means of a process called 'deduction'. Reasoning may also be framed by means of categories or frameworks of meaning found in our language. The resources we have to speak about our world help us to see and understand our world in particular ways. Our reasoning capacity also requires that we continually question the world, refining our arguments and subjecting our thinking and knowledge to critique. [*See*: Aristotle on higher forms of knowledge.[9]]

Critics of rationalism, or the commitment to the reasoning mind as the centre of knowledge, accuse it of logocentrism (prioritising abstract and formal logic over sensation, feeling and emotion) and anthropocentrism (putting humans at the centre of the universe, as though nothing else existed in the world, or as though everything other than humans was irrelevant). They also argue that it does not take sufficient account of cultural differences. Given the universal human capacity to think logically, it seems to imply that if they were to think hard enough and long enough, everyone should come up with the same rational answers. However, humans in different cultural contexts, and who speak different languages, think differently.

Canonical truths

Ways of knowing can also be based on canonical bodies of knowledge. Different areas of knowledge are captured in essence by disciplinary content. In schools, this becomes the basis for each subject area, and the substance of curriculum. For instance, canonical mother-tongue language teaching, such as the teaching of English in English-speaking countries, focuses on 'correct' pronunciation and usage that is not necessarily the same as the dialects, accents and forms of usage that children are used to at home. Taking 'language arts' involves learning formal writing in standard, official forms of the national language. It requires students to read great literature in order to imbibe the best style and the highest human spirit that, it is believed, is captured in great novels, plays and poetry. To give another example, the canonical discipline of history consists of a body of facts and dates, and an overall narrative that places significant people in the unfolding story of important events. History consists of a number of defined facts strung together into narratives. School history hands down to new generations what we already know about the past. Usually, it is just the one story, told in the way that people in powerful positions in society believe it should be told. To give still another example, science is a canonical body of knowledge that consists of lots of facts about the natural world and the theoretical or disciplinary frameworks that tie these facts together – physics or chemistry, for instance. And a final example: mathematics is a set of canonical rules, starting with learning our times-tables early in school, and concluding by the end of school with learning complex theorems and forms of proof.

Ways of knowing that rely on canonical bodies of disciplinary knowledge reflect a commitment to received wisdoms – what great writers have written and what great scientists have discovered, for instance. Students of these canonical truths learn them as proven facts, definitive theories that synthesise these facts, correct forms of expression and universal or national cultural ideals. The virtue of canonical knowledge is to select and synthesise content knowledge. And if all students learn the same things, we will end up having a shared body of knowledge as the basis for a common cultural heritage.

There are disadvantages in the canonical approach to knowledge, though. Empiricists argue that people should try to observe the facts for themselves rather than simply accept what others present to them as given. Rationalists put the case that you don't really understand a theory until you have figured it out for yourself. Empiricists and rationalists both argue that, by accepting canonical truths as presented, the learner is taking too passive a part in the knowledge process. They are allowing authorities to take control of knowledge. Learning, in the canonical view, is a process of authoritative content transmission and memorisation. The result is that knowledge remains abstract and distant, removed from everyday experience of the world. There is also an inherent conservatism in this approach to knowledge. The assumption is that canonical bodies of knowledge remain fairly stable over long periods of time. [*See*: Matthew Arnold on learning 'the best which has been thought and said'.[10]]

Dimension 2: Ways of learning

Each of these ways of knowing embodies a philosophy of learning and, with it, an often quite committed view of its practical effectiveness or rightness as teaching method.

Religious teaching has a significant non-rationalist and non-empiricist component. The fundamentals of existence are in God's control, and the sacred text is a far more important source of truth than anything that can be merely created by human reason or empirical observation. In the case of the Islamic sacred text, the *Koran*, this approach to learning sometimes extends to the point at which believers learn to recite the entire text by heart, in its original Arabic.

Empiricist ways of knowing assume that education should be based on learning observable facts. Sometimes this might be experiential – such as the case of an experiment or excursion during which students see things for themselves. However, empirically focused, didactic curricula are often full of facts handed down to students to learn and prove they had learnt, through tests.

Rationalist ways of knowing focus on logic, reasoning and the development of theoretical capacities. Some school subjects are more dependent on the rationalist knowledge framework than others, such as mathematics and physics. Critics argue that such an approach to learning and teaching tends to become overly abstract and removed from human realities and the practical purposes of knowing.

Canonical knowledge sometimes overlaps with the other approaches. In fact, religious knowledge is canonical – its peculiarity is that it prioritises sacred texts ahead of secular texts. Empiricism, which focuses on learning facts, relies on canonical bodies of fact; and rationalism often relies on canonical theories. [*See:* E. D. Hirsch on 'cultural literacy'.[11]]

A common tendency across all these committed ways of knowing is that, the more committed they are, the more exclusionary they tend to be of other ways of knowing and the more didactic their teaching methods. In other words, the balance of agency is heavily skewed towards authoritative knowledge sources and teachers. Learners are supposed to be relatively compliant absorbers of what they have been told. Of course, the proponents of each of these ways of knowing would argue that there is a strong element of volition – the act of faith of the religious learner, the observations of the empirical learner and the active reasoning of the rationalist learner. Often this is true, and when it is true, the approach is all the more powerful for that. However, when measured against the knowledge source and teacher, the level of agency of the learner as knowledge maker in strongly committed ways of knowing is, more often than not, relatively low.

There are, however, strengths in committed ways of knowing, and these strengths are the basis for forming powerful knowledge repertoires, as we discuss in the third part of this chapter. Religions prompt learners to ask themselves deep spiritual questions about human meaning that are sometimes neglected in the other ways of knowing. Empiricism teaches the learner to be an acute observer. Rationalism teaches reasoning, or thorough understanding of how one can come to a particular conclusion. Canonical knowledge requires that we become conversant with bodies of knowledge that encapsulate human understanding to date within discipline areas.

Dimension 3: Sites of knowing

Highly committed ways of knowing grant authority in the knowledge-making process to specialised groups of people.

The authors of sacred religious texts are people – sometimes anonymous and sometimes named – who have been the recipients of divine revelation. Priests and religious teachers are placed in powerful positions often formally ordained as qualified to interpret texts that are at times obscure or not written in the vernacular of believers. These texts also contain accounts of religious events and explanations of the world that are unbelievable on the basis of everyday experience, and thus require 'faith' to be believed. Religious knowledge creates an institutional separation between sites of knowledge creation and teaching (the sacred texts, the house of God, the instructional encounter with the priest or religious teacher) and the rest of life.

The creators of empirical knowledge are also members of a specialist group that uses its privileged access to knowledge-constructing techniques, which in turn puts it in a powerful position – the researcher who finds out and interprets the facts, the journalist who gets close to an incident or issue, or the textbook writer and teacher who presents the key facts of a subject to learners. In children's and adults' learning, the school, college or university is a key institutional conduit for the transmission of empirical knowledge, and the formation of a new generation of empirical knowledge workers.

So too, people who create and transmit reasoned argumentation – scientific theories or literary interpretations, for instance – are from a specialised group. They become influential and powerful for their privileged knowledge-creating positions in society. This institutional separation between knowledge making and knowledge using positions schools as key and specialist sites for the transmission of knowledge.

Facts and theories may be put together into canonical bodies of knowledge, created by people in privileged institutional positions, and passed on to new initiates through the mediating institution of schooling. This is how the textbook writer and the teacher become intermediaries in a knowledge-production system in which learners are recipients of knowledge.

In each of these models, the institutions of knowledge creation, knowledge transmission and the everyday lifeworld are relatively separate. The general direction of the flow of knowledge is from the institutions of knowledge creation, via a knowledge transmission system that includes education, to a broader society which absorbs that knowledge.

Knowledge relativism: More recent times

Some ways of knowing are less certain of their own rightness and less committed to the idea that their way of knowing is superior to others. Epistemological relativism, cultural relativism and postmodernism are three such ways of knowing, each overlapping with the other in significant ways.

Dimension 1: Ways of knowing

Epistemological relativism
Epistemology is the philosophy or theory of how people come to know. Religious faith, empirical observation, reasoned argumentation and accepting canonical truths are all epistemologies. They have within them a theory of knowing, and thus learning. Religion, empiricism, rationalism and canonical knowledge are all grounded in highly committed epistemologies.

Knowledge relativism, by contrast, is less certain about ways of knowing and their outcomes in the form of knowledge. Whatever you think you know is only ever relative to your experiences, your interests and your perspectives. This is why, from person to person, location to location and culture to culture, knowledge varies. The differences arise because everyone interprets the world in ways that reflect their viewpoint. Everything you know is relative to your way of knowing. You can only know what your way of knowing allows you to know. It follows that you can only learn what your way of learning allows you to learn.

Epistemological relativists concede that other people can and often do see things differently. This is one of their daily assumptions as they encounter others. Others may live by other truths. When the epistemological relativist encounters someone who lives by a different way to truth, they can say, 'I think I know what I know and you seem to know what you know, and if what we know is different it is because our ways of knowing are different. Our perspectives are different. But let's not argue about that. I am pretty sure of what is good for me. And what you think is good for you may in fact be good for you. How would I know if it wasn't? And who am I to have an opinion? You're welcome to your views, and I'll keep my views to myself.'

The epistemological relativist regards knowledge as provisional. Something that seems to be an accepted truth might be true for today practically speaking or it may be true for people living in a particular community. But certainties can always be shaken by change, conflict, debate and disproof. Knowledge, in this view, is fluid and contestable. You need to keep an open mind in case what you currently think might prove to be wrong. [*See*: Sextus Empiricus, the sceptic, on not being dogmatic.[12]]

Here are ways in which epistemological relativists approach some of the knowledge concepts and practices found in the more committed ways of knowing:

Facts: There is no such thing as a definitively proven fact. Facts are products of perspective. For example, the fact of the date of the 'discovery' of the Americas or Australia changes when one questions the notion of 'discovery'. The world is only a figment of our construction of the world, through our languages, imageries and ideologies, for instance.

Reason: The universal, reasoning individual does not exist. There is no universal person who can measure everything from the point of view of a single-minded 'reason', valid for all people and all times. Rather, there are interpretations in the plural, the products of different material (class, locale), corporeal (age, race, sex and sexuality, and physical and mental characteristics) and symbolic (culture, gender, affinity) attributes. There is no ultimate 'reason', just varied subjectivities and identity perspectives. [*See*: Nietzsche on the impossibility of truth.[13]]

Canonical texts, sacred and secular: We can only be suspicious of meta-narratives, or master narratives that try to present all-encompassing spiritual, scientific or historical stories. They have a habit of leaving out the knowledge and perspectives of those who are not powerful. Competing interpretations, moreover, seem to cancel the pretence each has to absolutism – how can the Darwinian view of natural history square up with the theory of intelligent design by God, when both purport to be definitively correct? The knowledge relativist warns us that we should approach any such texts with a warily critical eye, deconstruct or disman-tle their premises, trace their origins or genealogies and measure them against the practical stuff of culture, power and interests. Then we might be able to uncover the limitations and expose the totalising pretences of narratives that purport to be universally true. And what is the role of the reader, who may interpret the same text or theory in very different ways?[14] Canonical texts appear to speak unequiv-ocal, transparent truths, intended to be absorbed by readers and learners, and always with the same meaning. A person's reading of a text – what they see in it, and don't see in it – the epistemological relativist would retort, depends on their experiences, interests and reading position. Besides, who is to say that the canon has a special status? One person's canon is another person's irrelevance.

The stance of the epistemological relativist seems eminently reasonable, prag-matic, modest, undogmatic and generously flexible. It allows that other people with varying perspectives and interpretations might be right, even though from one's own, current perspective they may not seem right. If you are an epistemo-logical relativist, you're more open to the possibility that the other person could convince you that they are right. And if the person can't, or doesn't, or won't, you can still agree to differ and respect their right to differ.[15]

This relativist stance is also explicable in the light of our historical experience of committed knowledge frameworks. History provides sufficient cause to take fright at the consequences of dogmatic certainty – the technologists and scientists who knew their facts but didn't consider sufficiently the consequences of applying their knowledge; or the dictatorial leaders of imperialist, fascist or communist states who thought they knew what was best for their supposedly backward populaces; or the religious fundamentalists who have fanned the flames of sectarian violence. Relativism is a modest assessment of whatever we think we know. It makes for more careful and circumspect knowledge making. It is less arrogantly confident about what we know and our powers of knowing. It means we are less likely to want to impose our views on others.

However, relativism's critics argue that our everyday experiences tend to point to the existence of an underlying reality, a mundanely grounded truth with which it is hard to argue, ordinary things that are so unquestionable that people rarely do. If you touch something hot, you will get burnt. If you hit someone aggressively you will initiate or escalate conflict. These things are so basic that we almost know them instinctively.

The critics of epistemological relativism also point to the practical trust we have in expertise. Whenever we cross a bridge, we trust that the engineers have got their calculations right. Whenever we take medications, we trust the knowledge of chemistry and biology of the medical scientists who designed them and the pharmacist who dispensed them. In other words, we trust the knowledge of people who know more about a particular thing than we do. This can also apply to entire bodies of human knowledge. We could choose to accept that scientifically informed views are more powerfully proven than a layperson's casual opinions. So, for instance, if we choose to accept the Darwinian view of natural history because it is more widely held by the international scientific community than the theory of intelligent design, we move away from a position of epistemological relativism.

Still others claim that epistemological relativism avoids commitment in ways that are amoral and thus unconscionable. If nothing is any truer than anything else, how do we live? If no facts are ultimately more convincing than any others, we can't really argue with neo-Nazi sympathisers who deny the existence or scale of the Holocaust in which six million Jews were killed. If there are no spiritual interpretations of meaning that are more compelling than any others, then how do we live? If subjectivity is all there is, or as Nietzsche says, if it consists of nothing more than an ego-driven 'will to power', operating 'beyond good and evil', then what have we done to ethics? If there are no canonical texts, how do we discriminate reading works that are a waste of our time from brilliant literature, or profound and well-crafted films from junk TV? Is knowledge relativism so disruptive a choice that it wrecks human cultural traditions, or the idea that some knowledge is more deeply significant or useful than others?[16]

Cultural relativism

Cultural relativism is the view that everything is relative to a cultural context (a location) at a historical moment (a time). 'If that's the way your culture does things, that's fine for you.' 'If that's the way our grandparents did things, it must have been fine for them.' Committed knowledge tends to be less inclined to notice cultural differences, regard them as significant, or pay them the respect that they may deserve.

It's not that there are no truths in the ways of knowing of cultural relativism. For the cultural relativist, the truest you can get is what you know from your own lived experience, your feelings, your identity, your subjectivity. You act this way, think this way, are this way. Surely, that you know. If there is any truth at all, it is that to be true is to be true to yourself, to be authentic.

Language or discourse plays a big part in framing your self in a world of cultural relativism. It is one of the main conduits that connects the culture in which you are located with your singular personhood. Your ways of interpreting the world are shaped by the way you come to name and speak in the world – in English versus

Arabic, or through scientific discourse versus religious discourse, for instance. If there is truth in this sense, it is grounded in the play of language and the ways you have learnt to make meaning. [*See*: Wittgenstein on the way we make meanings with language[17]; Richard Rorty on truth and language.[18]]

Cultural relativism seems very reasonable. It is a way of knowing that promotes cultural respect and tolerance. It brackets or tries to set aside our own biases, to as great an extent as possible and at least for the moment, in order to avoid the blinkers of negative prejudgement, ethnocentrism (assuming that everyone sees things, or should see things the way you do in your culture) and racism (negative views of the inferiority of other racial or ethnic groups). It is a way of avoiding conflict and promoting peaceful co-existence.

Given the history of modern times – colonisation, the injustices committed by the nationalist state and the gross inequalities created in modern societies – cultural relativism seems a kinder, gentler way of knowing. Using this way of knowing it is possible to acknowledge the harm done to indigenous cultures and languages by colonisation, the pain inflicted upon less powerful or minority communities by groups with power, and the injustices of education systems that purported to provide a one-size-fits-all education but whose effects were not to fit all, thus perpetuating gross inequalities.

Cultural relativism, however, has its strong critics. Some say it is a formula for 'live and let live' complacency. It allows you to retreat into your own parochial little space, as though the rest of the world did not exist and did not matter. It's easy to say 'live and let live', but what do you do next, other than withdraw and indulge in your own prejudices? Cultural relativism is anti-intellectual insofar as it gives up on debate and discussion with an 'Okay, so that's what you think.' It is based on a form of recognition of difference, as though the differences are neutral and innocent and do not require action ('so that's life'). Insofar as differences also reflect relationships of inequality, a deeper recognition may also suggest an agenda of inclusion ('so let's do something about it'). You might be a woman and I might be a man, for instance, and it's not just a matter of recognising the differences, but going one step further and doing something about the historic inequalities that this recognition reveals. Cultural relativism, its critics argue, has a weak moral grounding, it is pragmatic to the point of opportunism and is based, in the final analysis, on the contingencies of self-interest. At times, its moral relativism is patronising – 'It may be fine for you, but I would not want to live that way'. And you may find that being tolerated is a less than satisfying form of engagement – 'You find me tolerable, you don't mind that I exist in my difference, but I know you don't feel comfortable with me and my way of being. When we relate, I get the sense that you have to put up with me and that you think you have to manage me carefully to get done with me what you want.' This can feel dehumanising.

Postmodernism
Postmodernism, as its name indicates, is a counterpoint to modernism. Often buried in difficult-to-read texts, the only thing that is clear about it on first

eading is what it is not: modernism. Modernism, the postmodernists argue, thought that the empirical world could be discovered through science. It thought technology was a route to progress, development and betterment for everyone on Earth. It created universal laws of human reason (the 'Enlightenment'), supposedly applicable to all human beings. It put 'man' and his interests at the centre of the universe, hence Descartes' famous 'I think therefore I am'. It created what it considered to be canonical knowledge in the form of agreed scientific theories and high culture as manifest in great literature and great art. These canonical texts, the postmodernists point out, are in fact the creations of 'dead white males' and carry with them all the biases and thus limitations connected with their cultural perspectives and discourses, and the interests connected with their positions of power and privilege.

Postmodernism is a way of knowing and a narrative describing the shape of contemporary life that incorporates elements of epistemological relativism and cultural relativism.[19] On the subject of contemporary life, postmodernism does not draw a distinction between high culture and low. It is as interested in the barrage of signs in the new media as it is in any other text. Who can judge what is better, a Shakespearean play or a five-minute sitcom on YouTube? If the number of people involved in cultural engagement on any one day is a measure, it may be the sitcom on YouTube. And who's going to be so elitist as to tell the YouTube viewers they are wrong?

Postmodernism also criticises what it regards to be the eurocentrism, or male-centredness, or heterosexual biases of Western culture.[20] Instead, it recognises and makes a virtue of decentring contemporary culture. There is no culture in the singular, just many cultures in the massively plural. This may be read as fragmentation. It may be interpreted as giving up on utopian social projects. But the postmodernist will tell you that utopian projects with totalising pretences all-too-easily end up as totalitarian nightmares, as did the communist utopias attempted in the 20th century.

When it comes to underlying ways of knowing, postmodernism does not allow that any single worldview could be better than any other. There are no intrinsically privileged forms of knowledge. Nothing is necessarily truer than anything else. Instead of modernism's 'logocentrism' or placing universal reason at the centre of everything, postmodernism recognises the many and varied forms and sites of feeling, subjectivity, desire and identity. Instead of modernism's faith in the methods of science or history, postmodernism cautions that you should never take the facts at face value. Behind every purported fact is a person or group in pursuit of their own interests. Don't trust abstract principles, because they are always the product of someone or other's concrete experiences. Don't trust the master narratives that try to tie all the facts and principles together, to universalise, to be all-encompassing and thus to totalise. They are only ever the product of a sectional interest and people who would wish that everyone could see the world in the way that suits them. There is no truth out there, just 'constructions'. There are no definitive knowledge sources, just discourses reflecting particular interests.

So if you are a postmodernist, what do you do? First, recognise that all you see is bricolage, lots of shreds and patches that happen to fall together as knowledge. Abandon the Enlightenment conceit that anyone can ever put together a bigger picture or a deeper picture. The most you can discover is that a bit of this (identity, experience, discourse) happens to sit beside a bit of that. If we want to find out some more, we might deconstruct, or work out which bit of identity sits beside what kind of discourse. We would do this, not in order to unveil any underlying truth, for that would be to fall into an Enlightenment trap. Nor would we do it because we thought we could know something beyond the scope of our own, immediate experience. 'Deconstruction', in fact, helps us find that the grand narratives are not so grand. Rather, they are the products of sectional perspectives, contingent interests and passing power plays.[21] Then, we might make postmodern knowledge by playful collage, paradoxical quotation and irreverent irony, juxtaposing one kind of meaning beside another and observing the not-much-more-than accidental cross-currents. In this pursuit, our knowledge-making mode is pastiche rather than the modernist's earnest consistency or commitment to one mode of cultural representation or discourse.[22]

Postmodernism has its vehement critics. They use much the same arguments as those used to attack epistemological and cultural relativism. And one more: for all its purported lack of commitment, postmodernism ends up looking pretty committed. Or, at least, this is how it seems whenever it faces down fundamentalist religions, or Western science, or pragmatists who trust their sense that something really exists in the world beyond the projections of our discourses. Then, postmodernism seems a quite definite position itself, a variant of Western liberalism as irritated by and intolerant of its others as any explicitly committed knowledge. Postmodernism plays a game of false modesty. It protests its lack of commitment too loudly.

Dimension 2: Ways of learning

Relativist ways of knowing embody an approach to learning that is quite different to ways of knowing that openly proclaim their commitment. In the classroom, the teacher may value the many points of view of their students. They may consider the 'popular culture' of the students to be of equal value as an object of study to the 'high culture' of the traditional curriculum. The teacher may go out of their way to incorporate the cultures and discourses that students bring to the classroom from their everyday lifeworld experiences. They may value different 'learning styles' or the varied ways in which learners feel more comfortable learning, such as getting a big-picture view from the theory first, compared to immersing oneself first in facts, experiences or practical problems. The teacher may also employ a 'critical pedagogy' in which students examine their own experiences and the knowledge sources they encounter for their biases, perspectives and ways of thinking about thinking (meta-cognition).

In the curriculum, different points of view might be presented, without insisting on the correctness of any one point of view, explicitly or even implicitly. This may require the neutral presentation of different interpretations. For instance, the curriculum may present evolution and intelligent design, as though they were equally valid perspectives and despite the fact that many scientists, on the one hand, and many fundamentalist Christians or Muslims, on the other, genuinely believe that the other interpretation is plain wrong.

Between one school and the next, a certain regime of relativism applies, too. A private or community school may have been established in order to inculcate its young learners with its epistemology and knowledge, and because it disagrees with the secular or relativist worldview presented in the public school. The teachers at the public school may say, 'That's fine, they're welcome to their way of teaching and learning. But we have our standards and principles of cultural relativism and critical pedagogy because we are an open, diverse, public school, and we are going to maintain these steadfastly.' [*See*: Aronowitz and Giroux on postmodern education.[23]]

These moves are typical of what we have called authentic education. However, they also bring with them difficulties that are common in this approach to teaching and learning. Are we addressing inequalities adequately? Are we being entirely honest if we do not consider this to be based in anything other than another, equally committed culture of knowledge and learning, the culture of relativism? [*See*: George Pell on the dictatorship of relativism.[24]]

Dimension 3: Sites of learning

As an approach to education, knowledge relativism seems eminently reasonable, sensible and just. It may, however, produce a fragmentation of learning. Schools feel like a shopping mall of knowledge in which learners can pick and choose their own ways and means. When education is based on knowledge relativism, it seems to be contributing to a broader state of fragmentation.

More seriously, however, this fragmentation may mask ongoing inequalities. School X is different to school Y because the students are different and the school is being true to their difference. But do the students from each school enjoy comparable outcomes? Course or subject X is different to Y, true to the interests of the students in each, but do its participants enjoy equal opportunities to further their education to comparable social effect once they have finished each course? Student X may be working on something close to their interests, and Student Y in the same classroom on something close to theirs, but will this produce equivalent results in the things that matter when it comes to measuring their learning outcomes? When Student X is studying popular culture (because that's what this student relates to closely in their lifeworld), and Student Y is studying 'the greats' of the canon (perhaps because this student has lots of books at home, and that's what their academically inclined parents value), will they necessarily end up getting the same results from their schooling? Perhaps it shouldn't be this way, but that's more often than not the way education turns out.

The key questions, then, are: To what extent do all our efforts to provide varied sites of learning and modes of engagement put a deceptively democratic gloss on what sometimes turn out to be pathways to inequality? When does our ostensible sensitivity to differences do differences an injustice?

Knowledge repertoires: New Learning

Another way of getting to know more than can be known from casual lifeworld experience alone, is to build a repertoire of different things you can do to know in order to gain deeper-than-ordinary knowledge. Building knowledge repertoires means to select, mix, match and test different knowledge-making methods and techniques developed for the more single-minded varieties of committed knowledge. It also tempers a commitment to absolute truth, or to the idea that some knowledge may be made in a way that we can trust and takes us closer to truth, with the reasonableness and caution that comes with a measure of knowledge relativism.

In everyday language, knowledge is stuff in your head. It is information or things you know. It involves 'understanding', or the capacity to work things out for yourself on the basis of logic and the patterns that underlie information. Knowledge, however, is a lot more than just what's in your head, or how your head perceives and what it figures is outside of it. Your head is at one with your body, and your body is a thing in and of the physical world. Your only mental experience is in your body, and your body is a part of the world of physical existence. Your mind's thinking is connected to the body's feeling, and these feelings are extensions of the body into the sensuous world – the sights, sounds, smells and tastes that comprise our everyday experience. Our whole bodies, not our minds alone, are gripped by emotion – happiness, sadness, love, hatred, fear, anger, surprise or curiosity – and these emotions are part of our deeply ingrained knowing processes.[25] Our bodies are also engaged in the business of representation or meaning. The mind cannot mean anything, either to others or to itself, without the body and its connections with the sensuous world: linguistic, visual, audio, gestural, tactile and spatial. In this sense, knowing is not just what you think. It is what you do and how you are.

Knowing is a set of capabilities, not just a set of mental capacities. It is a set of mental capacities that exist only in order to do things in the world – to hammer a nail or build a bridge, to cook a meal or travel to the moon, to solve a small problem or imagine a better future. Mental capacity is one part of the equation, but mental capacity is empty and meaningless without the capacity to do something with it. In this sense, knowing is not just what you can think; it is what you can do and who you can be.

Knowing is social, even though the physical bounds of the thinking brain might lead us to believe that it is an individual phenomenon. It is what you do as a result of what you have learnt from people with whom you have lived, people who have been doing things around you from the moment you were born. These are things that you have not simply observed but also taken part in. From the moment we are born, we find ourselves participating in a representational legacy: linguistic (a language that helps us make sense of the world), visual (the imagery of our surroundings and our culture), audio (from alerts to music that evokes emotion), gestural (bodily meanings), tactile (sensations of touch, smell and taste) and spatial (bodily positions such as teacher in relation to learner or shopkeeper and customer, and architecturally shaped meanings). Then whatever we do with this legacy as we make and remake our personal and social worlds, we do through a highly dependent series of social relationships. Our knowledge is nothing if it is not in relation to others. In this sense, our knowing is not just what we do by ourselves; it is what we are and do together.

So, if knowing is a kind of action that can be this ordinary, how might we distinguish everyday knowing from deeper knowing? We call the capability of deeper knowing 'knowledge-ability' and the product of that capability, to be 'knowledge-able'. Knowledge-ability is the specialised work and extra effort you put into knowing something. It entails a peculiar intensity of focus and specific knowledge-making techniques. As a consequence, others are able to trust that you are knowledgeable, and you are better able to trust your own knowledge. In practice, each of us cannot be knowledgeable about everything. We can trust our knowledge in some areas, but rely on the deeper knowledge of our fellow humans in other areas – experienced engineers, or doctors, or teachers, or mothers, or hikers, for instance. Not only do we rely on these others because they have become knowledgeable. We also respect their knowledge-ability, and the special techniques they have used to become knowledgeable. [*See*: Socrates' defence.[26]]

'Science' is a word that is often used to describe focused and deeper-than-everyday knowledge-ability. The roots of the word are in the Latin verb, '*sciens*', or 'knowing'. In modern English, the meaning of the word has narrowed, at its narrowest referring to the study of the natural world using a disinterested, empirical method of careful observation in order to determine 'the facts'.[27] There are some social sciences, too, such as sociology and political science, so named because they often use techniques of empirical observation similar to those of the natural sciences. In this narrow English definition, philosophy and the study of literature are not sciences; they are 'humanities'. And where is education in this narrow understanding of the term 'science'? The answer is ambiguous, halfway between the sciences and the humanities, perhaps.

We want to put the case for a broader understanding of science, one that is faithful to the Latin root and still to be found in many other languages, although not English. We want to talk about science as a certain kind of 'knowing'. We want to use the word to describe those deeper forms of knowing that are the purpose of education.

Science in this broader sense consists of things you do to know that are premeditated (you set out to know them, rather than know them as an incidental consequence of action); that involve out-of-the ordinary knowledge-making efforts with a peculiar intensity of focus; that entail special techniques or methods of knowing; that are connected with specialised traditions of knowledge-ability, bodies of knowledge and communities of knowers; that are broadly agreed to be more perceptive and penetrating than the everyday knowing in and of the life-world, insofar as many people simply rely on this knowledge as given; and that, as a consequence of their perspicacity, seem to be able to get more things done in the world and more effectively. [*See*: Husserl on the task of science, in and of the lifeworld.[28]]

Education, then, is the science of learning (and, of course, teaching). Its subject is how people come to know. In this sense, education is privileged to be the science of sciences. It is a discipline that develops knowledge about the processes of knowing. If knowledge is the product of learning, how does one learn? How does one become knowledgeable, and what knowledge-abilities does one need to develop to become knowledgeable? These are the central questions of the science of education.

Dimension 1: Ways of knowing

How, then, does one come to know? What is the range of knowledge-making actions that one could take to create out-of-the-ordinary knowledge? How does one develop deeper capacities for knowing that we have called 'science' in the broader sense?

We want to suggest four main types of engagement with knowing or knowledge processes that may contribute to the formation of a knowledge repertoire (see Figure 7.1). These are kinds of things you can do to know. Each of the four is no more than a rough grouping. In the real life of knowing, several of these modes of engagement in knowledge are indistinguishably connected. In this sense, they are orientations to knowledge rather than neat categories of knowledge-making activity.

Experiencing the known

We know from our lived experience. The lifeworld is a rich source of knowledge. Our experience of the known comes with a unique depth of feeling, duration of life experience, sense of intuitive truth, and a confidence that we can trust our emotions and judgements. The lifeworld gives shape and meaning to our identities. It is a reference point for our deepest wishes and desires. It gives meaning to our most subjective urges.

The knowledge process of experiencing the known adds a layer of science, or deeper knowing, to everyday lived experience. It explicitly recognises the influences of the sources of the self on what we know and the ways in which we know it – material (class, locale), corporeal (age, race, sex and sexuality, and physical and mental characteristics) and symbolic (culture, language, gender, family,

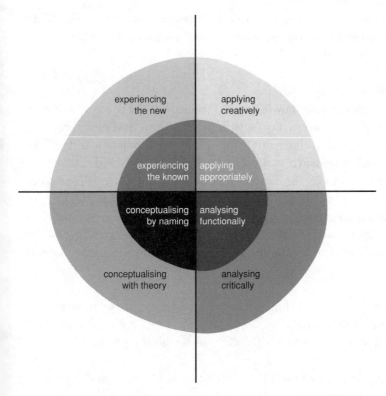

Figure 7.1: The four orientations to knowledge

affinity and persona). It entails conscious, reflective work on the lifeworld in order to interrogate one's perspectives, search for the sources of one's identity, deconstruct the forms of one's discourses and reflect upon the nature of one's thinking (meta-cognition). Deepening our experience of the known might also require us to reflect upon the ways our subjective interests can at times distort the knowledge we make. We might come to recognise the narrowness of our knowledge resulting from the limited range of our experience. Amongst the ways of knowing we have discussed earlier in this chapter, postmodernism predominantly uses this kind of knowledge process.

One danger of focusing too much on personal experience, however, is that you can become immersed in your perspective to the point where you don't raise yourself far beyond your own lifeworld experience. A one-sided focus on experiencing the known also brings with it all the difficulties of knowledge relativism and cultural relativism. A 'live and let live' complacency and scepticism may emerge. Why put extra effort into knowledge making when all you can achieve is to reflect your own perspective or express your own interpretation?

Learners using this knowledge process are encouraged to bring their (invariably diverse) experiences, interests, knowledge into the learning environment. They reflect on the sources of their knowledge and the interests that motivate it. They consider what they know and their knowledge-abilities, and what they might do to extend their knowledge based on a recognition of its limitations. [*See*: They knew much more than we realised.[29]]

Experiencing the new

We come to know by experiencing new things in the world – new objects or previously unremarked aspects of known objects, new situations and new facts that seem true enough. Becoming familiar with things that were previously unfamiliar is one of the ways in which we learn in an always-changing lifeworld.

Empirical science systematises the experiences that result in the exploration of the unfamiliar and discovery of the new. It aims to tell us more than we could normally learn from casual experience of something new. One example of empirical work is called 'scientific method' – drawn from a narrower understanding of the word 'science'. This is a kind of recipe for knowledge-action. Scientific method runs like this:

1. Focus: Decide what you want to find out and the things you are going to look at in the natural or social worlds.
2. Research: Find out what people have already seen who have looked in this place before.
3. Hypothesise: Suggest what you think you might see if you look, and explain why you think this is worth looking for.
4. Observe and/or Test: Now look hard. What can you see that you mightn't have seen at first glance; in other words, if you weren't looking so intently? Or experiment: do something and watch what happens.
5. Record: Your data could be quantitative, because you have counted or measured things. Or it could be qualitative, such as ethnographic data in which you join an unfamiliar social group and try as hard as you can to see the world the way they do, to speak, feel and think their world with them. The product is facts, as distinguishable from mere opinions or beliefs. Because you've done all that measuring and adding up, you can make conclusions about how the numbers stack up. Or because you've spent so much time in the other social setting tackling the question from this angle and then that, and hearing one person's perspective then another's, you can be pretty sure that your description of what you've seen is right.
6. Reason: Then you analyse your data and draw conclusions. You might say something like: 'We observed X a number of times, or carefully for a long time, from a number of perspectives, therefore we conclude that X must be generally true'. This is inductive reasoning, or drawing conclusions in the form of a general rule based on specific facts.
7. Corroborate: In case someone else doesn't believe your conclusion, you explain in enough detail what you did to create your knowledge. If another person were to repeat the operation (actually, or in their mind's eye), you would want them to be able to discover the same facts and come to the

same conclusions. In your formal knowledge-report, you explain what you observed and the way you observed it, how you recorded the facts, how you analysed the data and the reasoning you applied to come to your conclusions. You're not just expecting others to trust your judgement. You also say that they can verify your conclusions. If they looked in the same way, they should be able to find the same facts you found. The facts will speak for themselves.

Empirical method has its critics. In fact, its critics sometimes label it an 'ism', the ideology of 'empiricism' that pretends to be disinterested and objective but often hides the subjective interests of the knowledge maker. The facts don't necessarily speak for themselves, these critics point out, or at least not so clearly and unambiguously. The facts are not neutral. Rather, they are often the answers to the leading question you happen to have asked and a creature of your methods of observation. Nuclear scientists tend to think nuclear power is safe; anti-nuclear activists tend to think that it is not. Each has lots of 'facts' to prove their case. Scientific method looks disinterested, detached and objective. This is the impression that empiricism tries to create; an aura of authority the scientist exudes. The scientist tries to convey the impression that their science is true, and does this by trying to persuade you that they have objectively proven it. But can knowledge ever be removed from human interests and purposes? And why dismiss other ways of knowledge making as though they were less truthful?

Nevertheless, the extra effort entailed in empirical work, such as the 'scientific method', is often worth the trouble. It gives us a particular kind of confidence in our new knowledge. When they use this knowledge process as a part of their knowledge repertoire, learners will observe, interact with new factual information, and experience new things. They might not always engage in a fully fledged version of the scientific method. In fact, they might simply immerse themselves in new facts or a new situation. If their teaching is didactic, they might just be given facts that other people have already discovered. If it is authentic, they might be asked to experiment, observe and draw their own conclusions. In both cases, the epistemological presuppositions might be called empirical in a good sense, or empiricist for their narrowness. Transformative education suggests a broader knowledge repertoire of which empirical work is just one of a number of complementary things you can do to know.

Conceptualising by naming

In our everyday experience of the world, we name things, and by naming things we note similarities with other things, or draw distinctions. This is not that. (A chair is not a table.) This is an instance of that. (A chair and a table are both furniture.) This is part of that. (This chair and that table are parts of a dining room suite.) Young children, Vygotsky argues, think in complexes, whereby they connect chairs with tables because they are associated in everyday life. As they get older, they move into a stage of thinking and use language whereby 'chair' becomes a concept. There are many different kinds of chairs in the world, but even when they encounter a strange-looking chair, it deserves the name chair because the child has now grasped the abstracting concept, 'chair'.[30]

In the everyday experience of language in the lifeworld, there is much ambiguity to words and blurred edges between concepts. Some of the time, we only really know what a person is talking about in context, or because of our shared experience of the same situation.

Scientific conceptualising by naming makes distinctions that are clearer and less ambiguous than is often the case in the everyday lifeworld or natural language use. It creates higher levels of semantic precision and predictability of meaning. It makes clear distinctions (what's in a category and what's not; what the category consists of and what it is itself a part of). It creates explicit definitions for the purpose of a particular knowledge-making activity, abstracting meaning to identify the underlying functions of a concept so the precise extent of its applicability can be specified.

The dangers in such categorical work, its critics point out, are to become too rigid about classifications and too abstract about meanings. It becomes too dogmatic when it requires either/or classifications for the sake of conceptual clarity. Sometimes the drive to neat classification oversimplifies things. At other times the ambiguity is important, itself perceptive or revealing.

Notwithstanding these dangers, in conceptualising by naming, learners clarify, classify, group and distinguish – all essential parts of a knowledge-making activity. This is not just a matter of learning the meaning of words. It is a kind of action. Didactic teaching would have that we learn the proper names and definitions for things – atoms and verbs and constitutions. Conceptualising by naming, however, is a thing you do to know for yourself, and not just a dull list of labels you have to learn.

Conceptualising with theory
In our lifeworld experience, language puts concepts together into chunks of meaning. Putting concepts together is something we do all the time. Here's the theory of dining room suites: 'A dining room suite consists of a table and enough chairs to fit around the perimeter of that table.' Of course, in the everyday discourse of the lifeworld we'd never say something so stilted. However, by putting concepts together in this way, theories help us organise our experience in a way that is more explicit and understandable to strangers and learners who may not have encountered a particular phenomenon. Theories help us clearly describe patterns in the world.

Theory is a particular way of thinking and speaking, peculiar to the out-of-the-ordinary knowledge making that is science. Rarely in everyday experience do we even need to state the theory of dining room suites, or at least not expressed quite this abstractly. The theory is implicit in our experience of dining room suites, and we'd only need to state the theory if we went to purchase a new suite which, for instance, had too many chairs, or not enough. Scientific theories make the implicit explicit. They turn experience into useful generalisations that can be applied broadly and helpfully to new situations. They require a kind of thinking that helps us infer, predict and evaluate. When developing scientific theories, we put extra effort into making our thinking particularly clear and well organised. We also have a greater need to understand, make and apply theories when we are the creators of things rather than just users. Furniture manufacturers and interior designers creating new products and designing new spaces need the theory of furniture more than someone who happens to be sitting at a table as an incidental aspect of their lifeworld experience.

Science builds theories in order to model the world and provide frameworks that explain phenomena that are not immediately obvious. Patients feel sick, but doctors have theories about what could be wrong and what can be done about it. Travellers cross bridges, but engineers have theories that explain how to make bridges so they stay up. Learners learn, but teachers have theories of how learning happens.

Theories piece together concepts into mental maps or schemas. Theories come together into paradigms or larger interpretative frameworks, such as the paradigm of Western medicine compared to the paradigm of Chinese medicine, or the paradigm of didactic teaching compared to the paradigm of transformative education. Paradigms may be alternative ways to theorise a discipline, in these cases medicine or education. Theories not only help us identify and conceive patterns; they also help us draw conclusions based on the logic of regularity and irregularity. They help us figure out and explain what the patterns mean.

The danger of excessive reliance on conceptualising with theory, the critics of this knowledge process argue, is that we might allow our schemas to get ahead of experience, to be overly abstract or too readily accepting of presented theories as taken-for-granted when the concepts, facts they purport to represent or interests they reflect might be open to challenge. Theories always need to be left open to testing and possible disproof, not to be simply accepted as though by act of faith.

Using the knowledge process of conceptualising with theory, learners in an environment of didactic education will be presented with canonical theories – the periodic table, or grammar, or of the causes of war – which they need to learn and show they have learnt in their end-of-course tests. Authentic education will get learners to internalise theories or understand a theory by replication of an experiment or working through a proof. It will ask them to take apart and put back together the concepts that are used by a discipline. Transformative education asks learners to be active theory makers, within a larger repertoire of knowledge-making actions. Like authentic education, part of this theory making may involve figuring out canonical theories for themselves (working out how canonical science has come to a particular conclusion in order to understand its underlying logic). However, going one step beyond authentic education, transformative education also encourages learners to make theories that are their own, particularly as they consider their own lifeworld experiences, critically reflect on the knowledge they encounter, and apply that knowledge to real-world situations.

Analysing functionally

In our everyday lifeworlds, we continually find ourselves using reason, applying logic, figuring out cause and effect, deducing, inferring and predicting. All dining room suites contain a table and chairs. We know this. Now we have found a classified advertisement for a dining room suite, so we deduce that there must be chairs for sale as well as a table. So, we find we are working with a background or implicit theory of dining room suites. It's just that we don't do the theory as deliberately and systematically as we do when we perform the knowledge process of analysing functionally.

Science uses frames of reasoning based on the analytical tools of logic, inference and prediction. Deductive reasoning may, for instance, take the form of what is called a syllogism: If X is generally true, and Y is an instance of X, then Y must be true.[31] The fact of X (the premise) is assumed to be true and the knowledge-making work of this knowledge process is focused on the rational deduction from this premise.

The critics of this knowledge process label its unbalanced excesses 'rationalism' (applying arid, mechanical, disengaged, formal logic, whose premises are not questioned) and 'rationalisation' (providing a specious rationale for something whose premises cannot be justified). They argue that its danger is to develop systems of formal reasoning disengaged from human and natural consequences; technical control without adequate ethical reflection; a focus on the means for achieving certain ends at the expense of reflection on the value of the ends; and a narrow functionalism.

Using this knowledge process in a balanced knowledge repertoire, however, learners will systematically explore causes and effect and develop careful chains of reasoning that are closely connected with other knowledge processes.

Analysing critically

Suspicion that what you are being told may be deceptively slanted to serve the interests of the teller, or that what you seem to see at first glance may prove to be an illusion – these are critical instincts embedded in our most ordinary lifeworld experiences.

Science turns these instincts into a method – ways of reading the world through the always cautious eye of critical analysis and interrogating the interests, motives and ethics that may motivate knowledge claims. This is 'critique', the ever-vigilant process of meta-cognitive reflection. What are the conditions of thinking that might call to question possible limitations in that thinking? Rather than reacting with instinctive suspicion, the knowledge process of analysing critically involves a careful search for and comparison of rival hypotheses and conclusions, and interpretation of the underlying bases of disagreement. What are the key cultural, theoretical and political factors underpinning a particular knowledge claim? What motivates the claim? Analysing critically brings a significant measure of knowledge relativism and cultural relativism to the interpretation of knowledge. Different kinds of people are motivated by different things; different kinds of people are inclined to know the world in ways that produce different kinds of knowledge.

Critics of critique as an isolated knowledge process accuse it of occasionally ungenerous fractiousness, an inclination to debunk for debunking's sake, or intolerant resistance to other points of view. They may also accuse the bearer of critical messages of being a mere 'armchair critic', someone who is plenty willing to criticise but not so willing or able to take sufficient knowledge-making responsibility to come up with constructive alternatives.

Analysing critically is nevertheless a key knowledge process in which learners interrogate the interests behind an action, motives for expressing a meaning or reasons for highlighting a particular fact in a particular way. But analysing critically should not be left at that. It often requires that you do something in the world, or one of the applied knowledge processes. Critically review a fact or text or practice by all means. But surely your critical knowledge claim would be strengthened if it were part of a broader knowledge repertoire in which you also constructed a redesigned meaning or practice, or discovered and highlighted a new fact? Critical thinking is often too narrowly academic, interrogating the bases of knowing but failing to follow through with the action that necessarily follows from this knowing.

Applying appropriately

We intuitively know how to apply our knowledge because we do it in every waking hour. We apply what we know habitually.

Science also exists to be applied, but it is more focused and ordered in its processes of application. We mostly put in the extra effort that scientific knowing requires because we want to do something with that knowledge. The reason we put in this extra effort is to be sure that the application works and is useful. In the everyday lifeworld, by comparison, applications tend to be more hit and miss, and we allow for that when there's not too much at stake. Or they are predictable in their outcomes, so much so that the extra effort required in the more formal knowledge process of applying appropriately, is redundant.

Science is more conscious, premeditated and systematic in its methods of application. Applying appropriately involves practical forms of understanding in a setting in which that knowledge has immediately and specifically been designed to get things done. This kind of knowledge process is pragmatic, designing and implementing practical solutions that achieve technical or instrumental outcomes.

The critics of this kind of knowledge making accuse it of narrow technicism, an uncritical stance whereby it often leaves purposes and outcomes unexamined, and a pragmatism that borders on unreflective opportunism – if it works, it must be alright. But just because the application works, is it right?

Its particular value, however, is when it attempts to link other knowledge processes into practical applications. The theory of calculus makes more sense when we can see what we can do with it in the world. The theory of poetry (what it is and its characteristic features) makes more sense when we use its forms to say something we want to say. In a learning context, applying appropriately may involve learning by doing something in a predictable or to-be-expected way in a 'real world' situation, or a situation that simulates the 'real world'. Or it may involve transfer from theoretical understanding to a practical example of that theory in action. The learner's subsequent knowledge can then be evaluated against the application itself. Does the knowledge work? Is it apt to the context of application? Is it a useful solution to a known and agreed problem?

Applying creatively

Whether we recognise it or not, we transform the world in every moment of our acting and meaning. No one has ever done quite the things we have in our lives, or made quite the same contribution, or represented the world to others with quite the timbre of our voice and overtones of our experience. To innovate is in our natures. We take the objects and meanings of the world and rearrange them in invariably new ways. The innovations may be small, and we may hardly realise we are doing it, but innovating nevertheless we always are.

At its best, science is innovative in a premeditated, systematic and self-reflective way. Applying creatively is a knowledge process in which we attempt to make big leaps – to take knowledge from one context and apply it in a vastly different one; to solve big problems which hitherto seemed insurmountable; to come up with ingenious solutions to niggling little problems; to mix and match symbolic meanings in unusual, original and creative ways; to imagine new angles or perspectives; to take calculated but nevertheless significant risks; to imagine possibilities way beyond what currently seem realistic; or to conjecture pathways for action which seem improbable but may nevertheless prove realistic.

The critics of this knowledge process argue against its often-unrealistic over-confidence, its potentials to irrelevance and failure, its naive utopianism, its anthropocentric faith in humans' capacities to make progress and its sometimes stubborn lack of pragmatism.

As an aspect of a knowledge repertoire, however, applying creatively can engage learners in acts of imagination, risky but sometimes enlightening applications beyond their immediate comfort zones, strikingly original hybrid creativity, and transfer of their knowledge into distant sites of application. In so doing, applying creatively can engage learners in higher-order problem solving and to grasp a sense of how invention and innovation happen.

Dimension 2: Ways of learning

The more focused kind of knowing that we have called 'science' consists of a number of different kinds of action that produce deeper, broader, more trustworthy, more insightful and more useful knowledge. We have to concentrate on our ways of knowing to achieve this greater depth. We have to work systematically and more imaginatively at it.

School teaches us how to work at our knowing. The science of education is the science of these deeper and more discerning ways of knowing and how they are acquired through learning. Learning is coming to know. Education is the science of how we come to know. Doing education as a discipline and as a profession, we come to know how we come to know.

Knowledge, we have argued, consists of a variety of forms of action. It is not simply a process of thinking, a matter of cognitive understanding. Rather it is a series of performatives – acts of intervention as well as acts of representation, deeds as well as thoughts, types of practice as well as forms of contemplation. The deeper and broader knowledge that is the object of study of the science of education consists of the kinds of things we do (knowledge-abilities) to create out-of-the-ordinary knowledge. Fazal Rizvi calls these 'epistemic virtues'.[32]

We have roughly grouped the things we can do to know into four-times-two categories. Less important than the grouping itself is the idea that more purposefully deploying a broader range of knowledge processes can produce more cogent knowledge than a narrower and more ad hoc range. So, a careful empiricism in 'experiencing the new' is all the more powerful if measured with a cautious eye to interests and agendas by 'analysing critically'. 'Applying appropriately' or 'applying creatively' will be all the more powerful if they are founded on clarity and coherence of 'conceptualising with theory'. Science is more likely to be stronger if we use a balance of alternative knowledge moves or acts of knowing. Learning is likely to move the learner more powerfully if it involves an appropriate and balanced range of knowledge processes or activity types.

When your knowing is more partial, good science is aware of its partiality and able to justify it. Mathematics may at times stay entirely within the knowledge processes of 'conceptualising with theory' and 'analysing functionally'. This is because in some of its knowledge-making forms and processes, at least, there is no need to justify its activities in terms of application or criticaly review its purposes. A discipline may prioritise one or more knowledge processes or kinds of scientific moves over others, and this may be the source of its strength as often as it is a potential weakness.

Nor is there any need for a particular sequence or navigational path to scientific knowledge. Localised recipes for action such as the empirical 'scientific method' may prove handy. But the different knowledge processes may at times be tackled in any order, or even in a messy simultaneous way, whereby different orientations are combined in a particular knowledge-making activity. The most important thing is that learners make purposeful and appropriate knowledge-making choices according to their context, interests and needs.

The various modes of committed knowledge provide some hard-won paths to knowledge. There is much we can learn from these as we develop a broader knowledge repertoire, learning how to use a variety of tools for our knowledge-making trade. Knowledge relativism teaches us not to be over-zealous about any single path to knowledge. It suggests that we should be aware of our perspectives. We should look out for the differences in meaning between ourselves and other people whose lifeworld experiences and premises about knowledge may vary significantly. It suggests we should be careful, sensitive and tolerant of these differences. We should always be ready to concede that another perspective, or someone else's more thorough knowledge-work in a particular area, could challenge even our hardest-won confidences.

So, what do we do in schools? Knowledge repertoires are more open and more flexible whilst still being solidly grounded in a range of traditional practices in knowledge making. Some teachers, some learners, some schools, some cultures, some disciplines might prefer to emphasise some knowledge processes over others. Some might want to start with one knowledge process and end with another. However, viewed holistically, a balanced approach to building a knowledge repertoire draws on the strengths of the two conceptions of knowledge in education today, knowledge grounded in facts, theories, texts and reason, on the one hand, and the always-questioning stance of relativism and critical thinking on the other.[33]

Dimension 3: Sites of learning

Today, more than at any time in the recent, modern past, the processes of deeper knowledge making are more distributed, located in widely dispersed places.

Committed knowledge frameworks create special sites, institutions and roles for privileged forms of knowledge making. If we want to know more of what scientists, professionals or great writers knew, or even become one of these types of person by way of vocation, we would respectfully listen to their masters, their texts and their interlocutors in order to learn from them.

Relativist knowledge frameworks deconstruct the knowledge pretensions of these privileged sites, institutions and roles. The relativists highlight the equally valid truth in the life experiences of groups denied access to privileged forms of knowledge. As a counterpoint, they remark upon a certain kind of truth born of identity and deep personal experience. And they admit the everyday cultural truths of the mass media and popular culture.

So, what of New Learning? We argued earlier in this book that a momentous shift is underway in the balance of agency at work, in citizenship and in the everyday lifeworld of differentiated identities. So too, we are experiencing a shift in the balance of agency in the relationships of knowledge production. More people are knowledge makers and not just knowledge consumers – in the workplace, in community life and in the world of the new media. Sources of credible knowledge are now far more diffused across sites, institutions and social roles. Their credibility is based, not on their formal location and status, or at least not that alone. Rather, we come to trust the knowledge of others because of the hard work they have put into their knowledge making, and which we know they continue to put into that knowledge making.

The idea of a knowledge repertoire is the basis for a deepened and broadened conception of science (more resilient knowing). This is what we mean by the New

Learning (the way you come to know), and of a renewed science of education (knowing how you come to know). In the everyday practicalities of teaching, using a knowledge repertoire becomes a way of saying explicitly, 'Now I am using this particular way to know, and now I am using that other way, and this is the reason I did this, then that'. By the end of a learning experience, both learner and teacher are able to say, 'This is what we have done to know, this is where we have been, this is the knowledge we have picked up and the knowledge-abilities we have developed'. One reason for this approach is to be transparent about learning choices and quite clear about the learning outcomes – not necessarily to justify them as much as to evaluate them in order to work out what still has to be learnt, or to make the knowledge processes stronger next time. This requires a new kind of teacher, a new kind of profession for a world in which knowledge is made in more powerful and dynamic ways right across the society. A dynamically active conception of education is pivotal to the creation of a 'knowledge society' worthy of that name.

Summary

Knowledge and learning	Committed knowledge: The modern past	Knowledge relativism: More recent times	Knowledge repertoires: New Learning
Dimension 1: Ways of knowing	Strong commitment to one way of making knowledge and the body of knowledge that has been created that way; for instance, religious truths, empirical truths, rationalist truths and canonical truths.	Scepticism and caution about whether any one way of making knowledge can produce 'truth': epistemological relativism, cultural relativism and postmodernism.	Developing a range of things you can do to know. Purposefully balancing the methods of a range of committed knowledge approaches with the caution and respect for differences of knowledge relativism.
Dimension 2: Ways of learning	Following a method and learning its inherited truths.	Being authentic, true to one's own subjectivity, identity, self.	Social cognition and collaborative learning as aspects of human nature.
Dimension 3: Sites of learning	Special sites, institutions and roles for privileged knowledge making and formal learning.	Learning closely connected to, and influenced by, experience and identity.	Distributed knowledge, with more people as active knowledge makers, and trust based on the kind and amount of work they have put into their knowing.

190   *Part C: Responses*

Notes

1. Damasio 1994
2. Buddhist Pali Canon N. D. See extract at NewLearningOnline.com
3. Al-Ghazzali 1108 (2001), pp. 65–67, 98. See extract at NewLearningOnline.com
4. Schweber 2006, pp. 392–417. See extract at NewLearningOnline.com
5. Locke 1690 Book II, Chapter 1, p. 1; Book I, Chapter 1, p. 1; Book II, Chapter 1, pp. 2, 3, 4, 6, 22, 24. See extract at NewLearningOnline.com
6. Ibn Tufayl c.1170 (1907), pp. 29–37, 41–42, 47, 50–52, 58. See extract at NewLearningOnline.com
7. Descartes 1641 (1911), pp. 14–17. See extract at NewLearningOnline.com
8. Kant 1781 (1933), pp. 20, 22, 25, 27, 655, 653, 655–656, 329. See extract at NewLearningOnline.com
9. Aristotle 350 bce-c. See extract at NewLearningOnline.com
10. Arnold 1869, pp. viii, 7, 15–16, 41, 105, 108–110, 58, 67. See extract at NewLearningOnline.com
11. Hirsch 1988, pp. xiv–xv, xvii, 20–21, xiii, 115, 21, 23–24. See extract at NewLearningOnline.com
12. Empiricus c.200, Bk 1, pp. 1, 4, 6, 7. See extract at NewLearningOnline.com
13. Nietzsche 1888 (1915), p. 44. See extract at NewLearningOnline.com
14. Eco 1981; Barthes 1981
15. Blackburn 2005
16. Kalantzis and Cope 2006a, pp. 209–214
17. Wittgenstein 1958, pp. 2, 3, 5, 8, 11, 20, 15–16. See extract at NewLearningOnline.com
18. Rorty 1989, pp. 4–5, 6, 27, 51–52. See extract at NewLearningOnline.com
19. Lyotard 1979
20. Spivak 1999
21. Derrida 1976
22. Jameson 1991
23. Aronowitz and Giroux 1991, pp. 15, 93, 101, 81, 128–29, 133. See extract at NewLearningOnline.com
24. Pell 2005. See extract at NewLearningOnline.com
25. Damasio 1994
26. Plato c.399 347 bce See extract at NewLearningOnline.com
27. Chalmers 1976
28. Husserl 1954 (1970), pp. 205, 59, 51–52, 110, 152, 375. See extract at NewLearningOnline.com
29. Burrows, Cope, Kalantzis, Loi, Suominen and Yelland. 2006a. See extract at NewLearningOnline.com
30. Vygotsky 1962
31. Aristotle 350 bce-d
32. Rizvi 2007
33. Kalantzis and Cope 2004b, pp. 38–92; 2005

Chapter 8

Pedagogy and curriculum

Overview

In this chapter, we explore the processes for designing education that make it different from everyday, casual or incidental learning in the life-world. Education is learning that has been consciously designed. Education's designs can take curricular form by focusing on programs or courses of study; and they take pedagogical form by focusing on the learning tasks or activities in which learners engage as a part of this curriculum. The chapter discusses three approaches to pedagogy and curriculum: mimesis, synthesis and reflexivity.

Mimesis is imitation or copying, or learning by absorbing facts, theories, bodies of knowledge and literatures that have been presented to learners in a formal educational setting.

Synthesis is a process of gaining understanding in which learners figure out rules or discover facts through observation and experimentation, but mainly in order to get the 'right' answer in the artificial context of schooling and its assessments. The learner deconstructs then reconstructs knowledge without necessarily connecting closely to their own interests, motivations and experiences.

Reflexivity in education involves learners moving between different ways of knowing (developing a knowledge repertoire), connecting learning with their own experiences and identities, and applying their learning by doing things in the world which impact on that world.

Education's designs

Education is a social relationship of learning that has been consciously designed.

In our nature as humans, we learn anywhere and everywhere. Learning is an integral part of our life-world experience. The characteristic difference between the informal learning that is a casual part of life-world experience and the learning we call 'education' is that education is learning by design. The hallmarks of education are deliberate pedagogical actions, organised sequences of learning, specialised texts, dedicated teaching roles and specialised educational institutions. In this chapter, we examine these hallmarks of education through two dimensions of teaching – pedagogy and curriculum.

The practice of pedagogy involves a series of scaffolded performances of knowing; organised activity sequences that are localised in time and space, and with a narrative structure (orientation, journey, destination). Here is an example:

> *Orientation*: Students in classroom, teacher at the front of the room: 'Hey kids, today we're going to do the pyramids (or volcanoes, or whatever). Turn to chapter 11.'
>
> *Journey*: 'Let's read the chapter, talk about the chapter and find out more information from the library/Internet.'
>
> *Destination*: 'We're getting to the end now, so let's do the pyramids/volcanoes test.' Or, 'Finish your project now and hand it in.' The teacher then gives each student a mark for their efforts. The students know the narrative is over when the teacher says, 'Okay, now turn to chapter 12, on Ancient Rome (or rivers, or whatever).'

Here is another example, using the concepts developed in the 'Learning by Design' project[1]:

> *Orientation*: A group of students in the class has negotiated with their teacher to investigate the life cycle of a local pond, cognisant of formal standards and local curriculum requirements.
>
> *Journey*: The teacher is explicit about expected learning and performance standards and, together with students, designs a sequence of 'knowledge processes', or activities, including (in any particular order, moving backwards and forwards between different knowledge processes):
>
> Experiencing the known: Survey parents, other students on range of concerns about and everyday understanding of the ecosystem of the pond. What more do we need to know to develop a well-informed understanding of the pond?
>
> Experiencing the new: Visit the pond, examine it carefully, undertake some scientific tests, record data.

Conceptualising by naming: Research and define key scientific concepts that describe life cycles.

Conceptualising with theory: Develop a theory of life cycles in an ecosystem.

Analysing functionally: Model the life cycle diagrammatically.

Analysing critically: Model disruptions to the life cycle, such as pollution or the effects of development. Who is responsible for these? Investigate problem sources and plan possible solutions.

Applying appropriately: Write a scientific report of the findings.

Applying creatively: Develop a management plan for the pond and present it to the local council. Apply life-cycle concepts and theory to a new setting by examining a forest.

Destination: Self-assessment and peer assessment of activities as represented in a research report; external assessment by experts such as environmental scientists, representatives from local government or parents. Learning outcomes are aligned to individual and public expectations.

Curriculum is a larger framework for learning. If pedagogy in the earlier example was occurring within Chapter 11 (localised sequences of activity, such as read then answer the questions at the end of the chapter), then curriculum is all the chapters in the textbook (the whole course, and the test at the end of the year). Or, if pedagogy is the sequence of activities undertaken by students as they study the ecosystem of a local pond, the curriculum might be Grade 7 Biology. Curriculum ties the micro-sequences of pedagogy together into the larger frameworks or macro-sequences of learning design that we call courses or subjects. The product of curriculum making is sometimes called a 'syllabus', or program of learning.

In Chapter 2, we described three different kinds of experiences of education: didactic, authentic and transformative. In this chapter we discuss the design principles and processes that underlie each of these kinds of experience. These are, respectively, mimetic, synthetic and reflexive. We investigate each of these according to the dimensions of:

Dimension 1: Pedagogy

Dimension 2: Curriculum

Mimesis: The modern past

Mimesis is the process of imitating or copying. The Greek root of the word finds its way into English in the word 'mimic'. The ancient Greek philosopher, Aristotle, regarded all creative endeavour as a process of mimesis. The role of the artist was to exaggerate features of what they were copying to create tragic, comic or ennobling effect. [*See*: Aristotle on mimesis.[2]]

Dimension 1: Pedagogy

A mimetic pedagogy is one in which the learner acquires received knowledge and demonstrates this acquisition by repetition. As a learning relationship, mimesis is a system of knowledge transmission and reproduction.

In mimetic pedagogy, the teacher stands in an authoritarian relationship to the learner. In the 'Rule of St Benedict', the founder of Western Christian monasticism set out the relationship between the teacher in the monastery (the Abbot or the Superior) and the monks who had entered the monastery to learn the ways of God. Behind the teacher stands a body of knowledge, canonical texts and institutional structures, which represent a source of authority. St Benedict's Superior is subject to God's authority, as expressed in *The Holy Bible* and transmitted to believers through the ecclesiastical hierarchy. [*See*: St Benedict on the teacher and the taught.[3]]

Committed knowledge frameworks of the kinds discussed in Chapter 7 are mostly taught through a pedagogy of mimesis, including, for instance, pedagogies grounded in religious truths. Sacred texts may be taken to speak literal truths, such as that God created the world in seven days. Or they may be taken to speak to unbreakable rules of behaviour. To learn these truths, the faithful listen respectfully to the interpretation of a teacher-authority, in the person of the priest or the *imam*, for instance. They read the sacred texts diligently. They may also commit sections of the text to memory. The highest form of traditional Koranic learning is to be able to recite the whole of the sacred text by heart, from beginning to end and in the original Arabic. [*See*: Inside Pakistan's madrasas.[4]]

Pedagogies of empirical truth, also discussed in Chapter 7, may be mimetic, too. Learners are required to commit facts to memory (historical facts, scientific facts and the like). Empiricism can, in its more authentic moments, require greater engagement than this, by expecting that learners do their own empirical or fact-finding work. But when a pedagogy of empiricism is mimetic, the focus is on students learning acquired facts, or facts that have already been discovered for them by people who (must) know better. Learners prove that they have acquired this empirical knowledge by presenting the correct facts to teachers through tests. [*See*: Thayer, Learning about bark.[5]]

Pedagogies of rationalism (again, see Chapter 7), when they are mimetic in character, offer learners theories in the form of rules that must be learnt. Learners can prove they have learned these theories by repeating the rule, showing they can apply the rule in an example or solving a problem that requires application of the rule. Rationalism may also at times require learners to formulate their own theories and infer underlying rules (a more authentic pedagogy) – but in its mimetic form, it is primarily a process of knowledge transmission. Pedagogies of canonical text teach learners what is great about the idealised texts of 'high culture' and official knowledge, as expressed by famous writers and thinkers. [*See*: Confucius on becoming a learned person.[6]]

Mimetic pedagogy is a kind of learning design that weights the balance of agency in learning towards the teacher and their authoritative knowledge sources. The learner stands in a relatively passive relationship of knowledge acquisition. Committed knowledge frameworks tend to foster relationships of learning that are mimetic. [*See*: A morning at the Dong-feng Kindergarten.[7]]

Some mimetic pedagogical practices include whole-class recitation, learning things off by heart, question-and-answer routines whereby the learner takes a stab at the 'correct' answer, and factually oriented, multiple-choice tests. The tendency of this kind of pedagogy is to regard students as uniformly lacking in the new knowledge presented in the curriculum, and uniformly willing and able to absorb the new knowledge being presented. [*See*: Why should they look behind them?[8]]

However, mimetic pedagogy is never quite as it seems. Even in the most authoritarian of didactic pedagogies, the learner's subjectivity and identity are not entirely extinguished. Learning only occurs when the learner connects and listening is, in fact, an active process. Nor would any teacher, even a person like St Benedict, want or believe that learners are passive, empty vessels. Even the strictest of religious teachers, surely, would want the faithful to internalise as their own the knowledge they learn. Mimesis is not necessarily conducive to such internalised learning, but it is surely what any teacher would want. So, more-than-mimesis is what sometimes happens, though not reliably. This is because learners are never entirely passive. Readers and listeners never read and hear texts without their own experience producing a peculiar reading or hearing. Sometimes the reading or the hearing may not register, but at other times the reader or the listener does relate. Moreover, received texts and knowledges, no matter how insistent and dogmatic, are always open to some degree of reinterpretation by the receiver.[9] Indeed, as Gunther Kress points out, all representation or sense-making is transformative.[10] Representation is an act of appropriation of the world that never leaves the world precisely the way it was, and that includes representation to oneself in consciousness of what one is seeing or hearing.

Dimension 2: Curriculum

In curriculum, an epistemology of mimesis translates into the following view of knowledge: There are definite facts in the world. These are not directly accessible to learners in an educational setting. But they can be packaged into a digestible form, such as a textbook that covers the course. The textbook frames the reference point of learning, which is necessarily outside of the classroom – the facts of science, the events and dates of history, the places of geography, the formulae of mathematics. The book tells of these things of the outside world in a distant and distancing kind of way, condensed into theories that sum up what humans know, such as the narrative of history or the discipline of science.

Behind the textbook stands the syllabus, the course to be covered as mandated by an external agency. In earlier modern times, syllabi were mainly focused on areas of content knowledge (facts and theories). More recently, an approach of 'essential learnings' has specified in more general terms the learning outcomes expected in a particular area of curriculum and at a certain level.

The underlying message of mimetic curriculum is that the sources of definitive knowledge are external to the classroom. The learner acquires knowledge rather than makes knowledge. Not even the teacher is an expert. For much of the time, the teacher finds themself positioned as an interlocutor between the learners and the syllabus-making authority of the education system, or the content-knowledge authority of the textbook writer. As a consequence, the balance of agency in the processes of knowing favours a knowledge hierarchy, consisting of teacher, expert and discipline, over the learner. Mimetic curriculum determines the shape of the discipline, as revealed through general outlines of received bodies of knowledge, and abstract generalisations or syntheses of content areas. It condenses learning into core subject areas that all students should learn as part of a 'comprehensive' or 'general' education. The assumption, too, is that only experts possess the capacity to test and re-evaluate the theories and facts of disciplinary content, and that these bodies of knowledge remain fairly stable over long periods of time. [*See*: Michael Apple on ideology in curriculum.[11]]

Some educationalists argue that mimesis is an inappropriate basis for education in contemporary times – times in which the balance of agency has changed in our civic, working and personal lives. However, the mimetic frame also finds a number of seemingly comfortable places in today's world. One place is in the 'back to the basics' movement in education, which seeks to return to an earlier modernity when the rigour and standards of disciplined learning apparently ruled. It finds champions in the new and burgeoning social movements of fundamentalist religion. It is perhaps easier to do – educational inputs that show directly measurable results in educational outputs. It may also be the path of least resistance, given the expectations of parents who went to school some decades ago and the heritage institutional architectures of today's schools.

One sign of a back-to-the-future revival of mimesis has been a renewed emphasis on high-stakes, standardised testing in which the school undertakes the process of social sifting and sorting against a singular and supposedly universal measure of basic skills and knowledge. Another sign is the return to didactic, skill-and-drill curriculum, which jams in content knowledge to fit the tests. [*See*: A Japanese cram school.[12]]

In literacy, for instance, the skill-and-drill regime starts with phonics. When they come to write in English, children encounter 44 sounds and the 26 letters that represent these sounds. These can be learnt by rote – by repetition and association. However, literacy researcher James Gee questions just how intellectually challenging this is when, in the spaces of contemporary child culture, children quickly master immensely more complex systems without direct instruction by a teacher or conscious efforts to memorise (for example, the hundreds of configurations of Pokémon characters). The horizons of phonics are set so low and the results so easy to measure, he argues, that it's not hard to show improved results, even amongst children who come from communities and cultures that historically have not achieved well at school. Then comes the 'fourth-grade slump', when the test results return to more disappointingly predictable, unequal form.[13] The problem is that writing is not a transliteration of speech. It is a different mode with a significantly different grammar.[14] In the act of mimesis around sound–letter correspondences, the learners miss seeing the literacy forest for their focus on the phonic trees. Some kinds of learners seem to 'get it'; others don't. The more academic modes of written language make intuitive sense to some but not others. Some learners relate to the distinctive forms of written language as a cultural move – being a scientist and writing like one, or being an author and writing like one – but others do not. Learning to write is about forming an identity. Some learners comfortably work their way into that identity and others do not, and the difference has a lot to do with social class and community background. In the long run, Gee argues, phonics fails to bridge the deeper gaps, and thus fails learners who do not come from cultures of writing. Perhaps these learners may have been able to extend their repertoires into the mode of writing and its cultures if the starting point had been other modes and the entry points to literacy were more intellectually stimulating and motivating than sound–letter correspondences? Perhaps a pedagogy built on the multifarious subjectivities of learners might work better than drilling to distraction the ones who don't immediately 'get' the culture of writing?

Mimetic teaching makes a neat inside/outside distinction, drawing a line between the formalism of rote learning within the classroom and the outside cultures and social purposes to which learning connects. We may, however, need to connect the inside and outside more closely, particularly for those learners who do not immediately 'get' the connections between the formalism of education and real-world applications of schooled knowledge. In order to be more effective, we may also need to reduce the abstract formalism of the classroom and, in so doing, the distance between the culture of the classroom and the learners' experiences of the life-world. We may need to bring the subjectivities of learners into closer engagement with the sites of education and its processes of pedagogy and curriculum. This, however, involves disruptions to the neatly defined institutional order of things. Teachers who have grown comfortable with the mimetic mode may find this challenging.

Meanwhile, the public political rhetoric tells us that we are supposed to be creating learners for the knowledge economy, for new workplaces that place a premium on creativity and self-motivation, for citizenship that devolves regulatory responsibility to many layers of self-governing community and for an everyday life-world in which the balance of agency has shifted towards users, customers and meaning-makers. In this context, diversity, not measurable uniformity, prevails. The 'back-to-basics' movement, however, wants to take us back to the formalism of academic disciplines and the rigours of mimesis. This, its critics argue, may be misreading what today's society needs from education, and this even from the most conservative, systems-bolstering point of view.[15] The back-to-basics people might, in short, be wrong.

However, if there's some method in the apparent madness, it may be that back-to-basics mimetic curriculum is education on the cheap in the era of neoliberalism.[16] An education system grounded in the simple procedures of mimesis may be all that the politicians and the electorate understand and want to pay for. Education that moves beyond the horizons of didactic, mass-production, uniform, easy-to-measure teaching is something the users will have to pay for by sending their children to private schools. Anything more than the basics is only for those who can afford it. This is a bleak scenario, indeed. A politically more constructive and creative strategy might be to take at their word the more innovation-seeking politicians and business people. Whenever we find them talking the rhetoric of the knowledge society, we should press them about what they mean and convince them that they should mean something that departs from our heritage practices of education.

Synthesis: More recent times

In synthetic pedagogy and curriculum, the learner can deconstruct knowledge, and even reconstruct knowledge, but mostly in a way that leaves that knowledge more or less unchanged. The learner takes the building blocks of knowledge they have been given, takes them apart and reassembles them.

Dimension 1: Pedagogy

Synthetic pedagogy encourages learners to get actively involved in their learning. This may involve doing their own empirical work, such as conducting a scientific experiment, or showing their workings in such a way that they demonstrate they have 'understood' mathematical theory, or internalised the ethics, styles or sensibilities of the (for example, literary or musical) canon.

More than superficial repetition of knowledge in a pedagogy of mimesis, this synthetic work shows a deeper 'understanding', such that knowledge can be replicated based on its underlying logic or first principles. Synthetic pedagogy shifts the balance of agency towards the learner to some degree by allowing the learner space to appropriate knowledge for themselves. [*See*: Froebel on play as a primary way of learning for young children.[17]]

Synthetic pedagogy may also get the learner involved constructing knowledge according to a given formula and demonstrating their (mimetic) learning of the formulae. For example, following a prescribed experimental methodology in science and demonstrating a correct result and a correct process; applying a maths theory to get the correct answer, and also showing how they applied the theory.

The outcome of synthetic pedagogy is that you come to an accepted understanding of a part of a presented body of knowledge or discipline more knowingly than you would if you were simply presented with that knowledge as fact, theory or canonical text.

'Constructivism' is an instance of synthetic pedagogy. One of its sources is the work of the child psychologist, Jean Piaget. He made the case that knowledge is not simply absorbed by the child learner from what they are presented. Knowledge is, to a significant degree, constructed by the learner.[18] The learner internalises and builds their cognitive capacities as they progress from one developmental stage to the next. In other words, learners build their knowledge and knowledge-ability through engagement with the world. Learners are not simply given understandings. They build understandings. This is the basis for a learner-centred interpretation of the learning process. [*See*: Thayer, on making curriculum relevant.[19]]

A postmodern version of synthetic pedagogy is grounded in learners' identities. In recognising social differences and historically neglected or marginalised groups, teaching programs may be developed that bring the experiences and cultures of learners into the learning process. The raw material of learning may connect with learners more directly – one of the clear strengths of this kind of pedagogy. However, there is also a danger of restricting knowledge development and social access potentials. Would the learners have been better off if they had been studying the language of power or the methods of scientific reason, rather than wasting their time on stuff they already know? If the synthesis is just a deconstruction and reconstruction of existing subjectivities, identities and experiences, where does this take learners?

Synthetic pedagogy can also be criticised for placing the individual at the centre of learning processes at the expense of a balanced understanding of the complementary role of the social. Vygotsky, for instance, would claim that knowledge and learning are deeply social. A developing child's learning is shaped by the conceptual frame of reference in language they have learnt and continues to learn and the practical frame of reference of their culture.[20] The child doesn't simply invent the world for themselves. They reinvent a social world in which they are enveloped.

Synthetic pedagogy may involve lots of learner activity, but activity that does not necessarily promote deep intellectual growth. Its danger is to create 'busywork' in which the learners have their time filled with tasks but not ones that stretch their intellectual capacities or take them out of their zones of cultural comfort. At worst, this kind of pedagogy might be a waste of time. In the name of 'appropriateness' or relevance, it may serve to retard the progress of disadvantaged students. At best, it may be little more than another method for reaching traditional curricular and disciplinary ends, and this could have been achieved by means of the quicker and less circuitous route of mimetic pedagogy. Learners actively piece together bits of knowledge, but only from the clues that have been presented by the teacher. Their syntheses often amount to not much more than second-guessing what's in the teacher's head, or what will get the best marks in the test. Sometimes, it would have been easier and quicker just to have been told, learners might complain, and with some justification. Why bother with the activities when there is still really only one answer to each question, one solution to each problem and a rigidly singular body of knowledge to be learnt? And what is the role of the teacher other than a manipulative one – to lead the learners to their answers while avoiding telling them the answers directly? The cultural assumptions behind this kind of knowledge making are rarely spelt out, and favour some students ahead of others. Some learners thrive in ego-directed, individualised, inquiry learning, while others who come from different cultures of knowledge creation and whose learning styles are different, fall by the wayside.

Despite pretences to cultural openness, even the most democratic of synthetic curricula may be profoundly culture bound. The African-American educator Lisa Delpit highlights this kind of cultural disjunction at the level of classroom discourse. What appears to be an open, child-centred, democratic pedagogy is, she argues, a culture-laden imposition. In contrast to the culture of African-Americans, liberal discourse uses veiled rather than explicit commands. Under the cloak of child-centredness it is another discourse of adult authority. 'Would you like to do this next, Betty?' White children know that this means they are expected to do something. To African-American children, the White liberal teacher who operates in this discourse appears to have no authority, and the class reacts accordingly. The problem for African-American students is that they may misread the cues from the point of view of a discourse that expresses authority by other means. [*See*: Lisa Delpit on power and pedagogy.[21]]

Dimension 2: Curriculum

Synthetic curriculum gives teachers more scope to piece together learning programs at the school level. It allows them to customise the curriculum development process and create programs that fit the needs of their learners. [*See*: Bruner's theory of instruction.[22]]

The rhetoric that supports synthetic curriculum development includes terms like 'relevance', 'needs', 'diversity' and 'choice'. Curriculum is created to meet the needs of particular students in a particular community, as defined by their material, corporeal or symbolic attributes. It is also a curriculum that is more democratic. Instead of forcing official, disciplinary knowledge on learners, a locally appropriate synthesis of subject offerings and subject content is negotiated between learners, the community and teachers. This gives teachers more control over curriculum, and more responsibility, in a setup that is often called 'school-based curriculum'.[23] [*See*: There are moves that you make that you haven't given names to.[24]]

However, synthetic curriculum also attracts its critics. If the synthesis for schools in poorer communities happens to prepare students for certain kinds of non-professional destinations in the labour market, or to fill their time with 'Mickey Mouse' subjects, does this also mean that the curriculum has surrendered to inequality and doomed learners to a certain, limited kind of relevance? Does the negotiated, synthetic curriculum conspire to lower the sights of learners in the name of relevance and realism? It may engage learners, to be sure, but without extending their intellectual capacities or broadening their life horizons. Meanwhile, the privileged students in advantaged schools do subjects that will get them the marks to get into the more prestigious streams of higher education. Does this amount to school streaming by means of which curriculum participates in the reproduction of social stratification? To tread gently around the relationships of difference may seem democratic, but this kind of synthetic curriculum may also serve to rationalise social division, even when it is framed in the nicest-sounding rhetoric of relevance and diversity.

Despite the shift in the balance of agency, synthetic curriculum leaves the learner and their world substantially the way they are. Learners put things together, but only from what is given to them in the curriculum. They are active knowledge makers, but this rarely goes too far beyond second-guessing the teacher's, the curriculum's and the discipline's answers. They deconstruct knowledge but only to reconstruct it in more-or-less its received form. This is not enough for a society that now puts so much store on discernment, creativity, innovation, responsibility and participation.

Reflexivity: New Learning

As a part of the New Learning, we suggest a reflexive approach to pedagogy and curriculum that builds upon and extends the insights of mimetic and synthetic approaches. Relations between experts (teachers and authoritative texts) and novices (learners) are reconfigured. Agency is rebalanced. More than mere copying (mimesis), and more than pulling knowledge apart in order to put it back together again in much the same way that it was provided (synthesis), a reflexive approach involves backwards and forwards dialogue, a process of co-design of knowledge that draws on a range of resources and uses a broad repertoire of knowledge processes.

Dimension 1: Pedagogy

Pedagogy is series of activities consciously designed to promote learning – the creation of knowledge and the development of knowledge-abilities. Pedagogy has a characteristic dynamic that can be defined and described by tracing its sequence of movements. A distinctive beginning is followed by a middle and is drawn to a conclusion with an end, by which time a range of useful variations on a particular area of knowledge will have been explored.

Mimetic pedagogy taught facts assembled into disciplinary shape and unveiled to learners in a fixed sequence. In the 20th century, synthetic pedagogy emphasised experiential learning – through action, demonstration, experimentation or immersion – but did not necessarily allow more than one 'answer' or cater effectively to the differences amongst learners.

A reflexive pedagogy involves a more open-ended process of knowledge making, and more to-and-fro dialogue between learners and teachers, peers, parents, experts and critical friends. Reflexive pedagogy will engage learners in:

> *Activities that position the learner as the knowledge creator*. The 'answers' are not necessarily pre-determined (the 'answer' in the textbook or the teacher's head). Reflexive knowledge-creation processes link personal and local experience to more general bodies of human knowledge ('science', 'history' and the like) in such a way that all knowledge is both broadly social in its origins and new in its local application. Not only is the learner an agent in the knowledge-making process, they are always making new knowledge – the life cycle of a pond in their unique environment, or the impact of the Second World War on their family or community. The learner needs to be aware of the explicit links between their learning choices and knowledge outcomes. In this frame of reference, learners need to be understood as knowledge designers, using available conceptual and informational resources to be sure, but always remaking the world in the modulations of their own voice and connecting with their own, unique understandings and experiences. [*See*: Kress on meaning and agency.[25]]

> *Activities that are meaningful for being realistic and complex*. Reflexive pedagogy is either connected to life, or is life-like. Deep, disciplinary knowledge is most effectively acquired in contexts that focus on whole, socially realistic and meaningful tasks. In the case of literacy, for instance, learning to write is more effective when situated in the context of communication within a socially engaged community of writers and readers.

> *Activities that challenge the learner to develop more and more sophisticated and deeply perceptive conceptual schemas*. Experts in a subject domain typically organise knowledge into schemas and make sense of new information through processes of pattern recognition. Such knowledge representations are useful tools for understanding, knowledge making and knowledge communication.[26] At any particular point in a learner's development, intellectual movement involves building increasingly abstract intellectual schemas, capable of more penetrating interpretation of the world. To this end, reflexive pedagogy engages the learner as co-constructor of concepts – as definer, theory maker, critic and analyst. Applying this general principle to the domain of writing pedagogy, by way of example, writing performance is enhanced when students develop a meta-language with which to speak about their writing. This will not just be at the level of words and sentences (old-fashioned grammar), but also in

coming to terms with the overall structure of a piece of writing in such a way
that the learner can explain how the writing achieves (or does not achieve) its
communicative purpose.[27] In the cognitive development of a child, Vygotsky
regards the process of extending conceptual depth as critical. However, this
is only possible in a 'zone of proximal development'. Here, the learner is provided a conceptual scaffold whereby they can work just beyond – but never
too far beyond – their current conceptual capacity. [*See*: Vygotsky on the Zone
of Proximal Development.[28]]

Activities by which teachers and learners make explicit their thinking or knowl-
edge processes. Recent social–cognition research shows that thinking is more
efficient and effective when accompanied by processes of thinking about, mon-
itoring and reflecting upon one's own thinking.[29] Meta-cognition is the process
of thinking about thinking and meta-knowledge is the capacity to reflect upon
and articulate the processes of one's knowing.

Activities that deploy a variety of knowledge media, representing knowledge in
many ways. Until now, schooling has mostly divided modes of meaning neatly
into different subjects. Language was for text; art was for visuals. Schools
stripped away the richly multimodal life of pre-school children by separating
the mechanics of handwriting or phonics. Reflexive pedagogy uses synaes-
thesia – or mode shifting – as a pedagogical device. The new media make
this so much easier, and so much more excitingly close to the 'realness' of
contemporary media such as digital TV, video games and the Internet.[30] The
'multiliteracies' theory suggests that learner activities should involve a wide
variety of representational modes:

- *Written language*: writing (representing meaning to another) and reading
  (representing meaning to oneself) – handwriting, the printed page, the
  screen
- *Oral language*: live or recorded speech (representing meaning to another);
  listening (representing meaning to oneself)
- *Visual representation*: still or moving image, sculpture, craft (representing
  meaning to another); view, vista, scene, perspective (representing meaning
  to oneself)
- *Audio representation*: music, ambient sounds, noises, alerts (representing
  meaning to another); hearing, listening (representing meaning to oneself)
- *Tactile representation*: touch, smell and taste: the representation to oneself
  of bodily sensations and feelings or representations to others that 'touch'
  them bodily. Forms of tactile representation include kinaesthesia, physical
  contact, skin sensations (heat/cold, texture, pressure), grasp, manipulable
  objects, artefacts, cooking and eating, aromas
- *Gestural representation*: movements of the hands and arms, expressions of
  the face, eye movements and gaze, demeanours of the body, gait, clothing
  and fashion, hair style, dance, action sequences, timing, frequency, cere-
  mony and ritual. Here gesture is understood broadly and metaphorically as

a physical act of signing (as in 'a gesture to . . .'), rather than the narrower literal meaning of hand and arm movement. Representation to oneself may take the form of feelings and emotions or rehearsing action sequences in one's mind's eye

– *Spatial representation*: proximity, spacing, layout, interpersonal distance, territoriality, architecture/building, streetscape, cityscape, landscape.[31]

Activities that encourage dialogue and group collaboration. Powerful learning occurs in a context that fosters the formation of peer and broader communities for the construction of knowledge. At a localised, classroom level, this may take the form of reciprocal teaching[32] and the creation of communities of practice.[33] More broadly, learners will gain a sense of how to navigate a world in which knowledge is distributed, drawing on various sources of expertise, some of which are at hand and some at a distance. [*See*: Reggio Emilia educational principles.[34]]

A broad range of task options to cater for the diversity of learners. Not every student needs to be on the same page at the same time. They may bring different experiences to the learning and create knowledge that expresses something uniquely of who they are. Reflexive pedagogy needs to be sufficiently open to allow variations in the knowledge created, and the way in which it is created, from one learner to the next. In collaborative work, reflexive pedagogy builds on the complementarity of differences, or the knowledge that is constructed by the group, which is greater than the sum of its parts. Different students bring different perspectives, knowledge and ways of knowing to a piece of collaborative knowledge construction, contribute from their strengths, learn from others and together create knowledge that no individual could have created alone. The differences, in other words, work. And the learners see that they work.

A learning environment that gives learners continuous feedback on their learning. Reflexive pedagogy uses constant formative assessment, or assessment during the learning process which helps shape the learning process (as contrasted with only summative assessment, typically, the test at the end). Formative assessment can look like a conventional test, but often it will not: it may be a deliberate moment of self-reflection ('What do I know already, and what do I need to know to do this task?'), or more formal peer review, or comments and suggestions on work in progress sought from parents, experts or critical friends. Keys to reflexive pedagogy are regular and multiple forms of assessment and continuous feedback on learner performance – and not just tests that are left to the end. Summative tests do have a place in learning but they need to be clearly linked to the knowledge goals of the learning experiences.

Activities that represent a mix of knowledge processes. Reflexive pedagogy is a process of shunting backwards and forwards between different kinds of learning activities or 'knowledge processes'. [*See*: Cazden on pedagogical weaving.[35]]

To elaborate on this last point, in Chapter 7 we outlined a number of different ways of knowing. These knowledge processes represent a kind of conceptual

schema. By means of this schema, the flavour of a particular pedagogy can be identified, and then perhaps also justified. The schema is a way of identifying the epistemological underpinning of a particular piece of learning. [*See*: 'Learning by design knowledge processes'.[36]]

Translating this into lesson plans and learning resources, this schema can be embodied as a template or scaffold for designing, documenting and publishing learning content – not in a single, prescribed way, but in any way that suits a culture, a group of learners, a knowledge domain or a pedagogical orientation. [*See*: Learning by design in the Lanyon cluster.[37]]

This is a way of grouping the different kinds of things learners can do in order to know. They also describe the range of moves teachers can make as they design their pedagogy. These are the types of things you do, in a premeditated reflective way, which distinguish the pervasively everyday reality of 'learning' from the formal, systematic and focused form of learning that we call 'pedagogy'. [*See*: Planning strategically . . . pooling our pedagogies.[38]]

This is how the knowledge-process approach fits into the larger scheme of reflexive pedagogy:

Cultures: Some cultures, sub-cultures, institutions, situations or communities of practice may be driven more by one way of knowing than others.

Learners: Different individuals may feel more comfortable with, or inclined to use, one 'learning style' in preference to another: learning by immersion in experience; learning by getting a big-picture conceptual overview; learning by figuring out what something is for; learning whilst getting done the practical things that have to be done. These should not be the sum total of a learner's knowledge processes, but they may be their preferred starting point. [*See*: He didn't know what he didn't know.[39]]

Knowledge domains: Some content or discipline domains lend themselves more readily to one way of knowing over others: experiencing in the case of learning to read; conceptualising in the case of elementary particle physics; analysing in the case of social studies; applying in the case of learning a sport or a trade. Although these may well be the predominant emphases of a knowledge domain, they will rarely be the sum total of learning.

Pedagogies: Some forms of instructional design and teaching tend to emphasise certain knowledge processes in preference to others. Western knowledge systems vacillate between empiricist 'objectivism' (grounding in the 'facts' of external experience, the 'findings' of theory and the rights and wrongs of appropriate application) and relativist 'subjectivism' (grounding in the 'perspectives' of personal experience, the relativity of interests, and the creativity inherent in the process of applying what one knows). There have been fashions in pedagogy that have at times favoured some knowledge processes over others; there are disciplines that have traditionally relied on some knowledge processes more heavily than others; and the preferences of learners and teachers have also played a role. Teachers need to be self-aware and expert in the range of knowledge processes that produce learner transformation and ongoing performance. They need to have a wide pedagogical repertoire and to know when to plan, scaffold and deploy which knowledge process and for which learning goals.

Performance outcomes: Performance evaluation needs to ensure that learners meet agreed learning objectives and personal goals. This cannot simply be expressed as a mark, or score. Assessment needs to capture the substance of what has been learnt, demonstrating clearly the knowledge processes used.

In the educational environment of today, which we have called the New Learning, we may be reluctant to pass judgement upon cultures, learners, knowledge domains or pedagogies. Each seems to suit its own context. It is nevertheless important that teachers and learners are knowing participants in their knowing. They should be as clear about their ways of knowing (the approaches to knowing and their pedagogy) as they are about what they are knowing (their disciplines and subject matter). Not only should they become more knowing through the process of learning; they should also become more knowingly knowing – developing a parallel meta-knowledge alongside the content knowledge of the subject.

When they are clear about the ways of their knowing, they may consciously choose to broaden their repertoire of ways of knowing (or choose not to, but at least consciously choose their narrowness of focus). Reflexive pedagogy is not in itself defined by the choice to broaden the repertoire of ways of knowing. Rather, it is the business of knowingly making the choice amongst the range of possible knowledge processes. [*See*: You need to think about it! and Coaxing learners to think for themselves.[40]]

Dimension 2: Curriculum

A reflexive curriculum will allow alternative knowledge pathways to achieve social goals that are comparable, if not necessarily the same, from one learner to the next. Chapter 12 no longer has to follow Chapter 11. Reflexive curriculum, like with earlier forms, allows greater scope for teacher–learner negotiation of navigational choices at appropriate points. 'You've completed this,' the teacher may say to an individual learner or a group of learners, 'so where do you want to take this next? Here are some suggestions and advice from me.' In this way, curriculum becomes a negotiated design process. It is a dialogue between teacher-expert and learner-novice.

This may be an ideally open setup in some respects, though one which would never be without its challenges in practice. The politics of curriculum may constrain the range of realistic choices. The main arguments in the very public conversation about curriculum are about content and process. On the content side of the debate, just what should be taught, or what can learners be allowed to choose? Should all learners be exposed to the 'basics' that will help them get along in life – literacy, mathematics and science? What things should every student 'cover'? Should every learner undertake a 'comprehensive' or 'core' curriculum? Or will students be offered a broader range of curriculum choices according to their needs and interests? What is the place of multicultural education, or special education for learners with disabilities, or media education, or environmental education? None of these areas fit neatly into traditional disciplines, so are they to become extras in the form of electives or special classes? Or are the concerns of each area 'mainstreamed' into the core curriculum? If they are left to be electives, some would argue, this creates a 'smorgasbord', 'shopping mall' or 'crowded' curriculum. There can be no guarantee that anything is done in any depth and there is no common experience of learning. This produces a sense of fragmentation of knowledge and the learning community. On the other hand, 'mainstreaming' these areas of contemporary concern seems to reduce the rigour and seriousness of the traditional disciplines. Or, conversely, it can mean that the issues of concern that should be curriculum areas of their own get marginalised and lost in the mainstream curriculum.

Perhaps, however, the positions held by the proponents of the various sides of this debate may be at least to some degree reconcilable. You may be able to create alternative paths to comparable or equivalent knowledge and social ends. Comparable may not mean the same knowledge content. But to be equitable it does have to mean that the social usefulness of the learning is comparable – its capacity to open opportunities for well-paid work, to participate in civic life and to develop your person in everyday community life in ways that are different but equivalent to others. The outcomes of learning do not have to be the same to be equal. They do, however, need to be comparable.

There is also a process side to this debate. Where is curriculum made, and who makes it? Is it made in the school, or at the local, state or even national levels? Should government set 'standards' so schools all have a sense of what they should be achieving for their learners in different curriculum areas? How are these standards measured so the performance of one school can be measured against another, or even one country against another? What is the role of new technologies in learning? To what degree does this mean that curriculum can be self-managed? How does this change the role of the teacher and the nature of curriculum? And, finally, to what extent might learners themselves be co-creators of curriculum- – for instance, researching an area online and building a wiki that covers curriculum content – and thus effectively write the textbook for themselves?

In responding to these pressing questions, reflexive curriculum creates new inside/outside relations. The inside of the educational institution connects in new ways with the outside world of learner experiences and disciplinary knowledge. Education becomes ubiquitous, available anywhere and at any time, and in many forms – from online courses to help menus, and from the transformed learning relationships of the classroom to learner-directed activities increasingly located outside of the classroom itself.

Summary

Pedagogy, curriculum and education	Mimesis: The modern past	Synthesis: More recent times	Reflexivity: New learning
Dimension 1: Pedagogy	Acquiring received knowledge (facts, theories, literatures) and being able to repeat what one has acquired in a test.	'Understanding' as learners deconstruct and reconstruct knowledge and come up with the 'right' answers on 'their own'.	Shunting backwards and forwards between different things you can do to know, connecting with diverse learning experiences, creating deeper and broader knowledge, and reconnecting with the world in purposeful ways.
Dimension 2: Curriculum	Prescribed courses of study. A clear inside/outside distinction – outside knowledge copied inside the school.	School-based curriculum with a broader range of choice according to relevance, needs and diversity. Learner constructivism, the self-assembling individual knower; bringing in the outside of the school in a limited way through the recognition of differences, but often without addressing structures of inequality.	Alternative learning pathways to achieve comparable learning outcomes. Curriculum that supports a society in which agency has been rebalanced. Auto-production of knowledge; ubiquitous education.

Notes

1. Kalantzis and Cope 2005; 2006c
2. Aristotle 350 BCE-a. See extract at NewLearningOnline.com
3. St Benedict c.530 (1949). See extract at NewLearningOnline.com

4. Ali 2006, pp. 4–5. See extract at NewLearningOnline.com
5. Thayer 1928, pp. 8–9. See extract at NewLearningOnline.com
6. Confucius c.500 BCE, pp. 3–6. See extract at NewLearningOnline.com
7. Tobin, Wu and Davidson 1989, pp.72–79. See extract at NewLearningOnline.com
8. Cuban 1993, pp. 26–28. See extract at NewLearningOnline.com
9. Eco 1981; Barthes 1981
10. Kress 2000a, pp. 153–61
11. Apple 1979, pp. 63–64. See extract at NewLearningOnline.com
12. Peak 1992, pp. 58–60. See extract at NewLearningOnline.com
13. Gee 2004, pp. 9–10, 18–19; 2007
14. Kress 2003, pp. 27–34, 125–27
15. Peters and Beasley 2006
16. Apple 2006, pp. 21–26
17. Froebel 1895 (1985), pp. 244–46. See extract at NewLearningOnline.com
18. Piaget 1929 (1973); 1976
19. Thayer 1928, pp. 130–31. See extract at NewLearningOnline.com
20. Vygotsky 1934 (1986)
21. Delpit 1988, pp. 280–98. See extract at NewLearningOnline.com
22. Bruner 1966, pp. 49–53. See extract at NewLearningOnline.com
23. Boomer 1982
24. Burrows, Cope, Kalantzis, Morgan, Suominen and Yelland 2006b. See extract at NewLearningOnline.com
25. Kress 2000a, pp. 153–61. See extract at NewLearningOnline.com
26. Bransford, Brown and Cocking 2000; Pellegrino, Chudowsky and Glaser 2001
27. Cope and Kalantzis 1993
28. Vygotsky 1978, pp. 88, 89–90, 86. See extract at NewLearningOnline.com
29. Bransford, Brown and Cocking 2000; Pellegrino, Chudowsky and Glaser 2001
30. Kress 2003; Gee 2004
31. Cope and Kalantzis 2000b
32. Palinscar and Brown 1984, pp. 117–75
33. Lave and Wenger 1991; Wenger, McDermott and Snyder 2002
34. Edwards, Gandini and Forman 1993, pp. 56–58, 174–76. See extract at NewLearningOnline.com
35. Cazden 2006. See extract at NewLearningOnline.com
36. Kalantzis and Cope 2005. See extract at NewLearningOnline.com
37. See NewLearningOnline.com
38. Burrows, Cope, Kalantzis, Morgan, Suominen and Yelland 2006b. See NewLearningOnline.com
39. Ibid. See NewLearningOnline.com
40. Kalantzis and Cope 2005. See extract at NewLearningOnline.com

Chapter 9

Learning communities at work

Overview

This chapter explores different ways in which learning communities are organised. In the past, institutions of learning had neat and definable boundaries. Today, education can take place as a full-time activity at a particular time in your life and in a particular place, or as a part-time activity anytime in your life and anywhere you happen to be, such as at home or at work. Education is lifelong and life-wide.

One thing about education persists, no matter where and when it is and whatever its mode of organisation: it involves consciously designed, formally organised and explicit knowledge acquisition or knowledge making on the part of the learner. This makes it different from informal learning, which is an incidental and inevitable aspect of lifeworld experience. This chapter discusses three modes of organisation of formal learning or education.

Bureaucratic organisation of learning entails centralised and hierarchical control of the institution and the knowledge it distributes. Knowledge and authority are passed down from level to level, through chains of command – and eventually, at the bottom level, from teachers to learners in classrooms. This allows for little more than an 'assisted competence', in which teachers rely on curriculum content and disciplinary rules handed down to them, and learners rely on sources of authority to guide their action and as the source of their knowledge.

A more self-managing organisation of learning devolves a measure of self-direction to teachers in their work and learners in their knowledge making. This allows for an 'autonomous competence' in which teachers can take more control over pedagogy and curriculum, and learners can construct deeper, personal understandings of the knowledge they are presented.

Collaborative learning organisations regard themselves as knowledge-producing communities at every level, from the teachers who work collaboratively in the design of pedagogy and curriculum to the operation of the educational organisation. This organisation of learning extends as far as learners themselves, who come to understand themselves as makers of knowledge, who connect it with their own experiences and who explore applications for that knowledge in the 'real' or 'outside' world. This reflects a 'collaborative competence'.

Informal and formal learning

Educational spaces – be they formal institutions with physical locations or moments of time in which we do things that we might call 'educational' – have a peculiar manner of being in the world. They are about and for the world without quite being of that world. Their primary reason for being is outside of themselves. They refer to the world – now as mountains, then great deeds, then things to be enumerated. They shape human capacities, which can be used in the worlds of work, citizenship and community life. We call this 'exophoric' reference.

In language, an exophoric reference points out something. 'Look at that,' we might say in words, when we're both experiencing the sight of the mountain. The words mean very little without the shared experience, without our common understanding of what the sentence is pointing out. Education makes no sense until we have developed a shared understanding of what we are pointing out. Science education points out the natural world; history, the human past; literature, writing; art; visualisations; mathematics, things that can be counted, and so on. In education, we are forever referring to things in text or image that exist beyond the room or the page or the screen. This is one of the peculiar things about education. It never exists for itself. It always exists for purposes beyond itself. It points out at the world. Across the range of educational experiences, there is nothing in the world to which some bit of education does not point, or could not conceivably point. In these respects, there is nothing else quite like education. Of all the sciences and professions, education is uniquely 'other-worldly' and uniquely all-encompassing.

Learning, however, is not usually so other-worldly. It happens anywhere and everywhere, anytime and all the time, in our everyday experience of the lifeworld. It is embedded in the world with such pervasive subtlety that, much of the time, we are barely aware it is happening. After the event, we may be surprised by what we come to realise we have learnt. This becomes the stuff of judgement and intuition that lends strength to our convictions. The casual learning of the lifeworld is endogenous – intrinsic, arising from within and to be found throughout. This kind of learning is sometimes called 'informal'. It does not involve pedagogy, or curriculum, or social settings that might be called educational. This learning is amorphous. It happens in a haphazard way. It is an unorganised process – incidental and accidental, and often you end up having learnt something that you may not have expected to learn. Sometimes this learning is a roundabout process, whereby, in retrospect, you realise you could have learnt something quicker and more directly if you had been instructed. This learning is often so endogenous, so embedded in the lifeworld, that you barely realise you have learnt. It is organic, contextual, situational. The things you come to know this way mostly take the form of tacit, passive or background knowledge.

Education, by comparison, is more formal. It is deliberate, conscious, systematic and explicit. It sets out to be a more efficient way of becoming knowledge-able and acquiring specific knowledge. To this end, it is structured and goal-oriented. It is more analytical than everyday learning: abstracting, generalising and creating knowledge that will not only work for the setting in which it is found, but perhaps also be transferable from one context (the curriculum) to one or more other contexts (in the world). It is also a peculiarly focused kind of learning community, whose role, relationships and rules are directed in the first instance to learning, and only secondarily to the ends of this learning in the wider world.

Education, most importantly, is a peculiar form of learning which consciously creates an outside (the lifeworld) separate from the inside (the extra effort that is put into premeditated knowing). The two are intimately connected through lines of reference, to be sure – the methods of knowing that one may choose to use. But there are things about education that make it a different kind of learning process to everyday or casual learning in the lifeworld. One of the more obvious differences is tangible: we're in this classroom (inside) speaking about the world (outside). Another is the mode of speaking – external reference that speaks in a necessarily abstracting way about general phenomena for which there may be numerous instances. (In the lifeworld, we're mostly interested in the instances that stand before us.) It is, moreover, necessarily explicit. You can't say 'look at that' because the mountain stands before you as an awesome presence; instead, you have to name or picture or simulate what you are talking about explicitly, and this is so precisely because your referent is not there with you. The key is how you bring the outside inside. To achieve this there are specific roles, relationships (teacher/learner) and rules of engagement.

Today, the nature of inside/outside distinction that defines education is changing. In the past, it was geographically, institutionally and temporally defined. Today, education is becoming ubiquitous. A learner may be at home, engaged in an e-learning program. Or may be involved in a mentoring program at work. Or may be learning how to use a piece of software using a help menu or tutorial that is built into the software. The sites may be more dispersed, but there's something about the authority–novice relationship, about scaffolded learner activities and about the mode of inside-to-outside reference that still makes this form of learning specifically educational.

Informal learning occurs without conscious educational design. Formal learning or education is a process of learning by design. Learning communities that are specifically designed for that purpose may range from a traditional classroom to a mentoring relationship in a workplace, to an online program, to a school or a whole education system. They are unlike communities in which learning incidentally happens to occur, and this is because they establish specifically educational relationships between people and between people and knowledge. The following table characterises the differences between formal and informal learning.

	The casual, the everyday	*Knowledge and learning by design*
Knowing	Knowledge from lifeworld experience.	Science – extending the meaning of the world to include all systematic, conscious and deliberate acts of knowing.
Learning	Everyday learning, an incidental consequence of living (informal learning).	Education – pedagogy, curriculum and educational communities (formal learning).

In this chapter, we identify different kinds of learning communities, each with its own kind of inside/outside relations: bureaucratic, self-managing and collaborative. For each of these kinds of learning communities we analyse three dimensions of activity:

Dimension 1: Class management
Dimension 2: Curriculum planning and evaluation
Dimension 3: Educational leadership and management

Bureaucratic: The modern past

Social organisations are called bureaucratic when they are formally constituted with rule-bound roles and relationships and when they are hierarchically organised such that a person in a superior position in the organisation passes down orders and instructions to people in subservient positions. Earlier modern schools and education systems were mostly organised in a bureaucratic way. Some school systems, schools and classrooms remain bureaucratic in their orientation today. And even when they are not particularly bureaucratic, some educators in some learning communities, occasionally and under certain circumstances, may catch themselves at moments acting in a bureaucratic way. [*See*: Max Weber on bureaucracy.[1]]

Dimension 1: Class management

The classroom is a small learning community, or a learning community within a learning community. In schools that practise didactic teaching, the classroom is the smallest social unit of formal learning activity. It is a site of organisation that, in its own modest way, can be as bureaucratic as any larger organisation. [*See:* Rosabeth Moss-Kanter on nursery school bureaucracy.[2]]

The teacher-bureaucrat establishes a system of disciplinary roles and rules by which learners have to do certain things on the teacher's instruction (this activity, that test). This happens in part because they are themselves in a line of bureaucratic command. Power may have originated within the education system (itself a bureaucracy), and this in turn is delegated to the principal, who in turn delegates control to subject masters or division heads, who in their turn supervise the teachers under their command. This kind of bureaucratic structure applies as much to the control of knowledge as it does to person-to-person chains of command. The syllabus dictates to the textbook writer what they are to cover; the textbook writer then tells teacher what the syllabus means; the teacher tells the learners what they are to learn (facts, theories and the like), then at the last the parent, school and education system are told by the test results what the student has managed to learn. This is how the inside of the classroom connects with the outside world, via mechanisms that are by and large bureaucratic.

As the learner acquires knowledge in this setting, a kind of competence is developed, which we call 'assisted'.[3] The learner learns to know because there are lots of prompts and explicit directions around them – information provided in the textbook and the direct orders of the teacher (do precisely this first, then this next, then answer the test). Learners learn things, to be sure. But the underlying moral economy of the learning relationship is one whereby your competence depends on numerous props in the form of received knowledge, persons with knowledge authority and authoritative records of knowledge that can be looked up.

Relationships of assistance like this may be, at times, a good thing. You often need and appreciate these kinds of support when you move into a new or unfamiliar context. For a while, you need assistance, you need direct instruction, you need to be told some simple rules of what you should do until you find your feet in the new knowledge setting. You can be competent but only with assistance. And after you've been through a stage of assistance, you may be able to become a more autonomous or even collaborative member of the knowledge community.

Dimension 2: Curriculum planning and evaluation

In bureaucratic forms of educational organisation, teachers and schools have very little say over the syllabus, which is presented as a sequence of topics or areas of factual content that must be covered. In earlier modern bureaucratic education systems, you had to teach what your superiors instructed you to teach. These topics, you were told quite unambiguously, were to be covered in this particular year for this particular subject. This was standardised curriculum. If Henry Ford could say, tongue in cheek, 'Any colour you like as long as it is black' to the purchasers of his motor vehicles, so too the administrators of school systems could with similar justification say, 'Any topic you like so long as it is what we have determined to be the right topic for you to learn and the right stage in your education to learn it'.

As for evaluation, the teacher's success in a bureaucratic arrangement of curriculum is their learners' results, and this is measured by tests, sometimes devised by the teacher to fit the syllabus, sometimes externally written and administered 'standardised tests'. The more directly quantifiable the test results, the easier the test is to implement, such as multiple-choice tests with supposedly unambiguous answers. [*See*: No child left behind[4]; Kohn on standardised tests.[5]]

By means of these processes of curriculum planning and evaluation, teachers become intermediaries in a hierarchical command structure, middle managers in a system of line management.

Dimension 3: Educational leadership and management

Bureaucratic education systems were born of the same era that created the industrial system of Fordism, described earlier in this book. In the school, just as there was in any other workplace, there was a fine division of labour. In the secondary school, this particular teacher knew mathematics and so that's what they covered, and this other teacher knew history and so that's what they covered. This teacher taught this year level, separated by one-year age increments from other levels, and that teacher another. This person just did teaching, while that person, say, the principal, just did administration. Generic 'products' were created that were supposedly good for all learners, or at least all learners at a certain grade level or of a certain 'ability' – hence mass-production textbooks and mass-consumption curricula. Management was by bureaucratic command, with the sternly authoritarian principal at the head of the school. Their main function, so it appeared, was as the final arbiter of the most serious disciplinary infractions. The school was a cloistered, rule-bound place, with the look and feel of the prison or asylum, and cast in the same institutional mould. Beyond the school, the principal stood in a fixed and formal line management or hierarchical relationship to the equally bureaucratic apparatus of administration that ran the education system. [*See*: Thayer on the teacher-bureaucrat.[6]]

Self-managing: More recent times

Theories and practices of contemporary management have moved away from bureaucracy in the direction of many layers and sites of self-management.

Chapter 3 discussed this change in the larger world of work. This applies in educational organisations as much as it does elsewhere.

At the same time, the boundaries between the insides and outsides of educational institutions are blurred somewhat in the case of self-managing modes of education, both in institutional and curricular terms. [*See*: Jane Addams: Hull-House[7]; The future museum and the future school.[8]]

Dimension 1: Class management

Not only does the teacher in the self-managing classroom gain more professional independence and scope to design learning experiences for their learners. So, too, learners become progressively more independent or self-managing of their learning processes. This approach to classroom management fosters a kind of teaching and learning competence we call 'autonomous'. The autonomous teacher is in control of their own classroom. As for students, more than absorbing the facts and theories presented to them, the autonomous learner figures things out for themself. The students may come up with answers to which they have been guided, but they manage to do it more or less for themselves. Their learning is, in this sense, personalised – it is grounded in self-motivated inquiry. It might involve self-paced activity.

This stage in learning may emerge as you become more familiar with a subject or situation. You may need highly structured, scaffolded and explicit assistance at first, but once you've mastered the basics and feel comfortable, you can become a progressively more autonomous learner. Then you can take a greater personal responsibility for the next stage in your learning, and take initiative in finding facts, interpreting theories and solving problems. For the teacher, this entails a kind of classroom management style that has moved beyond direct instructional command of the bureaucratic variety. For the learners, the management of learning becomes, at least in part, a matter of self-management.

Dimension 2: Curriculum planning and evaluation

In self-managing systems of educational organisation, greater responsibility for curriculum planning and evaluation is placed upon teachers. Systems may set standards or specify essential learnings, but the business of meeting these standards is up to the teacher. Curriculum documentation planning is a task for teachers and schools. Sometimes, assessment is also school based, rather than standardised external examination. Other times, a hybrid of internal curriculum development and external assessment is used. Some of the critics of this hybrid model argue that the tail of external assessment invariably ends up wagging the dog of curriculum. It might look as though teachers have autonomy in their curriculum development, but pragmatically they have to 'teach to the test'.

Other critics of school-based curriculum argue that it loads an unrealistically onerous burden onto teachers. Workloads have grown as the old, highly scaffolded syllabus and textbook infrastructure of bureaucratic education systems has been replaced by school-based and teacher-designed curriculum. These pressures have made teaching a more challenging job. More than ever before, the breadth and depth of the teacher's knowledge and the lesson choices they make have a direct impact on levels of learner engagement and performance.

Dimension 3: Educational leadership and management

Schools are increasingly expected to be self-managing. Principals are ideally leaders who work with their communities to develop and articulate a shared vision. They build resilient self-governance structures, which give the broader community, the staff and learners a good deal of responsibility. They take financial responsibility and ask groups within the school to assume budgetary responsibility at a cost-centre level, too. With budgets devolved, or even with voucher systems in which 'clients' select the school of their choice, they are expected to work more like businesses. [*See*: Friedman on school vouchers.[9]]

Within the school, organisational arrangements are made along the lines of the post-Fordist workplaces described in Chapter 3. Teachers and educational administrators form project teams to address areas of educational need and concern. They develop an organisational culture that tends to find new entrants who will 'fit into' or be similar to the existing ethos and self-conception of the organisation (at the expense, often, of staff and faculty diversity). They require that people be multi-skilled or work cooperatively in teams. They build a common culture of learning (sometimes, too, at the expense of recognising the depth of learner diversity). They empower members of the community to take control of their own work and learning. [*See*: Caldwell and Spinks: The self-managing school[10]; Fullan on school leadership.[11]]

As schools have become self-managing organisations in these ways, educators have been provided with new opportunities. Schools have been able to differentiate themselves and provide offerings more closely aligned to the needs of local communities. [*See*: KIPP: 3D Academy, Houston[12]; El-Hajj Malik El-Shabazz Academy, Lansing, Michigan.[13]]

However, we might ask whether this has added to the burden of running the business of the institution as well as doing the teaching. Has education been too influenced by the logic of business and managerialism? A growing part of the educational process has literally been turned into a business as government reduces its overall contribution. Educators increasingly find they have to 'sell' the 'product' to fee-paying students, domestic or international. There has in recent times been a growth of partially self-funded, private and community based schools and, in some countries, the establishment even of for-profit schools built on private investment. Do we want to go back to the good old days when teaching was a quiet public service job?

Collaborative: New Learning

Today's educational institutions are increasingly required to blur the old inside/outside institutional boundaries. Education remains different to informal learning. It is by design rather than an incidental consequence of lifeworld experience. However, the inside/outside relations are being transformed. No longer are these inside/outside relations identifiable by time, space and formal institutional boundaries. Education can happen anywhere and at any time. What once were neat boundaries have been blurred by a mode of human engagement in which knowledge-abilities and bodies of knowledge are developed by teachers and learners working together and by design – explicitly, reflexively and collaboratively.

Dimension 1: Class management

More and more of the learning that once happened within the classroom is now happening beyond the classroom. This is because formal learning no longer needs to occur exclusively within the classroom. Students may leave the classroom to work whilst remaining within the orbit of class learning. If they are working online, there is no need for students to be within the four walls of the physical classroom to do it. If they are working in community linked learning activities, these may happen outside the school. [*See*: Virtual high schools.[14]]

Faced with the prospect of mixing the inside of formal learning with its geographical outside, teachers of the old school may worry about their duty of care. What could these learners get up to when they are out of the teacher's sight? The answer in part is that they can still always be within another kind of sight, if they have a mobile phone and geographical positioning system (GPS) device with them, for instance. Or what could they get up to on the Internet? What might they say publicly, and what dangers could they encounter? This time the answer, in part, is to be found in ways of tracking where learners have been on the Internet and what they have done there.

Apart from the audit trails – building systems of electronic surveillance whose lines of sight are the equivalent of the walls of the old classroom and the fences around the school – the new educational environments need to be built on unprecedented relationships of trust. Bureaucracies of old were intrinsically untrusting. Despite this, and for all their lack of trust, even in the strictest of bureaucratic regimes – the toughest of rules and the most authoritarian of teachers – some children still had enough initiative to pass subversive notes to each other, or to wag class, or to smoke in the toilets.

Teachers may need audit trails for classroom management in educational settings in which learners are not physically co-located. However, the classroom of today, virtual or physical, should be a site of learner collaborations. Not only are learners self-managing and autonomous; they can also help each other. A momentum can be achieved for each individual learner, which is at least in part derived from collective energies. As early as the beginning of the 20th century, Maria Montessori proved that this was possible from the earliest of ages.

The key to creating such an environment is to develop a group dynamic that focuses individual attention and active engagement in order to keep the learner on task for long enough to be able to learn. In the era of the new media, James Gee asks why learners who hate school will spend 50 to 100 hours playing what is in fact a highly intellectually demanding video game? They may play this on their own, but often they play this with others, who are either physically co-present or online. This is a space in which learners manage their own learning – within the framework of the scaffolds, prompts the game provides and in the case of multiplayer environments, the connections with other gamers. Gee analyses the dynamics of a variety of games, from the more benign 'civilisation' simulations to the most aggressive of 'first-person shooter' games. Common to all, he concludes, is an understanding of the nature of learning more engaging than most formal educational settings. This is particularly the case for today's learners who are used to the more active forms of engagement characteristic of today's media – being a character in the narrative, for instance, and not just a voyeur of characters created by an author. This kind of learning is highly active and intrinsically engaging. It recruits, challenges and morphs identity. Navigational paths are made by the player to the extent that the learner becomes an insider and producer, not just 'consumer'. The experience is multimodal, requiring the simultaneous or alternative manipulation of image, text, number, icon, artefact, space and sound. This learning is intrinsically critical, as the player looks for deception around every corner, or even attempts to outwit the game by breaking its rules. It is also staged, whereby mastery through levels involves a cycle of introducing challenging new skills followed by practice to make these automatic and reflexive. It is a learning environment that encourages risk in a context of safety, where real-world consequences are eliminated or reduced. It is a kind of learning that encourages the development of meta-knowledge because you get better at the game as you come to appreciate its design principles. And it is social, since you play with and against other players, and become part of a community of gamers. Conventional classrooms, Gee concludes, are for the most part not particularly good at any of these pedagogical moves.[15] [*See*: James Gee on video games and learning.[16]]

Video games are the stuff of sophisticated learning, to be sure, and this is learning quintessentially in the informal domain. Game-makers are not educators. They have nevertheless used some fundamental principles of learning to create an engaging product. However, the underlying principles they use are also the bases for effective, self-directed and collaborative learning.

Indeed, today we may well be at a turning point in education. Learners have become so used to the levels of engagement intrinsic to the new media that classroom management strategy of 'assistance' seems boringly inadequate, indeed. They have become so used to the sociability of learning environments that individualised learning seems sterile. It's not that all learning has to use the new media or require the level of investment in content development to be found in video games. Rather, education has to involve the same level of engagement with learner identity and allow as much scope for the learner in the co-design of knowledge and active collaboration in learning as to be found in contemporary cultural forms and media such as video games.

What kind of role does the teacher have in this context? If not the font of content knowledge, or the disciplinarian, or the bureaucrat, then what? Teachers are experts who design environments in which learners actively do their own learning. They build social environments within which learners can learn with and from each other as well as from the teacher. They can get learners motivated because the learning they design engages multifarious experiences and identities, and demonstrably means something in the form of potential life applications. They have deep and broad knowledge, but don't have to know everything – much can be learnt with and from the learners themselves, and their communities. However, they are intellectuals – working to build knowledge and knowledge-abilities for learners who will be connecting their learning in a world that will be very different within a decade, let alone five or eight decades hence.

Teachers are also researchers, reflexively applying and developing their 'science of education' – planning, implementing and measuring their effectiveness in terms of learner outcomes, then reworking their educational practices. They are members of a professional community, colleagues who share their professional understandings.

This is the environment, in other words, which fosters collaborative learning. Collaboration goes beyond the kind of learning that fosters autonomous, personal or individualised competence. Collaborative competence is a capacity to contribute something of your own experience and knowledge in a group learning context, where the sum of group knowledge is greater than the sum of the individual parts. Learners make the inside/outside connections, between education and the rest of their lives, and between their lives and other people's lives, in all their difference. Each learner has a sense of their unique perspective in relation to knowing, their perspective and the contribution they can make in the learning context. The learner is comfortable to be a teacher in one moment and a learner in another, and to work with people having in one moment more, and in another moment less, knowledge than them. They can work well in groups with diverse experiences and knowledge, negotiating in such a way that the differences are a strength rather than a problem. The learner is capable of offering constructive criticism and honestly articulating their without precipitating conflict. They can solve problems collectively that could not be solved individually.

Collaborative learning, in sum, creates conditions for making social knowledge. Much more than the stuff that's in your head, the key to this kind of knowledge is in the social connections – in the expertise of others that you can rely upon or the knowledge sources you can access to find things out. Knowledge-ability is a collaborative, social capacity.

Dimension 2: Curriculum planning and evaluation

Once, curriculum was a distinct space and time – a subject, course or program within a defined educational institution. Education today is becoming lifelong and life-wide. Soon, it may be ubiquitous.

Lifelong learning means that education is no longer located at a discrete time in your life, your one chance to learn, a time when you learn things that are sufficient for life. Specific skills and knowledge learnt today may be obsolete in 20 years' time, or even five years' time, and we will increasingly need to retrain and relearn throughout life. Formal educational institutions will not become less important in this new learning environment, but their role will change dramatically. No longer will they be so self-contained, so neatly separated as institutions. Future schooling will involve new locations, new relationships and new accountability measures. We may also see the emergence of hybrid mixes of formal and informal learning – in cases of the 'recognition of prior learning', for instance, in which certain levels of work or community experience are accredited as the equivalent of a formal qualification, or when formal learning supplements everyday informal learning.

In what we have called the New Learning, formal learning needs to be consciously contextualised in its informal setting. In practical terms, this means that, more than introducing the facts and theories of traditional mimetic pedagogy, formal learning needs to engage with the learner's experiential world, and to have them apply what they have learnt to that world. The domains of formal and informal learning need to be brought together more effectively in order to create the powerful and effective learning required in our contemporary world.

However, as much as we might wish to contextualise formal learning in the broader setting of informal learning, and even integrate the two so they complement each other, an important distinction needs to be maintained. Informal learning occurs without conscious pedagogical design. Formal learning is learning by design.

In the knowledge society, the role of formal learning is likely to become more significant, even if its sites and methodologies now stretch well beyond the walls of the conventional classroom – workplace training, e-learning, mentoring programs and the like.

The defining feature of formal learning is the nature of its 'design'. There is a nice ambiguity in the word 'design'. Design can denote morphology, the sense of invisible inner structures or inherent relationships of cause and effect. There is no imperative that such designs should have been consciously fabricated. Do the makers of the video games have a clearly understood and articulated theory of pedagogy when they make them? They may, but they need not, and most of the time they probably don't. The world of everyday learning is full of this kind of design. But it is designed nevertheless, if only from the point of view of questions we might want to ask after the event such as 'How did this learning occur?'

However, there's another important sense of the word 'design', and that is the act of planned and systematic fabrication, both mental and physical. Learning 'by design' refers to the agency and premeditation that is characteristic of education. These designs are the stuff of the self-conscious pedagogical moves, curriculum frameworks and organisational forms of education. They are also the stuff of specifically educational artefacts – curriculum plans, learning resources, assessment instruments, e-learning systems and the like.

In everyday parlance, we call the domain of formal learning 'education'. To be sure, education is built on the very ordinary (and extraordinary) fact of learning that is at the core of our natures. In its most powerfully effective moments, it builds upon and integrates itself with the learners' experiences in the domain of informal learning. Education, however, is different from everyday, informal learning insofar as it is deliberate – learning in a relatively conscious, systematic and explicit way. It sets out to be efficient; since the end is learning, the processes of engagement are designed to meet that end via as direct a route as possible. And its reference point is primarily exophoric. Although it is absolutely in the world, in an important sense education is not of the world. Education is not an end in itself. It is for use in the 'outside world' and refers to the 'outside world' as exactly that, positioning itself as externally representative and reflective of the world.

In each of these respects, everyday learning is different from education. Everyday learning happens in ways that are relatively unconscious, haphazard and tacit. It happens in ways that are often circuitous, incidental, fortuitous or even accidental. Everyday learning is deeply embedded within the world. The distinguishing feature of education (and curriculum and pedagogy) is that learning happens by design.

So what do we do when we design, implement and evaluate curriculum for the New Learning? One distinctive aspect of the New Learning may be to create carefully customised, student-centred, context-sensitive learning ecologies, whereby every group of learners feels that they belong to their learning environment because it connects with their needs and experiences, and every learning ecology is unique. The uniqueness of each learning environment emerges from the particular mix of experiences, identities and agendas brought to the learning mix. The balance of knowledge-making agency in such environments locates the teacher as the first amongst equals. The learning relationships – learner-to-learner and learner-to-teacher – become dialogical and collaborative, and in these senses more in sympathy with new media environments and knowledge systems. Curriculum design and evaluation are driven, not by external bureaucratic requirements so much as energetic horizontal communities of knowledge production and peer review.

An emerging feature of the emerging education scene is its 'ubiquity' – education that is available anywhere and any time, just enough and just in time. The new media create unprecedented opportunities for ubiquitous education. They allow greater accessibility for people who may have in the past found formal education to be too expensive of time or financial resources. It can allow hybrid or blended delivery whereby students switch from one mode to another as the need arises or their inclinations take them.

Digital learning management systems are not necessarily the answer. The medium is not necessarily the message. In fact, many e-learning systems attempt to replicate traditional teaching practices and relations – here's your topic, read about it online, talk about it in a chat room, now do the test and the machine will tell you your score. But e-learning does not have to be this way, a shadow of didactic teaching and minetic pedagogy. The participatory web of the Internet produces a different type of sociality to legacy media systems, and one that is very well suited to the creation of innovative pedagogies and more powerful learner engagement. Internet ecologies such as MySpace, YouTube, Facebook, Blogger, Flickr, Jigsaw and wikis are built on strongly collaborative social networks. E-learning ecologies and social networking tools provide means to support peer learning within such environments. 'Co-creation' is a key in the new online environment – energetic horizontal communities that aren't constrained by rank. The logic of the co-construction of knowledge is a keystone both to the knowledge economy and the new education that will support it.[17]

The transformation, in fact, runs as deep as the transformation of the knowledge systems in the broader society. Online environments are frequently driven by lateral rather than vertical energies. They entail collaborative knowledge construction rather than content transmission from authoritative sources. These reflect deeper changes in knowledge ecologies outside of education, including, for instance, the 'learning organisation', which is capable of creating knowledge and learning as an integral part of the organisation's development.[18] [*See*: The School of the Future.[19]]

How do we know what has been learnt in these new environments? How do we assess student learning? A thorough and holistic approach to assessment may include some or all of the following. As a general rule, the more multifaceted the assessment the more valid (relevant to the intended outcomes of the learning) and reliable (a trustworthy measure of actual outcomes) it will be:

Formative or diagnostic assessment: Finding out what a learner already knows and doesn't know in relation to a planned area of learning.

Portfolio assessment: Keeping a record of what students create during the learning process, with teacher, peer or parent review and rating.

Summative assessment: A specially designed assessment task at the end of a period of learning, to find out what individual students or whole groups of students have learnt. This could range from a short, in-class test to external assessment.

Program evaluation: Examining the effectiveness of a curriculum or a learning organisation in achieving educational standards and meeting learner needs.

This offers an evidence-base, which provides learners with feedback to assist them in the learning process, and for teachers and educational institutions, information on how well both teachers and learners are doing. This information is a crucial part of the accountability of educators to learners and the larger community.

What are the principles that should underlie assessment practices? Following the contours of contemporary assessment theory, three foundational elements are present in effective assessment:

1. *Knowledge representations*: A cognitive model of how learners represent knowledge, which reflects competence in a domain of learning. This is the measure of what constitutes achievement and what is assessable in a particular domain.
2. *Observable tasks*: Activities that can demonstrate levels and forms of learner competence.
3. *Interpretation*: Assessing the quality of student responses to tasks and the thinking that underlies it, using a rubric based on the knowledge representations.[20]

Today, these are the foundational principles that underlie valid (fair) and reliable (consistent) summative, or end-of-course assessment. In the near future, however, we envisage assessment that is much more closely connected to learning, assisted by the new information technologies. Formative assessment will provide learners with immediate feedback on their learning – some of which will be provided by machines in e-learning environments. Much more valuable feedback, however, is likely to be available to learners when lateral 'social networking' energies are unleashed, not only by the affordances in web-based working environments, but by the horizontal energies of reflexive pedagogies. Imagine a learning environment in which every task and every piece of student work is undertaken for, and anticipating feedback from, multiple sources: teacher, peers, parents, experts, critical friends and self (thinking aloud in moments of self-reflection and self-assessment).

With so much accessible formative data and the possibility of machine aggregation and interpretation of this data, we might even be able to do away with conventional summative assessments. We might, in other words, be able to make exams redundant precisely because we have so much, and such rich data representing the reflexive relationships between every learner and the feedback they get. We will be able to assess the progress the learner makes in their learning, with the assistance of the feedback they have been given. Every student will have an instantly accessible record of their own progress, complete with an explanation of what that progress demonstrates – and so will teachers and parents. Teachers and education systems will be able to aggregate this data to see how particular demographic groups, and schools and classes are progressing.

Dimension 3: Educational leadership and management

The organisation of education today requires that learning communities go beyond a uniformly shared vision, to a productive diversity of the variety we discussed in Chapter 3. This approach to management brings differences together into a negotiated common ground of mutual learning. Such learning organisations do not demand new teachers and learners 'fit' into the educational culture beyond a commitment to share their experiences and learn from each other in a collaborative way. Their organisational ethos is based on recognition of diverse knowledge and experiences, establishing lateral relationships of complementarity in a collaborative learning context and extending one's knowledge and learning repertoire. Differences in learner outcomes are measured, not according to fixed standards, but through the comparability of their effects in terms of levels of access to material resources, social participation and personal fulfilment.[21]

Today's learning communities also need to regard themselves as organisations in which 'knowledge management' is pivotal. Knowledge management adds system and rigour – active learning by design – to the knowledge that is implicit and informally learnt within organisations.[22] It involves transforming personal knowledge into common knowledge, implicit and individual knowledge into explicit and shared understandings and everyday common sense into systematic designs. [*See:* Using action research to improve education.[23]]

Teaching in modern times has been a talking profession, at least so long as the primary information architecture was the four-walled classroom. What happens in the classroom is ephemeral in the sense that the spoken word disappears once spoken. Except for the learners' marks, the classroom is a private, even secret place because the door is closed. There is not a lot of professional sharing. However, self-paced and e-learning environments require the teacher to document more, to record learning processes explicitly. And once they do this, teachers can share their lesson plans or learning resources with other teachers. Teaching becomes a more collaborative profession. The school becomes a knowledge-producing community. Using the new digital media, in particular, educators can share their pedagogical choices, document their learning programs, share effective practices and write up jointly developed learning community goals. Students can themselves participate in this collaborative, knowledge-building culture, by digitally publishing portfolios of the work they have created, either individually or collaboratively – such as a course wiki to which students have contributed different components, or a digital portfolio. The result will be greater transparency and accountability amongst those who share responsibility for education. In this way, the traditionally closed door of the classroom is thrown open, and its primarily oral – and thus its private and ephemeral – character is transformed. Its knowledge-producing actions and learning processes are recorded in such a way that they become publicly visible to peers, to the educational organisation, to parents and communities.

At the level of whole-school organisation, it is the project of knowledge management to ensure that collaboration is institutionalised and that knowledge sharing does occur. As a result, wheels are not needlessly reinvented. Lessons from mistakes are learnt once. And the knowledge of the organisation or community is not dangerously depleted when a key person departs. In short, the extra work of organising knowledge should create less. This is the basis of the 'learning organisation' the sum of whose knowledge is greater than the individual components of knowledge in the heads of individuals. [*See*: We talk about teaching, not trivia;[24] and The role of collegial support.[25]]

Summary

Learning communities at work	Bureaucratic: The modern past	Self-managing: More recent times	Collaborative: New learning
Dimension 1: Class management	Towards assisted competence.	Towards autonomous competence.	Towards collaborative competence.
Dimension 2: Curriculum planning and evaluation	Standardised.	Personalised.	Multifaceted and holistic.
Dimension 3: Educational leadership and management	Line management.	Vision, culture and 'fit'.	Blurred institutional boundaries; education spreads its wings.

Notes

1. Weber 1922 (1968), pp. 956–58, 999–1001. See extract at NewLearningOnline.com
2. Moss-Kanter 1972, pp. 186–212. See extract at NewLearningOnline.com
3. Cope, Kalantzis, Luke, Morgan, McCormack, Solomon, Slade and Veal 1993; Cope and Kalantzis 1997a
4. President Signs Landmark No Child Left Behind Education Bill, Hamilton High School Hamilton, Ohio, 8 January 2002. http://www.whitehouse.gov/news/releases/2002/01/20020108–1.html. See extract at NewLearningOnline.com
5. Kohn 2000, pp. 17–18. See extract at NewLearningOnline.com

6. Thayer 1928, pp. 14–16, 165. See extract at NewLearningOnline.com
7. Addams 1990, pp. 61–64, 244. See extract at NewLearningOnline.com
8. Sotiriou 2006. See extract at NewLearningOnline.com
9. Friedman 1975, pp. 273–81. See extract at NewLearningOnline.com
10. Caldwell and Spinks 1988, pp. 5, 71, 88. See extract at NewLearningOnline.com
11. Fullan 2003, pp. 1–3. See extract at NewLearningOnline.com
12. http://www.kipphouston.org/.kipp/Default_EN.asp. See extract at NewLearningOnline.com
13. http://shabazzlearning.com. See extract at NewLearningOnline.com
14. Chaika 1999. See extract at NewLearningOnline.com
15. Gee 2003
16. Gee 2006. See extract at NewLearningOnline.com
17. Knobel and Lankshear 2007; Yelland 2006
18. Senge 1990
19. Hurdle 2006
20. Kalantzis, Cope and Slade 1989; Mislevy 2006, pp. 257–305; Pellegrino, Chudowsky and Glaser 2001
21. Cope and Kalantzis 1997a.
22. Kalantzis 2004, pp. 1827–33; Cope and Kalantzis 2002, pp. 1–15
23. Kemmis and Wilkinson 1988, p. 21. http://education.qld.gov.au/students/advocacy/equity/gender-sch/action/action-cycle.html. See extract at NewLearningOnline.com
24. Burrows, Cope, Kalantzis, Morgan, Suominen and Yelland 2006.
25. Burrows, Cope, Kalantzis, Morgan, Suominen and Yelland 2006.

Conclusion

Futures of education

Changing society, New Learning

The changes occurring in the world around us are pervasive. The challenges we face as educators, profound.

Take something so ordinary and pervasive as narrative. In everyday family and community life, the narratives of gaming have now become an even bigger business than Hollywood. From the most impressionable of ages, children of the Nintendo, PlayStation and X-Box generation have become inured to the idea that they can be characters in narratives, capable of determining or, at the very least, influencing the story's end. They are content with being no less than actors rather than audiences, players rather than spectators, agents rather than voyeurs, users rather than readers of narrative. Not content with programmed radio, these children build their own play lists on their iPods. Not content with programmed TV, they read the narratives of DVD and Internet-streamed video at varying depth (the movie, the documentary about the making of the movie) and dip into 'chapters' at will. Not content with the singular vision of sports telecasting of mass TV, they choose their own angles, replays and statistical analyses on interactive digital TV. And not content with being mere receivers of media content, they are creators and sharers of identity laden content, at MySpace, Facebook, YouTube, or on blogs.[1]

Old logics of teaching and learning are profoundly challenged by a social context in which these changes in media are mere symptoms of a broader and deeper change. Old-style schools are bound to fall short, not only for disappointing young people whose expectations of engagement are greater, but also for failing to direct their energies to developing the kinds of persons required for the new domains of work, citizenship and personality. At work, school leavers will find that the crude command structures that their parents experienced in the past are being replaced by a more sophisticated cultural co-option – the co-option of teamwork, vision, mission and corporate culture, in which everyone is supposed to personify the enterprise, to think and will and act the enterprise. 'Any colour you like, so long as it's black,' said that heroic command personality, Henry Ford. Not only did he order his workers around, and get away with it. He also ordered around the consumers of his products. Today, there can be no entrepreneurial heroism because the customer is always right and products and services need to be customised to mesh with the multiple subjectivities of niche markets – the big SUVs, the smart sports cars, the spacious family cars, the environment-friendly hybrid cars, the micro cars for crowded cities, cars of any hue and trim – so many permutations, in fact, that sometimes an individual order has to be placed before a vehicle is manufactured. This is why Fordist mass production is being displaced by today's mass customisation.

Whether it be in the domain of work, governance or cultural life, the command society is giving way to the society of reflexivity in which agency is more evenly balanced. Or so we might say in moments of strategic optimism. In moments of pessimism, we might experience these same phenomena as fragmentation, ego-centrism, randomness, ambiguity and anarchy. And when this pessimism turns to fear, we might want to return to earlier, simpler command structures – in nations, workplaces, households and schools.

Pessimists and optimists alike might agree that we are in the midst of a transformation that is creating new forms of subjectivity and new kinds of personality. These transformations can be viewed both from within a systems perspective and beyond it. From a systems point of view, these are the kinds of governance structures, the kinds of organisations and the kinds of people required today, for the most conservative, small government and pro-enterprise points of view. We hear these points of view expressed in the public rhetoric of innovation and creativity, the knowledge economy and individual autonomy and responsibility. Notwithstanding the high-sounding rhetoric, left to run their course these transformations may only legitimate and even exacerbate systemic inequities.

History, however, is more open-ended than that. Inevitably, human systems are so complex that they allow possibilities outside the scope anticipated by their progenitors and apologists. For every moment that the ideologues of small government succeed in shrinking the state, there is another moment in which people learn the civilities of self-government in their various communities of practice; for every moment that command structures in workplaces are replaced by structures asking workers to 'fit' in with the workplace culture, there is another moment in which people acquire the collaborative competencies of socially directed work; for every moment that compliant personalities are replaced by the egocentrism of individualism, there is another moment in which new relationships of co-dependence and mutual reliance are created and the bonds of sociability are extended and deepened. Whatever the domain, there is a shift in the balance of power and in the moral economy of agency that favours egalitarianism and liberty. And this, despite and beyond prevailing systems and structures of power. From this something genuinely new could emerge.

The trends, however, are always contradictory. Just as agency is passed over to users and consumers, power is also centralised in ways that become more disturbing with time. The ownership of commercial media, communications channels and software platforms is becoming alarmingly concentrated.[2] Besides, to what extent are the new media, such as games, an escape from reality? And for every dazzling new opening to knowledge and cultural expression in the new 'gift economy' of the Internet (whereby content can be accessed for free) – and Google is a prime example of this – there are disturbing new possibilities for the invasion of privacy, cynically targeted advertising and control over knowledge sources and media.[3]

Meanwhile, differences that had been hidden away in private lives are now being exposed more publicly. Everything has become a potential subject for media discussion. Discourses that were once confined to the private domain – the sexual lives of public figures, discussion of repressed memories of child abuse and intimate moral struggles about life, sexuality and relationships, for instance – are now made public in all their sometimes compelling, other times lurid detail. Important issues are at stake, and often they need a public airing. In more and more ways people speak publicly to their identities – when, for example, something once so introspective as a diary becomes a web log for the world to see. Some of this can be regarded as cynical, manipulative, invasive and exploitative, as discourses of private life and community are appropriated to serve commercial ends. At other times, it can be regarded as an opportunity to air matters of moral inclination and concern that were once suppressed, repressed or ignored. The result is that a thousand and more identities find voice and a thousand lives make their differences poignantly felt.

Against the comforting simplicities and certitudes of the older modernity, some fear irretrievable social fracturing; the creation of worlds unto themselves without any of the former geographical constraints and assurances of locality. Others see a lowering of barriers to access, where more and more communities can become media creators rather than media consumers. The auto-creative potentials of the digital media and the 'semantic web' have been opened by the Internet. These potentials create new economies of cultural scale, geographies of distribution and balances of cultural power. The costs of owning the means of production of widely communicable meaning have been hugely reduced and, with this, the small and the different have become as viable as the large and the generic.[4]

With this, we witness a burgeoning of cultural diversity in any number of guises – more and more finely grained ethnic diasporas, professional associations, coalitions of expertise and affinity groups of fad and fetish. The tools of self-creation allow lifeworlds a degree of autonomy not possible in the earlier media regime. Over time, these communities diverge – by way of knowledge, style and modes of representing the world. The challenge is to make space available so that different lifeworlds can flourish; to create spaces for community life whereby local and specific meanings can be made. To harness the new forms of agency for scientific breakthroughs, economic solutions and cultural creativity that produces cohesive sociality and sustainable communities.

In a bleak view of these differences, they remain as that; as fragmented and fragmenting. Cultures in the plural make for a voluntary form of apartheid spurred on by isolationisms and separatisms of one kind or another; from the ethno-nationalisms of the post-Cold War world, to drop-out communities and new-age alternatives, to defeated, defiant and lawless ghettoes. And insofar as persons invariably live in many, now deeply personalised, sub-cultures, personality heads in the direction of a metaphorical schizophrenia. Underlying all of this is an increasingly fractured and de-centralised consciousness. The individual subject of an early modernity often found themselves submitting to the authority of mass culture. They were a person more spoken to than speaking. However, the rise of the new more active subject is also accompanied by cultural relativism, with all the chaos and amorality of 'anything goes' and 'live and let live'. In the world of high culture, this form of consciousness is often labelled 'postmodern'.

The moment one allows more scope for agency, one invariably finds oneself facing layer upon layer of difference – in workplaces, markets, self-governing communities, amongst, between and within personalities. One discovers agencies actually existing in the massively plural, and not in the fabrications and falsifications of the command society with its one-people, one-state nationalism, its regime of mass production and uniform mass consumption, and the pretensions to cultural homogeneity of the old mass media and mass culture. These go far deeper than simple demographics, uncovering deep and ever-diverging differences of experience, interest, orientation to the world, values, dispositions, sensibilities, social languages and discourses. And insofar as one person inhabits many lifeworlds (home, professional, interest, affiliation), their identities are multilayered.

If diversity is a fundamental fact of our moment in modern times, an integrating inclusiveness is a necessary antidote to this fragmentation. Diversity may become the paradoxical basis for cohesion. In personal life, the place to start is with the person as a social being, and the integrating potential of multilayered identities. This is a strategically optimistic response to the end of mass culture and the increasing fragmentation of community.

The more autonomous lifeworlds become, the more people seem to be free to move in and out; whole lifeworlds go through major transitions; there is more open and productive negotiation of internal differences; there are freer external linkages and alliances. The more scope we are given to be ourselves, the more different we make our selves. The more different we can be, the more sociable we become. The more we are allowed to be the source of our selves, the more we connect with others.

This logic of divergence linked to tighter and more expansive sociability has become a paradoxical universal, a distinctive characteristic of our times. The kind of person who can live well in this world is someone who has acquired the capacity to navigate from one domain of social activity to another, who is resilient in their capacity to articulate and enact their own identities, who can find ways of entering into dialogue with, and learning, new and unfamiliar social languages and who is able to reinvent themself as contexts and circumstances change.

One of the fundamental challenges schools face today is to create the conditions or learning that support the growth of this kind of person, a person comfortable with themself, as well as flexible enough to collaborate and negotiate with others who are different; to work on common projects and forge shared interests, and able to learn and to transform themself in new and changing situations.

In a world of endemic divergence, the old, one-size-fits-all, on-the-same-page curriculum is no longer a good idea. Heritage modern schooling did all it could to remove or ignore differences. With the teacher at the front of the room and the test at the end of the term, everyone had to be working on the same thing at the same time. This was the communicative basis of its key technologies of homogenisation – separatism (by age, 'ability', culture, language, social destiny) and assimilation (remember this stuff, demonstrate you can think this way, become the kind of person we want you to be).

Look at all the differences in school today, so visible and so insistent: material (class, locale), corporeal (age, race, sex and sexuality, and physical and mental characteristics) and symbolic (culture, language, gender, family, affinity and persona). The New Learning has little alternative but to recognise the social realities of pluralism and develop strategies for inclusion that are without prejudice to that diversity.

Using digital media, for instance, all learners do not have to be on the same page. At any one time, each can be doing what is best for them given what they already know. And how can a teacher know what a learner knows? A much more graphic, realistic and detailed view is possible in a digital environment in which actual performance is recorded in portfolios rather than by means of bald test scores. Complex, multi-perspectival assessment is possible, which continuously feeds back into the process of appropriate learning design for that student. If students are knowledge creators, they can be asked to link the particularities of their life experiences closely into the knowledge that is being made. By this means, their knowledge making becomes re-voicing, not replication. Students can also work together more readily in digital sharing environments. Lesser or greater contributions are visible for what they are (and this could be appropriate), and differential perspectives and knowledge can be valued as the basis for collective intelligence.

Belonging and transformation

A transformative, inclusive, reflexive New Learning starts with the facts of diversity. It allows you to be yourself. But it also creates conditions in which you can become more than yourself. Here, two fundamental conditions of learning come into play: belonging and transformation.

Belonging occurs in an educational setting when formal learning engages with the learner's lifeworld experience, when their learning interacts with the learner's identity. Such learning builds on their knowledge, experiences, interests and motivations. In any learning community, the range of differences is broad, and this is because the everyday lifeworlds from which students come are always varied. Successful engagement must recognise difference and actively take account of the diverse identities of learners.

Our challenge as educators is to identify the kinds of educational environments in which these conditions of learning are met. In order to learn, the learner has to feel that the learning is for them. The learner has to feel a sense of belonging in the content, and that they belong in the community or learning setting; they have to feel at home with that kind of learning or way of getting to know the world. In other words, the learner's subjectivity and identity must be engaged. Learners have to be motivated by what they are learning. They need to be involved as interested parties. They have to feel as though that learning is for them. The learning has to include them. And if they are learning in a formal educational setting such as a school, they also have to feel a sense of belonging in that social and institutional context. The more a learner 'belongs' in all these senses, the more thet are likely to learn.

Belonging to learning is founded on three things: the learning ways, the learning content and the learning community. From the learner's point of view, the 'learning ways' question is: 'Do I feel comfortable with this way of knowing the world?' (Or, do I feel at home with this style of thinking or way of acting? Do I feel it can work for me? Do I know it can help me know or do more?). The learning content question is: 'Do I already know enough about an area of content to want to know more?' ('Do I already know so much about something that I naturally want to know more?' Or 'Has my appetite been sufficiently whetted by what little I already know to want to know more?'). And the learning community question is: 'Do I feel at home in this learning environment?' (Or 'Do I feel sufficiently motivated to take on the learning tasks required by this environment as my own and feel safe enough in this space to be able to risk moving into new domains of knowledge and action?')

The learner's subjectivity, however, is always particular, and it is this particularity that must be engaged. Here, the concept of 'difference' is helpful because it highlights some dimensions of learner particularity. Differences arise from the everyday lived experience that the learner brings to a learning setting. It is the person they have has become through the influence of family, local community, friends, peers and the particular slices of popular or domestic culture with which he or she identifies. It is a place in which the learner's everyday understandings and actions seem to work, and so much so that their active participation is almost instinctive – something that requires not too much conscious or reflective thought. The lifeworld is what has shaped the learner. It is what has made the learner who they are. It is what they like and unreflectively dislike. It is who they are.

The underlying attributes of lifeworld difference form the basis of identity and subjectivity. These attributes are the fundamental bases of a learner's sense of belonging in an everyday or formal learning setting, and their levels of engagement. We are creatures of subjectivity, identity and motivation – intuitive, instinctive and deeply felt. The lifeworld is the ground of our existence, the already learned and continuously being-learnt experience of everyday life. This lifeworld is deeply permeated by difference; in fact, we live in a myriad of diverging and interacting lifeworlds. The individual is uniquely formed at the intersection of many group identities; they are is a unique concatenation of many group identities, and lives in and through multiple or multilayered identities.

In all its variability, the lifeworld is the first site of learning, not only in the chronological sense (babies and young children), but also in the extended sense that it is always prior to, or the foundation of, any education in the formal sense, or learning by design. It is from the start and always remains a place of deep learning, albeit in primarily amorphous, unorganised and endogenous ways. The lifeworld is the ground of all learning, including the secondary processes of learning by design. As learning occurs through engagement, that engagement must be with learners in their lifeworld reality, a reality that is marked by extraordinary difference.

Education, however, is not simply about recognising and affirming difference. There's much more to effective education-for-diversity than that. Staying where you are is not education. Education is a journey away from the learner's comfort zone, away from the narrowness and limitations of the lifeworld. As much as education needs to affirm identity and create a sense of belonging, it is also a process of travelling away from the familiar, everyday world of experience. This journey is one of personal and cultural transformation. Education takes the learner into new places, and along this journey acts as an agent of personal and cultural transformation.

Transformation occurs when a learner's engagement is such that it broadens their horizons of knowledge and capability. Effective learning takes the learner on a journey into new and unfamiliar terrains. However, in order for learning to occur, the journey into the unfamiliar needs to remain within a zone of intelligibility and safety. At each step, it needs to travel just the right distance from the learner's lifeworld starting point.

This educational journey takes two paths, along two axes. Both of these journeys are away from who you are, and sometimes in unsettling ways. The first is a depth axis, or learning what's not immediately or intuitively obvious from the perspective of everyday lived experience. This may challenge everyday assumptions – that the Earth is flat, for instance, or that certain unreflectively held values such as racism or sexism are socially sustainable. The second is a breadth axis, by which you travel to unfamiliar places in the mind and perhaps also in reality. This is a kind of cross-cultural journey, and deeply so because it involves a genuine crossover. The place to which you travel becomes part of you, an addition to your repertoire of life experience, indeed another aspect of your identity.

These journeys can be understood as narratives of sorts. They are life narratives of self-transformation and growth. But they are only that when the learner is safely and securely in the centre of the story. Retrospectively, the learning story runs like this: who the learner was, where they went, the things they encountered, and what, as a consequence of their learning, the learner has (knowingly) become. In this story, learning is the key thread in what turns out to be a kind of cultural journey.

If the lifeworld is the place of belonging, the place from which learners depart, the new world of knowledge might be called the 'transcendental' – a place above and beyond the commonsense assumptions of the lifeworld.[5] The learning journey from the lifeworld to the transcendental takes the learner into realms that are necessarily unfamiliar but never too unsettling in their unfamiliarity. Education will not result in learning if the landscape is unseeable, unthinkable, incomprehensible, unintelligible, unachievable. Learners must travel into cultural territories that take them outside of their comfort zones, but never to the point at any particular stage of the journey where the learner finds themself in places that are so strange as to be alienating. The journey will involve risk, but the risk can only be productive if the learning environment feels safe, if it is a place in which the learner feels they still belong, even if only as a traveller. The learner needs scaffolds – learning prompts or support – which reassure them as the learner faces the risks of alienation and failure in the realm of the unfamiliar. Vygotsky calls this the 'zone of proximal development'.[6]

Educational settings ideally scaffold or provide support as learners move into a zone of partial but as-yet-incomplete intelligibility. With all the motivation in the world to learn Chinese, there's no point for a beginner to start in the third year of the program, or for an aspiring mathematician to try to learn calculus before arithmetic. This brings us back to the first learning condition, the need to engage with identity. The second learning condition, transformation, now tells us that this engagement has to be achievable as well as aspirational. It also reminds us of the necessity to engage with the complex particularity of different learners, as well as the educational necessity to a journey into strange places, adding something genuinely new to that particularity. For every student in every learning setting, the comfort zone of proximal development is going to be different. Herein lies the key dilemma of the whole educational project.

Those who succeed best in a particular learning setting will do so because that setting is right for people like them. The level of risk in moving into a new area of learning is one they are comfortable to take. Those who do not succeed so well, find that they struggle when the distance between who they are and what they are learning is too great, when they don't feel they belong in the content or the setting and when the risks of failure outweigh the benefits of engagement.

All too often, however, learning seems to gel for some kinds of students (such as the 'mainstream' learner, attuned to dominant educational values) and not for others. The challenge for educators – learning designers – is how to make learning gel for each and every student.

And why do we need to learn? What is the role of formal, institutionalised learning? Why is the educational project so important to us? Why do we bother with learning by design when the lifeworld is already so profoundly a site of learning? The answers to these questions are as much practical as they are idealistic. Education can transport you into new lifeworlds. It provides access to material resources in the form of better-paid employment; it affords an enhanced capacity to participate in civic life; it promises personal growth. Upon education rests one of the key promises of modern societies. The world is tragically unequal, and for practical purposes people much of the time regard this inequality as inevitable. Education, however, assures us equity. Inequality, in this limited view, is not unjust because education affords all people equivalent chances.

There is no equity in education, however, unless the two learning conditions are met. Learning has to engage with students' identities, and these identities must be recognised as different. It must take people into unfamiliar places, and at each stage in the journey these places have to be unfamiliar in just the right measure. That measure can only be based on precisely who the learner is – all the lifeworld attributes combine to define who they are as an individual. Success is achieved when the measure of distance is appropriate to the learner. Failure occurs when the measure of distance is inappropriate to the learner. If the distance between the lifeworld and the learning designs is too great, the educational effort will be misdirected, compromised or ineffectual. And if there is no distance between the lifeworld and what is to be learnt, learning will be diminished or illusionary. The distance between the lifeworld and what is to be learnt must be productive.

Belonging is a generalised condition of learning, whether learning is endogenous to the everyday lifeworld, or whether it is by conscious design. In the case of the former, belonging usually comes easily. In the case of learning by design, belonging needs to be a conscious endeavour. Spaces of formal learning are strangely not of the world, and for some learners at some times, they prove just too strange.

Transformation, of course, is not the exclusive preserve of education. It may occur in the lifeworld when, for instance, surroundings radically change. Migration is a case in point, as are other willed or unwilled, traumatic or relief-giving changes in lifeworld circumstances. Transformational learning in these cases is incidental to circumstantial change.

Elements of a science of education

The questions we face as educators today are big, the challenges sometimes daunting. How do we, for instance, ensure that education fulfils its democratic mission, through quality teaching, a transformative curriculum and dedicated programs that address inequality? Targeting groups disadvantaged and 'at risk' is an essential responsibility of educators, not on the basis of moral arguments alone, but also because of the economic and social dangers of allowing individuals and groups to be excluded.

The issue, however, is not merely one of quantity, of simply providing more education for more people. While many nations persevere with educational structures founded in the 19th century or earlier, the new economy demands different and creative approaches to learning. Schools, at least in their traditional form, may not dominate the educational landscape of the 21st century. Neat segregations of the past will crumble. Givens will give. A radical restructuring of learning is required to prepare students, workers and citizens of the 21st century.

Are we, as educators, well enough equipped to answer the questions and address the challenges? Does our discipline provide us with the intellectual wherewithal to face changes of these proportions? Our answer is that it could, but only if we conceive education to be a science as rigorous in its methods and as ambitious in its scope as any other.

We use the word 'science' in quite a pointed way, as some proponents of 'educational science' today refer to narrow forms of measurement (What do the tests results show?) rather than bigger social, political or ethical questions (Should we change the tests?). Their interest is to measure 'objectively' changes in learners' test scores after some modification in one group of learners' curriculum, by comparing the results with another ('control') group that has not been through the same program. The model used by these proponents of 'educational science' is drawn from what they understand, too simplistically at times, to be the methodology of medical science, whereby one statistically significant group is given a new pill, and another group is given a placebo. None of the participants is told which group they are in, and so the results are 'scientific'. By this kind of 'scientific' methodology, the most didactic teaching and mimetic pedagogy can be shown to work. The larger question of whether it is appropriate to our times, however, is not asked. In this educational paradigm, scientific evidence means narrow empiricism.[7] It is science in a certain, methodological sense – a business of careful observation and interference. But in a broader sense, it is not necessarily good science. It will measure various classroom inputs in relation to learner outputs in tests in an empiricist and instrumentalist kind of way without critically examining the broader frame of reference of the classroom in a changing society, or the relevance of the outputs. For its methodical procedures, it calls itself science. But what of a science which attempts no more than minor re-engineering of an educational system? What if education is in need of a more thoroughgoing overhaul?

One possible rejoinder is that education can never be like a science – the model of controlled experimentation offered by laboratory natural science is unachievable in education and if anything unethical.[8] We're dealing with human beings with interests, desires, identities and agency, not just brains and clinically isolatable pedagogical moves.

Another rejoinder is that the natural and technological sciences are themselves more 'ideological' – more subject to contestation around axes of human interest – than the narrow understanding of science proffered by the proponents of such 'evidence-based' research seem able to comprehend. Whether it is bioethics, or the politics of climate research, or the debates around Darwinism versus intelligent design, or the semantics of computer systems, questions of politics and ideology are bound closely to the evidence. Any pretence to simple-minded empiricism no longer works, not even in the natural and technological sciences.

Nor are narrowly unambitious and apolitical horizons any longer sufficient to the challenges at hand. Maybe there's something fundamentally wanting in the institutional inheritance that is today's schools? Perhaps the 'back-to-basics' movement is flawed at its core? Maybe our contemporary social conditions ask of us something quite different and much better?

Meanwhile, medical scientists are trying to tackle the seemingly impossible – multiple sclerosis, Alzheimer's disease and cancer. None of them seems to know the answers, but their ambitions are high and their risks great as they try to come up with something fundamentally new, radically innovative, shockingly transformative. Any such ambitions would be way beyond the bounds of a narrowly 'evidence-based' view of science.

What, then, is a science? Some of the studies of the social comfortably and habitually call themselves 'sciences', but others do not. In the case of education, there's a good deal of discomfort about the applicability of the term, particularly given the way it is used by the advocates of a narrow empiricism.

As we said in Chapter 6, the English word 'science' derives from the Latin *'sciens'*, or knowing. The meaning of science has been narrowed in English to mean empirical method applied without any potentially prejudicial interest to the natural or human world. Return to the expansiveness of this root and the study of human learning must have claim to that word equal to the other social sciences and the natural sciences.

'Science' in a broader and deeper sense implies an intensity of focus and a concentration of intellectual energies greater than that of ordinary, everyday, commonsense or lay 'knowing'. It relies on the ritualistic rigour and accumulated wisdoms of disciplinary practices.

Wherever science is to be found, it is more than casual knowing. It involves a kind of systematicity that does not exist in casual experience. Husserl draws the distinction between the 'lifeworld' and what is 'transcendental' about science.[9] The 'lifeworld' is everyday lived experience. It is a place in which one's everyday understandings and actions seem to work instinctively – not too much conscious or reflective thought is required. The 'transcendental' of science is a place above and beyond the commonsense assumptions of the lifeworld. In counter distinction to the relative unconscious, unreflexive knowledge in and of the lifeworld, science sets out to comprehend and create designs that are beyond and beneath the everyday, amorphous pragmatics of the lifeworld. Science, by contrast, is focused, systematic, premeditated, reflective, purposeful, disciplined and open to scrutiny by a community of experts. At its best it is experiential and conceptual and critical and applied.

What is a discipline? Disciplines are fields of deep and detailed content knowledge, communities of professional practice, forms of discourse (of fine and precise semantic distinction and technicality), areas of work (types of organisations or divisions within organisations such as academic departments or research organisations), domains of publication and public communication, common experiences of learning through induction as apprentices into the community, methods of reading and analysing the world, epistemic frames or ways of thinking, and even ways of acting and types of persons. 'Discipline' delineates the boundaries of intellectual community, the distinctive practices and methodologies of particular areas of rigorous and concentrated intellectual effort, and the varying frames of reference used to interpret the world. Medicine is the science of human physiology; archaeology is the science of ancient human traces; history is the science of the human and natural past; psychology is the science of mind. The discipline of education is the science of learning in informal and formal settings.

Education's agenda is intellectually expansive and practically ambitious. It is learner-transformative (the enablement of productive workers, participating citizens and fulfilled persons). And it is world-transformative as we interrogate the human nature of learning and its role in imagining and enacting new ways of being human and living socially – shaping our identities, framing our ways of belonging, using technologies, representing meanings in new ways and through new media, building participatory spaces and collaborating to build and rebuild the world. These are enormous intellectual and practical challenges.

The science of education is a domain of social imagination, invention and action. It's big. It's ambitious. And it's determinedly practical.

Book summary

Changing education	The modern past	More recent times	New Learning
Chapter 1: New Learning	What modern education has been	What modern education has been slowly becoming	New Learning: Education for the near future
Chapter 2: Life in schools	Didactic education	Authentic education	Transformative education
Chapter 3: Learning for work	Fordism	Post-Fordism	Productive diversity
Chapter 4: Learning civics	Nationalism	Neoliberalism	Civic pluralism
Chapter 5: Learning personalities	From exclusion to assimilation	Recognition	Inclusivity
Chapter 6: The nature of learning	Behaviourism	Brain developmentalism	Social cognitivism
Chapter 7: Knowledge and learning	Committed knowledge frameworks	Knowledge relativism	Knowledge repertoires
Chapter 8: Pedagogy and curriculum	Mimesis	Synthesis	Reflexivity
Chapter 9: Learning communities at work	Bureaucratic	Self-managing	Collaborative

Notes

1. Kalantzis 2006, pp. 7–12
2. Jenkins 2004, pp. 33–43
3. Lanchester 2006, pp. 3–6
4. Cope and Kalantzis 2004, pp. 198–282
5. Husserl 1954 (1970)
6. Vygotsky 1978
7. Schwandt 2005, pp. 284–305; Erikson and Gutierrez 2002, pp. 21–24
8. Popkewitz 2004, pp. 62–78
9. Cope and Kalantzis 2000a, pp. 203–34; Husserl 1954 (1970)

References

Addams, Jane. 1990. *Twenty Years at Hull-House*. Urbana IL: University of Illinois Press.

Al-Ghazzali, Abu Hamid. 1108 (2001). *Deliverance from Error and Mystical Union with the Almighty*. Washington, DC: Council for Research in Values and Philosophy.

Ali, Farhana. 2006. 'Inside Pakistan's Madrasas.' *Terrorism Focus* 3:4–5.

Anderson, Benedict. 1991. *Imagined Communities: Reflections on the Origin and Spread of Nationalism*. London: Verso.

Anderson, Perry. 1974a. *Lineages of the Absolutist State*. London: NLB.

Anderson, Perry. 1974b. *Passages from Antiquity to Feudalism*. London: NLB.

Apple, Michael. 2002. 'Educating the "Right" Way: Schooling and the Power of Conservative Modernization.' *International Journal of Learning* 9:1–23.

Apple, Michael W. 1979. *Ideology and Curriculum*. London: Routledge.

Apple, Michael W. 2006. 'Understanding and Interrupting Neoconservatism and Neoliberalism in Education.' *Pedagogies: An International Journal* 1:21–26.

Aristotle. 350 BCE-a. *Poetics*. The Internet Classics Archive, MIT.

Aristotle. 350 BCE-b. *Politics*. The Internet Classics Archive, MIT.

Aristotle. 350 BCE-c. *Posterior Analytics*. The Internet Classics Archive, MIT.

Aristotle. 350 BCE-d. *Topics*. The Internet Classics Archive, MIT.

Arnold, Matthew. 1869. *Culture and Anarchy: An Essay in Political and Social Criticism*. Oxford: Project Gutenberg.

Aronowitz, Stanley and Henry Giroux. 1991. *Postmodern Education: Politics, Culture and Social Criticism*. Minneapolis MN: University of Minnesota Press.

Asimov, Isaac. 1951 (1973). 'The Fun They Had' in *The Best of Isaac Asimov*. New York: Doubleday.

Barraga, Natalie (ed.). 1983. *Visual Handicaps and Learning*. Austin TX: Pro-ed.

Barthes, Roland (ed.). 1981. *Theory of the Text*. Boston: Routledge and Kegan Paul.

Battiste, Marie and James Henderson. 2000. *Protecting Indigenous Knowledge and Heritage: A Global Challenge*. Saskatoon, Saskatchewan: Purich Publishing.

Bauman, Z. 1992. *Intimations of Postmodernity*. London: Routledge.

Bean, Robert Bennett. 1932. *The Races of Man: Differentiation and Dispersal of Man*. New York: The University Society.

Beecher, Catharine. 1829. *Suggestions Respecting Improvements in Education: Presented to the Trustees of the Hartford Female Seminary, and Published at their Request*. Hartford CN: Packer & Butler.

Bell, Daniel. 1999. *The Coming of Post-Industrial Society*. New York: Basic Books.

Bernstein, Basil. 1971. *Class, Codes and Control: Theoretical Studies Towards a Sociology of Language*. London: Routledge & Kegan Paul.

Bernstein, Richard. 1994. *Dictatorship of Virtue: Multiculturalism and the Battle for America's Future*. New York: Alfred A. Knopf.

Binet, Alfred. 1905 (1916). 'New Methods for the Diagnosis of the Intellectual Level of Subnormals' in Alfred Binet and Theodore Simon (eds) *The Development of Intelligence in Children*, New York.

Bishop, Dorothy V. M. and Laurence B. Leonard (eds). 2000. *Speech and Language Impairments in Children: Causes, Characteristics, Intervention and Outcome*. Hove, East Sussex: Psychology Press.

Blackburn, Simon. 2005. *Truth: A Guide*. Oxford: Oxford University Press.

Boomer, Garth (ed). 1982. *Negotiating the Curriculum: A Teacher–Student Partnership*. Sydney: Ashton Scholastic.

Bourdieu, Pierre. 1973. 'Cultural Reproduction and Social Reproduction.' pp. 71–112 in R. Brown (ed.) *Knowledge, Education and Social Change: Papers in the Sociology of Education*. Tavistock, UK: Tavistock Publications.

Bowe, Frank. 1978. *Handicapping America: Barriers to Disabled People*. New York: Harper & Row.

Bowles, Samuel and Herbert Gintis. 1976. *Schooling in Capitalist America: Education Reform and the Contradictions of Economic Life*. New York: Basic Books Inc.

Bramfield, Theodore. 1965. *Education as Power*. New York: Holt, Rinehart, Winston.

Bransford, John D., Ann L. Brown and Rodney R. Cocking (eds). 2000. *How People Learn: Brain, Mind, Experience and School*. Washington DC: National Academy Press.

'Brown v. Board of Education.' 1954. p. 483: US Supreme Court.

Bruegmann, Robert. 2005. *Sprawl: A Compact History*. Chicago: University of Chicago Press.

Bruner, Jerome. 1977. *The Process of Education*. Cambridge, MA: Harvard University Press.

Bruner, Jerome S. 1966. *Toward a Theory of Instruction*. Cambridge, MA: Harvard University Press.

Buddhist Pali Canon. N. D. 'Magga-vibhanga Sutta: An Analysis of the Path' in *Samyutta Nikaya*.

Burrows, Peter, Bill Cope, Mary Kalantzis, Daria Loi, Kieju Suominen and Nicola Yelland. 2006a. 'Data from the Australian Research Council Learning By Design Project.' Unpublished Manuscript.

Burrows, Peter, Bill Cope, Mary Kalantzis, Les Morgan, Kieju Suominen and Nicola Yelland. 2006b. 'Data from the Australian Research Council Learning By Design Project.' Unpublished Manuscript.

Caldwell, Brian J. and Jim M. Spinks. 1988. *The Self-Managing School*. London: Falmer Press.

Candland, Douglas Keith. 1993. *Feral Children and Clever Animals: Reflections on Human Nature*. Oxford: Oxford University Press.

Carroll, Janell L. and Paul Root Wolpe. 1996. *Sexuality and Gender in Society*. New York: HarperCollins.

Castles, Stephen, Bill Cope, Mary Kalantzis and Michael Morrissey. 1992. *Mistaken Identity: Multiculturalism and the Demise of Nationalism in Australia*. Sydney: Pluto Press.

Cavalli-Sforza, Luigi. 2000. *Genes, Peoples and Languages*. Berkeley CA: University of California Press.

Cavalli-Sforza, Luigi and Francesco Cavalli-Sforza. 1995. *The Great Human Diasporas*. Cambridge MA: Helix Books.

Cazden, Courtney B. 2006. 'Connected Learning: "Weaving" in Classroom Lessons' in *'Pedagogy in Practice 2006' Conference*. University of Newcastle.

Chaika, Gloro. 1999. 'Virtual High Schools: The High Schools of the Future?' in *Education World*.

Chalmers, A. F. 1976. *What is This Thing Called Science?* St Lucia: University of Queensland Press.

Chomsky, Noam. 1959. 'Review of Verbal Behavior, by B.F. Skinner.' *Language* 35:26–58.

Chomsky, Noam. 1972. 'I.Q. Tests: Building Blocks for the New Class System.' *Rampart* 24–30.

Chomsky, Noam. 2000. *New Horizons in the Study of Language and Mind*. Cambridge: Cambridge University Press.

Chomsky, Noam. 2002. 'Chomsky's Revolution: An Exchange.' Pp. 64–65 in *New York Review of Books*.

Christian, David. 2004. *Maps of Time: An Introduction to Big History*. Berkeley, CA: University of California Press.

Churchill, Winston. 1960 (1930). *My Early Life*. London: Oldhams.

Confucius. c.500 BCE. 'The Great Learning.' MIT Internet Classics Archive.

Connell, R.W. 2005. *Masculinities*. Sydney: Allen and Unwin.

Cope, Bill. 1993. 'Schooling in the World's Best Muslim Country.' *Education Australia* 20–23.

Cope, Bill. 2001. 'Globalisation, Multilingualism and the New Text Technologies.' pp. 1–15 in Bill Cope and Gus Gollings (eds) *Multilingual Book Production*. Melbourne: Common Ground.

Cope, Bill and Mary Kalantzis (eds). 1993. *The Powers of Literacy: Genre Approaches to Teaching Writing*. London and Pittsburgh: Falmer Press (UK edition) and University of Pennsylvania Press (US edition).

Cope, Bill and Mary Kalantzis (eds). 1997a. *Productive Diversity: A New Approach to Work and Management*. Sydney: Pluto Press.

Cope, Bill and Mary Kalantzis (eds). 1997b. 'White Noise: The Attack on Political Correctness and the Struggle for the Western Canon.' *Interchange* 28:283–329.

Cope, Bill and Mary Kalantzis (eds). 1998. 'Multicultural Education: Transforming the Mainstream' in Stephen May (ed.) *Critical Multiculturalism*. London: Falmer Press.

Cope, Bill and Mary Kalantzis. 2000a. 'Designs for Social Futures.' pp. 203–234 in Bill Cope and Mary Kalantzis (eds). *Multiliteracies: Literacy Learning and the Design of Social Futures*, London: Routledge.

Cope, Bill and Mary Kalantzis (eds). 2000b. *Multiliteracies: Literacy Learning and the Design of Social Futures*. London: Routledge.

Cope, Bill and Mary Kalantzis (eds). 2002. 'Manageable Knowledge: Communication, Learning and Organisational Change.' pp. 1–15 in Bill Cope and Robin Freeman (eds) *Developing Knowledge Workers in the Printing and Publishing Industries: Education, Training and Knowledge Management in the Publishing Supply Chain, from Creator to Consumer*. Melbourne: Common Ground.

Cope, Bill and Mary Kalantzis (eds). 2004. 'Text-Made Text.' *E-Learning* 1:198–282.

Cope, Bill, Mary Kalantzis, Allan Luke, Bob Morgan, Rob McCormack, Nicky Solomon, Diana Slade and Nancy Veal. 1993. 'The National Framework of Adult Language,

Literacy and Numeracy Competence.' Melbourne: Australian Committee for Training and Curriculum.

Crawford, James. 1992. *Hold Your Tongue: Bilingualism and the Politics of English Only*. Reading, MA: Addison-Wesley.

Crystal, David. 2000. *Language Death*. Cambridge: Cambridge University Press.

Cuban, Larry. 1993. *How Teachers Taught: Constancy and Change in American Classrooms, 1890–1990*. NY: Teachers College Press.

Cummins, Jim. 1986. 'Empowering Minority Students.' *Harvard Educational Review* 56.

Cummins, Jim and Merrill Swain. 1986. *Bilingualism in Education: Aspects of Theory, Research and Practice*. London: Longman.

Damasio, Antonio R. 1994. *Descartes' Error: Emotion, Reason and the Human Brain*. New York: Penguin Putnam.

Darwin, Charles (ed). 1892. *The Autobiography of Charles Darwin and Selected Letters*. New York: D. Appleton and Company.

Datnow, Amanda and Lea Hubbard. 2002. *Gender in Policy and Practice: Perspectives on Single-Sex and Coeducational Schooling*. New York: Routledge Falmer.

d'Augelli, Anthony R. and Charlotte J. Patterson (eds). 2001. *Lesbian, Gay, and Bisexual Identities and Youth: Psychological Perspectives*. Oxford: Oxford University Press.

de Beauvoir, Simone. 1952 (1993). *The Second Sex*. New York: Knopf.

Deacon, Terrence W. 1997. *The Symbolic Species: The Co-evolution of Language and the Brain*. New York: W.W. Norton.

Delpit, Lisa D. 1988. 'The Silenced Dialogue: Power and Pedagogy in Educating Other People's Children.' *Harvard Educational Review* 58:280–298.

Deng Xiaoping. 1984. 'Building Socialism with a Specifically Chinese Character' in *The People's Daily*. Beijing.

Department of Immigration and Multicultural Affairs (DIMA). 1998. 'Charter of Public Service in a Culturally Diverse Society.' Canberra: DIMA.

Derrida, Jacques. 1976. *Of Grammatology*. Baltimore: Johns Hopkins University Press.

Descartes, René. 1641 (1911). *Meditations On First Philosophy*. Cambridge: Cambridge University Press.

Dewey, John. 1902 (1956). *The Child and the Curriculum*. Chicago: University of Chicago Press.

Dewey, John. 1915 (1956). *The School and Society*. Chicago: University of Chicago Press.

Dewey, John. 1916 (1966). *Democracy and Education: An Introduction to the Philosophy of Education*. New York: Free Press.

Dewey, John. 1938 (1963). *Experience and Education*. New York: Collier Books.

Dewey, John and Evelyn Dewey. 1915. *Schools of Tomorrow*. New York: Dutton.

Dickens, Charles. 1854 (1945). *Hard Times*. London: Collins.

Donald, Merlin. 1991. *Origins of the Modern Mind*. Cambridge, MA: Harvard University Press.

Donald, Merlin. 2001. *A Mind So Rare: The Evolution of Human Consciousness*. New York: W.W. Norton.

Dreger, Alice Domurat (ed). 1999. *Intersex in the Age of Ethics*. Hagerstown, MD: University Publishing Group.

Drucker, Peter F. 1993. *Post-Capitalist Society*. Oxford: Butterworth Heinemann.

Eco, Umberto. 1981. *The Role of the Reader: Explorations in the Semiotics of Texts*. London: Hutchinson.

Edwards, Carolyn, Lella Gandini and George Forman. 1993. *The Hundred Languages of Children: The Reggio Emilia Approach to Early Childhood Education*. Norwood, NJ: Ablex.

Elmhirst, L. K. 1961 (1925). 'Siksha-Satra' in Rabindranath Tagore and L. K. Elmhirst (eds) *Rabindranath Tagore, Pioneer in Education: Essays and Exchanges between Rabindranath Tagore and L.K. Elmhirst*. London: John Murray.

Empiricus Sextus. c.200. *Outlines of Pyrrhonism*.

Erikson, Frederick and Kris Gutierrez. 2002. 'Culture, Rigor and Science in Educational Research.' *Educational Researcher* 31:21–24.

Evans, Tony. 1998. *Human Rights Fifty Years On: A Reappraisal*. Manchester, UK: Manchester University Press.

Eysenck, H.J. 1971. *Race, Intelligence and Education*. London: Temple Smith.

Ford, Henry. 1923. *My Life and Work*. Sydney: Angus & Robertson.

Foucault, Michel. 1979. *Discipline and Punish: The Birth of the Prison*. New York: Vintage Books.

Fraser, Steven (ed.). 1995. *The Bell Curve Wars: Race, Intelligence, and the Future of America*. New York: Free Press.

Freire, Paulo. 1972. *Pedagogy of the Oppressed*. Harmondsworth, UK: Penguin.

Friedman, Milton. 1975. *There's No Such Thing as a Free Lunch*. LaSalle, IL: Open Court.

Friedman, Thomas L. 2006. 'The Exhausting Race for Ideas.' pp. 10–12 in *Newsweek Special Edition: Issues 2006*.

Froebel, Friedrich. 1895 (1985). *Friedrich Froebel's Pedagogics of the Kindergarten: Or, His Ideas Concerning the Play and Playthings of the Child*. New York: D. Appleton.

Fullan, Michael. 2003. *The Moral Imperative of School Leadership*. Thousand Oaks, CA: Corwin Press.

Gandhi, Mahatma. 1949. *Gandhi, An Autobiography*. London: Phoenix Press.

Gardner, Howard. 1993. *Multiple Intelligences: The Theory in Practice*. New York: Basic Books.

Gardner, Howard. 2006. *Multiple Intelligences: New Horizons*. New York: Basic Books.

Gates, Bill. 2005. 'Remarks on Education' in *National Education Summit on High Schools*. Washington DC.

Gee, James Paul. 1992. *The Social Mind: Language, Ideology, and Social Practice*. New York: Bergin & Garvey.

Gee, James Paul. 1996. *Social Linguistics and Literacies: Ideology in Discourses*. London: Taylor and Francis.

Gee, James Paul. 2000. 'New People in New Worlds: Networks, the New Capitalism and Schools' in Bill Cope and Mary Kalantzis (eds) *Multiliteracies: Literacy Learning and the Design of Social Futures*. London: Routledge.

Gee, James Paul. 2003. *What Video Games Have to Teach Us about Learning and Literacy*. New York: Palgrave Macmillan.

Gee, James Paul. 2004. *Situated Language and Learning: A Critique of Traditional Schooling*. London: Routledge.

Gee, James Paul. 2005. *Why Video Games are Good for Your Soul: Pleasure and Learning*. Melbourne: Common Ground.

Gee, James Paul. 2006. 'Are Video Games Good For Learning?' in *Technical Paper*. Madison, WI: Games and Professional Simulation Group, University of Wisconsin.

Gee, James Paul. 2007. *Good Video Games + Good Learning: Collected Essays on Video Games, Learning and Literacy*. New York: Peter Lang.

Gellner, Ernest. 1983. *Nations and Nationalism*. Ithaca, NY: Cornell University Press.

Gellner, Ernest. 1994. *Conditions of Liberty: Civil Society and Its Rivals*. London: Hamish Hamilton.

Gilmore, David, Crain Soudien and David Donald. 1999. 'Post-Apartheid Policy and Practice: Educational Reform in South Africa.' pp. 341–350 in Mazurek Kas, Margaret Winzer and Czeslaw Czeslaw Majorek (eds) *Education in a Global Society: A Comparative Perspective*. Boston: Allyn and Bacon.

Gould, Stephen Jay. 1981. *The Mismeasure of Man*. New York: W.W. Norton.

Habermas, Jürgen. 1998. 'Learning by Disaster: A Diagnostic Look Back on the Short Twentieth Century.' *Constellations* 5:307–320.

Halasz, George, Gil Anaf, Peter Ellingsen, Anne Manne and Frances Thomson Salo. 2002. *Cries Unheard: A New Look at Attention Deficit Hyperactivity Disorder*. Melbourne: Common Ground.

Handy, Charles. 1994. *The Age of Paradox*. Boston: Harvard Business School Press.

Harvey, David. 1996. *Justice, Nature and the Geography of Difference*. Cambridge, MA: Blackwell.

Harvey, David. 2005. *A Brief History of Neoliberalism*. Oxford: Oxford University Press.

Hausman, Bernice L. *Changing Sex: Transsexualism, Technology and the Idea of Gender*. Durham, NC: Duke University Press.

Herbert, Jeannie. 1998. 'Making the Links' in *Making the Links: Aboriginal Pedagogy Conference*: Department of Education, Western Australia.

Herdt, Gilbert. 1994. *Third Sex, Third Gender: Beyond Sexual Dimorphism in Culture and History*. New York: Zone Books.

Herrnstein, Richard and Charles Murray. 1995. *The Bell Curve: Intelligence and Class Structure in American Life*. New York: Free Press.

Hilton, Isabel and Anthony Barnett. 2005. 'Democracy and openDemocracy.' London: OpenDemocracy.

Hirsch, E.D. 1988. *Cultural Literacy: What Every American Needs to Know*. New York: Vintage Books.

Honderich, Ted. 2004. *On Consciousness*. Edinburgh: Edinburgh University Press.

Hurdle, Jon. 2006. 'Philadelphia Opens High-tech School of the Future.' in *Reuters, 7 September*.

Husserl, Edmund. 1954 (1970). *The Crisis of European Sciences and Transcendental Phenomenology*. Evanston: Northwestern University Press.

Ibn Tufayl, Muhammad. c.1170 (1907). *The Awakening of the Soul*. London: The Orient Press.

Illich, Ivan. 1973. *Deschooling Society*. Harmondsworth, UK: Penguin.

Jameson, F. 1991. *Postmodernism, or, the Cultural Logic of Late Capitalism*. Durham, NC: Duke University Press.

Jardim, Anne. 1970. *The First Henry Ford: A Study in Personality and Business Leadership*. Cambridge, MA: The MIT Press.

Jenkins, Henry. 2004. 'The Cultural Logic of Media Convergence.' *International Journal of Cultural Studies* 7:33–43.

Kalantzis, Mary. 2000. 'Multicultural Citizenship.' pp. 99–110 in Wayne Hudson and John Kane (eds) *Rethinking Australian Citizenship*. Melbourne: Cambridge University Press.

Kalantzis, Mary. 2001. 'Civic Pluralism and Total Globalisation.' pp. 110–123 in Brad Buckley and John Conomos (eds) *Republics of Ideas: Republicanism, Culture, Visual Arts*. Sydney: Pluto Press.

Kalantzis, Mary. 2004. 'Waiting for the Barbarians: "Knowledge Management" and "Learning Organisations".' *International Journal of Knowledge, Culture and Change Management* 4:1827–1833.

Kalantzis, Mary. 2006. 'Changing Subjectivities, New Learning.' *Pedagogies: An International Journal* 1:7–12.

Kalantzis, Mary and Bill Cope. 1988. 'Why We Need Multicultural Education: A Review of the "Ethnic Disadvantage" Debate.' *Journal of Intercultural Studies* 9:39–57.

Kalantzis, Mary and Bill Cope. 1989. *Social Literacy: An Overview*. Sydney: Common Ground.

Kalantzis, Mary and Bill Cope. 1993. 'Histories of Pedagogy, Cultures of Schooling.' Pp. 38–62 in Bill Cope and Mary Kalantzis (eds) *The Powers of Literacy: A Genre Approach to Teaching Literacy*. London: Falmer Press.

Kalantzis, Mary and Bill Cope. 1999. 'Multicultural Education: Transforming the Mainstream.' Pp. 245–276 in Stephen May (ed.) *Critical Multiculturalism: Rethinking Multicultural and Anti-Racist Education*. London: Falmer/Taylor and Francis.

Kalantzis, Mary and Bill Cope. 2001. 'New Learning: A Charter for Australian Education.' Canberra: Australian Council of Deans of Education.

Kalantzis, Mary and Bill Cope. 2004a. 'A Short History of Meaning.' *International Journal of the Humanities* 2:2245–2250.

Kalantzis, Mary and Bill Cope. 2004b. 'Designs For Learning.' *E-Learning* 1:38–92.

Kalantzis, Mary and Bill Cope. 2005. *Learning by Design*. Melbourne: Victorian Schools Innovation Commission.

Kalantzis, Mary and Bill Cope. 2006a. 'Big Change Question – Taking into Account Mainstream Economic and Political Trends, Can/Should School Have a Role in Developing Authentic Critical Thinking? A Question of Truth: The Role of the "Critical" in Pedagogy.' *Journal of Educational Change* 7:209–214.

Kalantzis, Mary and Bill Cope. 2006b. 'On Globalisation and Diversity.' *Computers and Composition* 31:402–411.

Kalantzis, Mary and Bill Cope. 2006c. *The Learning by Design Guide*. Melbourne: Common Ground.

Kalantzis, Mary, Bill Cope and Andrew Harvey. 2003. 'Assessing Multiliteracies and the New Basics.' *Assessment in Education* 10.

Kalantzis, Mary, Bill Cope, Greg Noble and Scott Poynting. 1991. *Cultures of Schooling: Pedagogies for Cultural Difference and Social Access*. London: Falmer Press.

Kalantzis, Mary, Bill Cope and Diana Slade. 1989. *Minority Languages and Dominant Culture: Issues of Education, Assessment and Social Equity*. London: Falmer Press.

Kalantzis, Mary, Diana Slade and Bill Cope. 1990. 'Minority Languages and Mainstream Culture: Problems of Equity and Assessment.' pp. 196–213 in John H.A.L. De Jong and Douglas K. Stevenson (eds) in *Individualising the Assessment of Language Abilities*. Clevedon, England and Philadelphia: Multilingual Matters.

Kant, Immanuel. 1781 (1933). *Critique of Pure Reason*. London: Macmillan.

Kemmis, Stephen and Mervyn Wilkinson. 1988. 'Participatory Action Research and the Study of Practice' in Bill Atweh, Stephen Kemmis and Patricia Weeks (eds) *Action Research in Practice: Partnership for Social Justice in Education*. London: Routledge.

Knobel, Michele and Colin Lankshear (eds). 2007. *The New Literacies Sampler*. New York: Peter Lang.

Koch, Christof. 2004. *The Quest for Consciousness: A Neurobiological Approach*. Engelwood, CO: Roberts and Company.

Kohn, Alfie. 2000. *The Case Against Standardized Testing: Raising the Scores, Ruining the Schools*. Portsmouth, NH: Heinemann.

Kress, G.R. 1995. *Writing the Future: English and the Production of a Culture of Innovation*. Sheffield: National Association of Teachers of English.

Kress, Gunther. 2000a. 'Design and Transformation: New Theories of Meaning.' pp. 153–161 in Bill Cope and Mary Kalantzis (eds) *Multiliteracies: Literacy Learning and the Design of Social Futures*. London: Routledge.

Kress, Gunther. 2000b. 'Multimodality.' pp. 182–202 in Bill Cope and Mary Kalantzis (eds) *Multiliteracies: Literacy Learning and the Design of Social Futures*. Melbourne: Macmillan.

Kress, Gunther. 2003. *Literacy in the New Media Age*. London: Routledge.

Labov, William. 1972. *Language in the Inner City: Studies in the Black English Vernacular*. Philadelphia: University of Pennsylvania Press.

Lanchester, John. 2006. 'The Global Id.' *London Review of Books* 28:3–6.

Lave, Jean and Etienne Wenger. 1991. *Situated Learning: Legitimate Peripheral Participation*. Cambridge: Cambridge University Press.

Lee, Yan Pho. 1887 (1914). 'When I was a Boy in China.' pp. 214–221 in Eva March Tappan (ed.) *The World's Story: A History of the World in Story, Song, and Art*. Boston, MA: Houghton Mifflin.

Lo Bianco, Joseph. 2000. 'Multiliteracies and Multilingualism.' pp. 92–105 in Bill Cope and Mary Kalantzis (eds) *Multiliteracies: Literacy Learning and the Design of Social Futures*. London: Routledge.

Locke, John. 1690. *An Essay Concerning Human Understanding*.

Lorde, Audre. 1982 (1996). *Zami: A New Spelling of My Name*. London: Pandora.

Lyotard, Jean-François. 1979. *The Postmodern Condition: A Report on Knowledge*. Manchester, UK: Manchester University Press.

Marika-Munuggiritj, Raymattja and Michael J. Christie. 1995. 'Yolngu Metaphors for Learning.' *International Journal of the Sociology of Language* 113:59–62.

Marx, Karl. 1976. *Capital: A Critique of Political Economy*. Harmondsworth, UK: Penguin.

Marx, Karl and Frederick Engels. 1848 (1973). 'Manifesto of the Communist Party.' pp. 62–98 in David Fernback (ed.) *Karl Marx, Political Writings: The Revolutions of 1848*. Harmondsworth, UK: Penguin.

Masuda, Yoneji. 1980. *The Information Society and Post-Industrial Society*. Washington: World Future Society.

McCalman, Janet. 1984. *Struggletown: Public and Private Life in Richmond, 1900–1965*. Melbourne: Melbourne University Press.

McGuinness, Diane. 1985. *When Children Don't Learn: Understanding the Biology and Psychology of Learning Disabilities*. New York: Basic Books.

McLaren, Peter. 2003. *Life in Schools: An Introduction to Critical Pedagogy*. Boston: Pearson Education.

Miles, Robert. 1989. *Racism*. London: Routledge.

Mislevy, Robert J. 2006. 'Cognitive Psychology and Educational Assessment.' pp. 257–305 in Robert L. Brennan (ed.) *Educational Measurement*. New York: Praeger.

Mitchell, Juliet. 1971. *Woman's Estate*. Harmondsworth, UK: Penguin.

Montessori, Maria. 1912 (1964). *The Montessori Method*. New York: Schocken Books.

Montessori, Maria. 1917 (1973). *The Montessori Elementary Material*. New York: Schocken Books.

Mortimer, Jeylan T. and Reed W. Larson (eds). 2002. *The Changing Adolescent Experience: Societal Trends and the Transition to Adulthood*. Cambridge: Cambridge University Press.

Moss-Kanter, Rosabeth. 1972. 'The Organization Child: Experience Management in a Nursery School.' *Sociology of Education* 45:186–212.

National Center for Education Evaluation and Regional Assistance. 2003. 'Identifying and Implementing Educational Practices Supported by Rigorous Evidence.' US Department of Education, Institute of Education Sciences.

Neill, A.S. 1962. *Summerhill*. Harmondsworth, UK: Pelican.

Neville, A.O. 1947. *Australia's Coloured Minority: Its Place in the Community*. Sydney: Currawong Publishing.

New London Group. 1996. 'A Pedagogy of Multiliteracies: Designing Social Futures.' *Harvard Educational Review* 66:60–92.

New South Wales Department of Education. 1951. 'Helping the New Australian Child.' *The Education Gazette*: 317–320; 350–352.

New South Wales Department of Education. 1983. *Our Multicultural Society*. Sydney: Directorate of Special Programs, NSW Department of Education.

Nietzsche, Friedrich. 1888 (1915). 'Twilight of the Idols' in Oscar Levy (ed.) *Complete Works of Friedrich Nietzsche*. Edinburgh: T.N. Foulis.

Nolan, James. 1996. *The American Culture Wars: Current Contests and Future Prospects*. Charlottesville, VA: University Press of Virginia.

Organisation for Economic Cooperation and Development (OECD). 2003. *Health at a Glance: OECD Indicators 2005*. Paris: OECD.

Organisation for Economic Cooperation and Development. 2005. *Education at a Glance: OECD Indicators 2005*. Paris: OECD.

Orwell, George. 1949 (2003). *Nineteen Eighty-Four*. New York: Plume.

Orwell, George. 1968 (1953). 'Such Were the Joys.' in *The Collected Essays, Journalism and Letters of George Orwell: Volume 4, 'In Front of Your Nose', 1945–1950*. Harmondsworth, Middlesex: Penguin.

Palinscar, Annemarie Sullivan, and Ann L. Brown. 1984. 'Reciprocal Teaching of Comprehension-Fostering and Comprehension-Monitoring Activities.' *Cognition and Instruction* 1:117–175.

Pavlov, I.P. 1941. 'The Conditioned Reflex.' pp. 166–185 in W. Horsley Gantt (ed.) *Lectures on Conditioned Reflexes: Vol. 2. Conditioned Reflexes and Psychiatry*. New York: International Publishers.

Peak, Lois. 1992. 'Formal Pre-Elementary Education in Japan' in Robert Leestma and Herbert Walberg (eds) *Japanese Educational Productivity*. Ann Arbor, MI: The University of Michigan Press.

Pell, George. 2005. 'The Dictatorship of Relativism: Address to the National Press Club.' Canberra.

Pellegrino, James W., Naomi Chudowsky and Robert Glaser (eds). 2001. *Knowing What Students Know: The Science and Design of Educational Assessment*. Washington DC: National Academies Press.

Peters, Michael A. and Tina A.C. Beasley. 2006. *Building Knowledge Cultures: Education and Development in the Age of Knowledge Capitalism*. Oxford: Rowman & Littlefield.

Peters, Thomas J. and Robert H. Waterman Jr. 1984. *In Search of Excellence: Lessons from America's Best-Run Companies*. New York: Harper & Row.

Phillips, D.C. and Nicholas C. Burbules. 2000. *Postpositivism and Educational Research*. New York: Rowman and Littlefield.

Phillipson, Robert. 1992. *Linguistic Imperialism*. Oxford: Oxford University Press.

Piaget, Jean. 1929 (1973). *The Child's Conception of the World*. London: Paladin.

Piaget, Jean. 1971. *Psychology and Epistemology: Towards a Theory of Knowledge*. Harmondsworth, UK: Penguin.

Piaget, Jean. 1976. *An Introduction to Jean Piaget Through His Own Words*, edited by Sarah F. Campbell. New York: John Wiley & Sons, Inc.

Piaget, Jean. 1997. *How the Mind Works*. New York: Norton.

Piaget, Jean. 2002. *The Blank Slate: The Modern Denial of Human Nature*. New York: Viking.

Pinker, Steven. 1995. *The Language Instinct*. New York: HarperPerennial.

Piore, Michael J. and Charles F. Sabel. 1984. *The Second Industrial Divide: Possibilities for Prosperity*. New York: Basic Books.

Plato. c.399–347 BCE. *The Apology [Defense] of Socrates*: Wikisource.

Polanyi, Karl. 1975. *The Great Transformation*. New York: Octagon Books.

Popkewitz, Thomas S. 2004. 'Is the National Research Council Committee's Report on Scientific Research in Education Scientific?: On Trusting the Manifesto.' *Qualitative Inquiry* 10:62–78.

Post, Robert and Michael Rogin. 1991. *Race and Representation: Affirmative Action*. New York: Zone Books.

Preves, Sharon E. 2003. *Intersex and Identity: The Contested Self*. New Brunswick, NJ: Rutgers University Press.

Rasmussen, Mary Louise, Eric Rofes and Susan Talburt (eds). 2004. *Youth and Sexualities: Pleasure, Subversion, and Insubordination in and out of Schools*. New York: Palgrave Macmillan.

Reagan, Ronald. 1989. 'Ronald Reagan's Farewell Address to the Nation.' in *Reagan Presidential Library*. Simi Valley CA.

Reynolds, Henry. 1995. *Fate of a Free People*. Melbourne: Penguin.

Reynolds, Henry. 1996. *Aboriginal Sovereignty: Reflections on Race, State and Nation*. Sydney: Allen and Unwin.

Rival, Laura. 1996. 'Formal Schooling and the Production of Modern Citizens in the Ecuadorian Amazon.' pp. 153–167 in B. Levinson, D. Foley, and D. Holland (eds) *The Cultural Production of the Educated Person*. Albany, NY: State University of New York Press.

Rizvi, Fazal. 2007. 'Internationalization of Curriculum: A Critical Perspective' in M. Hayden, D. Levy and J. Thomson (eds) *Handbook of International Education*. London: Sage.

Roeser, Ross J. and Marion P. Downs (eds). 2004. *Auditory Disorders in School Children*. New York: Thieme.

Roosevelt, Eleanor. 1930. 'Good Citizenship: The Purpose of Education.' pp. 4, 94, 97 in *Pictorial Review*.

Rorty, Richard. 1989. *Contingency, Irony and Solidarity*. Cambridge: Cambridge University Press.

Rose, Steven. 2005. *The Future of the Brain: The Promise and Perils of Tomorrow's Neuroscience*. Oxford: Oxford University Press.

Rousseau, Jean-Jacques. 1762 (1914). *Emile, or Education*. London: J. M. Dent & Sons Ltd.

Sahllins, Marshall. 1974. *Stone Age Economics*. New York: Aldine.

Sapir, Edward. 1921. *Language: An Introduction to the Study of Speech*. New York: Harcourt Brace.

Schmidt, Eric and Hal Varian. 2006. 'Google: Ten Golden Rules.' pp. 42–46 in *Newsweek Special Edition: Issues 2006*.

Schwandt, Thomas A. 2005. 'A Diagnostic Reading of Scientifically Based Research for Education.' *Educational Theory* 55:284–305.

Schweber, Simone. 2006. 'Fundamentally 9/11: The Fashioning of Collective Memory in a Christian School.' *American Journal of Education* 112:392–417.

Searle, John R. 2002. 'End of the Revolution.' *New York Review of Books* 49.

Searle, John R. 2004. *Mind: A Brief Introduction*. Oxford: Oxford University Press.

Sedgwick, Eve Kosofsky. 1990. *Epistemology of the Closet*. Berkeley, CA: University of California Press.

Senge, Peter M. 1990. *The Fifth Discipline: The Art and Practice of the Learning Organization*. New York: Doubleday Currency.

Sennett, Richard. 1998. *The Corrosion of Character: The Personal Consequences of Work in the New Capitalism*. New York: Norton.

Shavelson, Richard J. and Lisa Towne (eds). 2002. *Scientific Research in Education*. Washington DC: National Academies Press.

Sheehan, Paul. 1998. *Among the Barbarians: The Dividing of Australia*. Sydney: Random House.

Shoumatoff, Alex. 1985. *The Mountain of Names: A History of the Human Family*. New York: Simon and Schuster.

Skinner, B.F. 1968. *The Technology of Teaching*. New York: Meredith Corporation.

Skutnabb-Kangas, Tove. 1997. 'Language Attrition, Language Death, Language Murder – Different Facts or Different Ideologies?' in *'Strong' and 'Weak' Languages in the European Union Conference*. Thessaloniki, Greece: University of Roskilde, Denmark.

Smith, Adam. 1776 (1976). *An Inquiry into the Nature and Causes of the Wealth of Nations*. Oxford: Clarendon Press.

Smith, Helen, Mary Kalantzis and Bill Cope. 2006. 'Australian Research Council Digital Literacies Project.' Unpublished Manuscript.

Sotiriou, Sofoklis A. 2006. 'Taking Education from Sci-fi to Sci-fact' in *IST Results*.

Spencer, Herbert. 1862. *First Principles*.

Spivak, Gayatri Chakravorty. 1999. *A Critique of Postcolonial Reason: Toward a History of the Vanishing Present*. Cambridge, MA: Harvard University Press.

Spock, Benjamin. 1958. *Child and Baby Care*. London: The Bodley Head.

St Benedict. c.530 (1949). 'The Holy Rule of St. Benedict.'

Suggs, David N. and Andrew W. Miracle (eds). 1999. *Culture, Biology and Sexuality*. Athens, GA: University of Georgia Press.

Swan, William D. 1844. *The Grammar School Reader, Consisting of Selections in Prose and Poetry, with Exercises in Articulation, Designed to Follow the Primary School Reader, Part Three, Improved Edition*. Philadelphia: Thomas Cowperthwait and Co.

Sykes, Brian. 2001. *The Seven Daughters of Eve*. New York: W.W. Norton.

Tatum, Beverly Daniel. 2007. *Can We Talk about Race?* Boston: Beacon Press.

Taylor, Charles. 1994. *Multiculturalism: Examining the Politics of Recognition*. Princeton: Princeton University Press.

Taylor, Frederick Winslow. 1911. *The Principles of Scientific Management*. New York: Harper Brothers.

Thatcher, Margaret. 1987. 'Interview for "Woman's Own" ("No Such Thing as Society")' in *Margaret Thatcher Foundation: Speeches, Interviews and Other Statements*. London.

Thayer, V.T. 1928. *The Passing of the Recitation*. Boston: DC Heath.

Thompson, E.P. 1998. *'Alien Homage': Edward Thompson and Rabindranath Tagore*. Delhi: Oxford University Press.

Tobin, Joseph, David Wu and Dana Davidson. 1989. *Preschool in Three Cultures: Japan, China, and the United States*. New Haven: Yale University Press.

Tyack, David B. 1974. *The One Best System: A History of American Urban Education*. Cambridge, MA: Harvard University Press.

Verran, Helen. 2001. *Science and an African Logic*. Chicago: University of Chicago Press.

Vetterling-Braggin, Mary. 1982. *Femininity, Masculinity and Androgyny: A Modern Philosophical Discussion*. Totowa, NJ: Rowman and Littlefield.

Vygotsky, L.S. 1978. *Mind in Society: The Development of Higher Psychological Processes*. Cambridge, MA: Harvard University Press.

Vygotsky, Lev. 1934, trans. 1962 (1986). *Thought and Language*. Cambridge, MA: MIT Press.

Wadsworth, Barry J. 1996. *Piaget's Theory of Cognitive and Affective Development*. White Plains, NY: Longmans.

Ward, Russel. 1952. *Man Makes History*. Sydney: Shakespeare Head Press.

Watson, John B. 1914. *Behavior: An Introduction to Comparative Psychology*. New York: Henry Holt and Company.

Weber, Max. 1922 (1968). *Economy and Society: An Outline of Interpretive Sociology*. New York: Bedminster Press.

Wenger, Etienne. 1998. *Communities of Practice: Learning, Meaning and Identity*. Cambridge: Cambridge University Press.

Wenger, Etienne, Richard McDermott and William M. Snyder. 2002. *Cultivating Communities of Practice: A Guide to Managing Knowledge*. Cambridge, MA: Harvard Business School Press.

Whorf, Benjamin Lee. 1956. *Language, Thought and Reality: Selected Writings of Benjamin Lee Whorf*. Cambridge, MA: MIT Press.

Wittgenstein, Ludwig. 1958. *Philosophical Investigations*. New York: Macmillan.

Wolf, Naomi. 1991. *The Beauty Myth: How Images of Beauty are Used Against Women*. New York: W. Morrow.

Wollstencraft, Mary. 1792. *A Vindication of the Rights of Woman: With Strictures on Political and Moral Subjects*. London: J. Johnson.

Womack, James P., Daniel T. Jones and Daniel Roos. 1990. *The Machine that Changed the World*. New York: Rawson.

Yelland, Nicola. 2006. *Shift to the Future: Rethinking Learning with New Technologies in Education*. New York: Routledge.

Index